(continued from front flap)

Kapleau explores topics we all tend to ignore or find too uncomfortable to approach. With sections focusing on meditations, living wills, hospices, and funerals, as well as do's and don'ts for consoling the bereaved, THE WHEEL OF LIFE AND DEATH is an honest and real yet touching treatment of a subject that at one time or another affects us all.

PHOTO BY DAVID SACHTER

Philip Kapleau spent thirteen years of ardent Zen training in Japan. His other books include *Zen: Merging of East and West* and *The Three Pillars of Zen*, the latter having remained in print for over twenty-five years. He has established Zen centers throughout the world and now spends his time at the centers in Rochester, New York, and Santa Fe, New Mexico.

THE WHEEL OF LIFE AND DEATH

"THE WHEEL OF LIFE AND DEATH"

A Practical and Spiritual Guide

PHILIP KAPLEAU

DOUBLEDAY

NEW YORK   LONDON   TORONTO   SYDNEY   AUCKLAND

PUBLISHED BY DOUBLEDAY

a division of Bantam Doubleday Dell Publishing Group, Inc.,
666 Fifth Avenue, New York, NY 10103

DOUBLEDAY and the portrayal of an anchor with a dolphin are trademarks
of Doubleday, a division of Bantam Doubleday Dell Publishing Group, Inc.

Library of Congress Cataloging-in-Publication Data
Kapleau, Philip, date
The wheel of life and death : a practical and spiritual guide /
by Philip Kapleau. — 1st ed.
        p.   cm.
    Bibliography: p.
    Includes index.
    1. Death.   2. Karma.   3. Reincarnation.   I. Title.
BD444.K34   1989
291.2'3—dc19   88-25751
                            CIP

ISBN 0-385-26058-X
APRIL 1989
FIRST EDITION

BG

Even as night darkens the green earth
the wheel turns, death follows birth.
Strive through the night with every breath
that you may wake past day, past death!

CONTENTS

TWO: DYING

THREE: KARMA

FOUR: REBIRTH

FIVE: SUPPLEMENTS

INTRODUCTION

Anyone researching the literature on death and dying confronts a prodigious array of books and articles on these inescapable human experiences. In the past decade their number has ballooned to include controversial suicide manuals, accounts of near-death experiences, and articles on how to execute a living will. This vast literary output obviously feeds a deep human need: the need for answers to the perennial questions "Where did I come from when I was born and where will I go when I die? What meaning has my life, my death?"

To be human is to ask these questions, which reflect our greatest doubts, our deepest alienation from Self. Without answers that satisfy, there remains in the heart a gnawing angst that sours the sweetest of life's experiences. For with the mass of humanity it is still an article of faith that death is the greatest of human misfortunes, and dying the final and agonizing struggle against extinction. At the same time the incomprehensibility of death, its presumed finality, has awed and terrified men and women since the dawn of consciousness.

Why yet another book on death and dying? And how does this one differ from the rest? Valuable as these numerous studies have been in shaping constructive and compassionate social attitudes toward the fatally ill and in clarifying our ways of thinking about our own life and death, most of them nevertheless lack a spiritual dimension—a religious attitude toward life and death —and practical guidance in what may be called the art and religion of dying.

A religious orientation to dying involves, among other things, an understanding and deep acceptance of causation and the continuity of life. It also implies a recognition of the value of rites of passage—funeral services which, when conducted with passion and conviction, help facilitate the smooth transition from this life to future cycles of existence. Many people feel that funerals today are brief, hurried events devoid of true spiritual significance even when conducted by clergy—that they fail to acknowledge the reality of death, loss, and grief.[1]

Sociology professor Robert Fulton and others have noted that over the past generation a tremendous secularization of death has taken place, that now "people die ascetically in aseptic hospitals rather than aesthetically in their homes." The physician has replaced the priest; he is today's magician with the power to extend life; he is our new escort from this vale of tears. For this confusion of values we pay a high price. In his book *Modern Man in Search of a Soul*, Carl Jung (1875–1962) spells out the cost:

> Among all my patients in the second half of life—that is to say, over 35—there has not been one whose problem in the last resort was not that of finding a religious outlook on life. It is safe to say that every one of them fell ill because he has lost that which the living religions of every age have given to their followers, and none of them has been really healed who did not regain his religious outlook.[2]

A religion of dying need not involve dogmas or creeds or moral absolutes; like the air we breathe, it is inseparable from life. Long ago the Egyptian *Book of the Dead*, the later Tibetan *Book of the Dead*, and the medieval Christian text *The Art of Dying* provided such practical guidance. But these ancient texts have the disadvantage of presenting arcane data couched in terms too esoteric or quaint for modern readers.

A viable art of dying in our own day could go a long way toward relieving the dehumanized atmosphere of the average hospital death, which has become a tragic sign of our times. Inherently, medical practice expresses deep compassion, but that compassion seems to have gone increasingly astray as the art and religion of dying have become drowned in the science of prolonging life at any cost.

Today the science and technology of lengthening the life of the fatally ill have reached dizzying heights of efficiency. "Technology today," says Dr. Irwin Frank, medical director of Strong Memorial Hospital in Rochester, New York, "has provided an enigma—we can keep people alive in a state where there is no chance for them ever to be a member of society again."[3] Huge, costly diagnostic machines and life-sustaining high-tech apparatus have become medical surrogates, with medical personnel largely relegated to the role of technicians. But while the medical profession can now prolong life in areas once thought impossible, it can also prolong suffering. To provide maximum treatment in life-threatening illnesses, hospitals now utilize intensive care units, transplants, renal dialysis, cardiopulmonary resuscitation, and powerful chemotherapeutic agents. Such heroic measures have sometimes reversed the underlying disease to the extent that the patient has recovered to lead a normal existence for months or years. Predicting the exact episode which will result in death can be a tricky business, however, and physicians are understandably reluctant to withhold treatment when death does not appear to be imminent. As a consequence, patients are likely to meet their end in a sedated or comatose state, betubed and bewildered. Equally worrisome, hospital care has become frightfully expensive.

Commenting on the detrimental effect of artificially prolonging life, W. Y. Evans-Wentz in his preface to *The Tibetan Book of the Dead* writes:

> To die in a hospital, probably while under the mind-benumbing influence of some opiate, or else under the stimulation of some drug injected into the body to enable the dying to cling to life as long as possible, cannot but be productive of an undesirable death, as undesirable as that of a shell-shocked soldier on a battlefield. Even as the normal result of the birth-process may be aborted by malpractices, so similarly may the normal result of the death-process be aborted.[4]

Studies have shown that when the mental state of dying patients is not disturbed by sedation or other medication—in other words, when they are fully conscious and capable of responding to their environment with awareness unimpaired—their predominant emotion is not fear but calmness, the more so if they have established belief in the continuity of life.[5]

In fairness to the medical profession it should be said that the practice of thwarting the death process through powerful chemical agents and other means reflects a cultural pattern which not only sees all pain as pointless but also looks upon death as the last great enemy, to be outwitted and subdued at all costs. Death, which ought to be welcomed as natural and inevitable, becomes the Grim Reaper, and dying the terror of all terrors. If modern men and women are again to "preside at their own passing" and not be cheated out of their own death, they must recover their sovereignty as autonomously acting individuals and, while physically active and mentally clear, write the script and set the stage for the drama of their own exit, resisting manipulation by familial and other forces pressing upon them. Remarking on the individual's impotence in the contemporary world to act in this manner, the French historian Phillipe Ariés writes:

> Death in the hospital is no longer the occasion of a ritual ceremony, over which the dying person presides amidst his assembled relatives and friends. Death is a technical phenomenon obtained by a cessation of care, a cessation determined in a more or less avowed way by a decision of the doctor and the hospital team. Indeed, in the majority of cases the dying person has already lost consciousness. Death has been dissected, cut to bits by a series of little steps, which finally makes it impossible to know which step was the real death, the one in which consciousness was lost, or the one in which breathing stopped.[6]

Today dying in the average hospital in America has even less dignity and cohesiveness, I believe it is fair to say, than it had fourteen years ago, when Ariés' observations were first published. And hospital care itself has become more dehumanized. In part this is due to the stressful conditions under which doctors, nurses, and other hospital personnel are obliged to work. "It is now one of the world's most poorly kept secrets," a national newsmagazine commented recently, "that anxiety, depression, loneliness, and burnout are major factors in the lives of doctors."[7] But there are other reasons. One is the pervasive Western attitude of actively trying to influence events instead of letting them take their own natural course. It is summed up in the expression "Don't just sit there—do something!"

The experience of a doctor friend of mine dramatically illustrates this attitude. One day while he was working as a resident in a large hospital, an elderly lady in a comatose condition was carried into the emergency room, where he was on duty. She had not been in an accident but was dying of a fatal illness. As he began to examine the lady, a senior doctor appeared, took one look at her, and ordered my friend to have her brought quickly into intensive care. "Wait," my friend pleaded. "We both know she's dying. Let me sit with her, hold her hand, and try to comfort her until she dies, which can't be more than an hour or two." Fixing my friend with a withering look, the senior doctor rebuked him with "How can you be so cold and uncaring, Doctor?" and called for an orderly to take the woman to intensive care. "I thought he was uncompassionate," commented my friend, "and he thought I was. How perceptions differ!"

But there is also the good news. The growing hospice movement, dedicated to more personal and sympathetic care of the terminally ill, and the living will movement are hopeful signs of changing attitudes toward death and the dying. Furthermore, changes in the curricula of a number of medical schools in the United States and abroad are focusing not only on treating the dying but on giving them emotional support as well. While the revalidation[8] of the doctrines of karma (the law of cause and effect and of willed action and its fruits on a moral plane) and palingenesis (successive rebirths) have made great strides in the West in recent years, a "lyrical acceptance" by a science-oriented public still seems distant. Nonetheless, many people, convinced that these teachings have substance and meaning and fulfill the yearnings of the heart, have searched among writings of East and West for further knowledge of the revolving phases of life and death. Happily, these individuals have begun to breach the barriers, the intellectual taboos, constructed by the scientific-minded, many of whom find the notion of "rebecoming" unbelievable because it is resistant to proof.

Perhaps the main obstacle to an even wider acceptance of the doctrine of life after death is the difference in philosophical outlook between the cultures of the East and West. "The attitude of Western philosophy is . . . what is *not proved* is to be treated as false," writes Professor P. J. Saher. "The attitude of Eastern philosophy is . . . what is *not proved* may be accepted as true until proved to be false."[9] And yet abundant evidence exists to convince any reasonable mind of the validity of rebirth—a doctrine that needs to be distinguished from both reincarnation and the notion of an afterlife. (See "Rebirth" section, and other passages in this book quoting the psychiatrist Carl Jung, Leo Tolstoy, and other distinguished persons who have written of their past-life experiences.)

Unlike the linear theology of the West, Buddhism, for example, teaches that life and death present the same cyclic continuity observed in all aspects of nature.[10] Buddhism says that the life and death of animate matter is, in each instance, merely the seen aspect of an unending stream of cause and effect which, though appearing to emerge from and sink into the earth at two points, nonetheless has an unseen subterranean existence and appears at other places, in other times, and in other shapes.

The assertion that nothing precedes birth or follows death is largely taken for granted by those who have a here-and-now approach to life. But however widely believed, it is still absurd from an Eastern viewpoint. Such a contention rests on the blind assumption—in its own way an act of faith—that life, of all things in the universe, operates in a vacuum. It asks us to believe that this one phenomenon, the invigoration of supposedly inert matter, springs out of nowhere and just as miraculously disappears without a trace. Most people who hold such views consider themselves "rational," and yet in this question of life and death they deny the principle of the conservation of matter and energy, one of the essential laws of physics, as it applies to the psychic energy of consciousness.

Any explication of the doctrine of karma that ignored rebirth would be as imperfect as a scissors with one blade. Accordingly, much new material, largely from Western sources, on both these subjects has been included in this volume to aid the reader in understanding these subtle yet vital doctrines.

The "Dying" section, besides providing crucial spiritual guidance to the dying and the family, includes detailed instructions on how to conduct meaningful funeral and memorial services and how to relieve the sorrow of grieving relatives during the mourning period. Moreover, I have tried to put into a wider perspective what may be called the practice of daily dying and I have also provided simple exercises that facilitate the attainment of this highly desirable state. These day-to-day deaths—total immersion to the point of self-transcendence—can through training be perfected and turned into genuine religious experiences. Without the submersion of ego, however, such dyings cannot take place. And so I have found it desirable to deal at length with the nature and source of ego and its role in death and dying; for ultimately a serene or fearful death, like a joyous or painful life, is not unrelated to the subordination or dominance of the ego-I. In the "Dying" section I have also discussed suicide and euthanasia—two subjects which are increasingly claiming the attention of sociologists, psychologists, and religious leaders, given the spectacular rise in self-inflicted death among the elderly as well as the young.

Another subject examined in some detail is the fear of death —a fear that especially haunts the young, many of whom have come to believe that they may not live out their lives in full in our age of potential nuclear holocaust, mass executions and imprisonments, wars of annihilation, rebellions, and worldwide terrorism.

Closely allied to daily dyings are the meditations on death— exercises to enable the reader to reflect on the omnipresence of the twin phenomena of birth and death.

Also included are five brief inspirational biographies of people who have faced death uncringingly, even with sublime indifference.

In the Supplements I have provided information on living wills

and the growing hospice movement, do's and don'ts for consoling
the bereaved, a checklist of what to do upon someone's death,
and instructions on the basics of meditation.

Unlike *The Wheel of Death* (the ancestor of the present volume),
which relied mainly on Buddhist and Hindu sources, this volume
is more broadly based. My research assistant and I have combed
Eastern and Western religious literature, as well as the philosophic, scientific, and humanistic traditions, for writings on
death and dying that have the unmistakable ring of truth, and
these have been interwoven with insights growing out of my own
religious experiences. Instead of describing, this material aims
at *exemplifying* the perennial teachings of the masters. It also
encourages the reader to think about death in terms of his own
departure and not in the abstract as the fate of the human race.

Although this book has been divided into four main sections—
namely, Death, Dying, Karma, and Rebirth—in reality the life
force cannot be divided into categories. These convenient yet
artificial divisions really represent movements or expressions of
the one nameless "It"; each is part of a larger whole and at the
same time the whole itself. When life is truly lived and not
conceptualized, such mental constructs as life, death, rebirth
evaporate.

The basic aim of this volume can be summed up in these words:
to help the reader learn to live fully with life at every moment
and die serenely with death. Such an affirmative rapport with
life and death is possible, however, only if one has discerned that
death closes the circle on life just as life prepares the way for
death, and that death therefore has a validity and a raison d'être
of its own. Such acceptance, moreover, makes it possible to face
death courageously and to wisely take from it what it has to offer:
a means to replace a worn-out, pain-racked body with a new one
and, foremost, a once-in-a lifetime chance to awaken to the true
nature of existence. No wonder Socrates inveighed against the
notion that death is the greatest of all evils, and Pliny Earle
(1809–92) poeticized:

> What is it, then, to die,
> That it should be essential to our happiness?
> It is to throw off all things worldly,

> All the dross that man is heir to,
> And go forth again clad in the vestment of
>   immortal life . . .[11]

Beings come and beings go, but the flame of life, the generating impulse animating all existences and underlying the whole of creation, neither comes nor goes; it burns eternally, with no beginning, with no end. Aglow with this enlightened awareness, one can die not like someone being dragged kicking and screaming to the scaffold, but like one about to embark on an enticing adventure. Such an exemplary death, let me emphasize, is causally related to a life artfully lived, a life dedicated to the fulfillment of one's physical, mental, moral, and spiritual potential.

The sacred texts and modern commentaries in this book, if carefully studied, can help the dying person achieve an easy death and even liberate him from painful bondage to birth and death. And they can hearten the living by making them realize that death, like life, is also transitory.

At a workshop on death and dying I gave several years ago, a management consultant, a dance instructor, several psychotherapists and homemakers, a sociologist, a nurse, a psychologist, and two computer programmers were active participants. Much of the format of *The Wheel of Life and Death* involves the dialogue between these workshop participants and me. The material for this book is drawn not only from this workshop but from my lectures through the years at colleges and universities, as well as from workshops at the Zen Center of Rochester, growth centers, encounter groups, and the like. Also included are reconstructions of free-wheeling conversations—the substance of which I later recorded in shorthand—following an evening lecture at a college or university. In addition, throughout I have added passages from the writings of well-known authors that seemed pertinent to the subject matter.

A NOTE ON THE DRAWINGS

Wheel: an elemental device that evolved from the circle. The circle symbolizes, among other things, oneness, the indivisibility of all life. Nothing can be added to or subtracted from a circle: it is perfect in itself. In the same way, man in his Essential-nature is whole and complete.

The wheel is one of the principal symbols of Buddhism. The eight-spoked wheel is emblematic of the Noble Eightfold Path leading to enlightenment.

Skull rosary: the skull, which survives the disintegration of the flesh and sinews, symbolizes both the impermanence of the body and the indestructibility of Buddha-nature.

Flame passing from lamp to candle: indicates that dying and death lead to rebirth.

Endless knot: stands for the infinite network of interrelationships between all forms of life.

Phoenix: a mythical bird of great beauty which lived for five hundred years in the desert. It immolated itself on a funeral pyre and then rose from its own ashes in the freshness of youth, living another cycle of years; it represents death and regeneration.

One: DEATH

So live that when thy summons comes
To join the innumerable caravan
Which moves to that mysterious realm
Where each shall take his chamber
In the silent halls of death
Thou go not like the quarry slave at night
Scourged to his dungeon
But sustained and soothed by an unfaltering trust
Approach thy grave like one
Who wraps the drapery of his couch about him
And lies down to pleasant dreams.

—WILLIAM CULLEN BRYANT

1. EXISTENTIAL ASPECTS OF DEATH

WHAT IS LIFE, WHAT IS DEATH?

What is life? What is death? To the casual observer the answers are obvious: When the heart beats, the blood circulates, the lungs breathe, the brain perceives—that is life. When one eats and sleeps, works, makes love, feels pain and joy, one is alive.

Death, of course, is that condition in which there is a permanent cessation of all the vital functions: respiration ceases, the heart stops beating, the brain no longer reacts to stimuli, and the vital tissues have degenerated beyond any function—in short, one can no longer experience, think, or feel. With death one becomes immobile, a corpse: if buried, fit only for worms to feed on; if cremated, a puff of smoke, then ashes. Nothing before birth, nothing after death.

But is such a view of the human condition the only reality? The two selections that follow—and my comments on them—present a wholly different scenario of human destiny: physical birth is not a beginning, physical death is not an end.

The first selection is from the book *The Romeo Error*, subtitled *A Matter of Life and Death*, by the biologist Lyall Watson. The book represents fifteen years of research and embodies his own theories and experiences. In it he discusses what is known about the biology of life, and therefore of death. Born and raised in South Africa, Dr. Watson was educated there and in Britain, taking his Ph.D. degree in biology at the University of London in 1963. He is the author of a number of books, among them *Supernature*, *The Living World of Animals*, *Gifts of Unknown Things*, and *Lifetides*.

What distinguishes Dr. Watson from many other scientists is his vision that scientific investigation and mystic revelation can be reconciled. In the introduction to *The Romeo Error* he writes that he carries the heavy handicap of ten years' training in the sciences, and that he feels compelled to search for some way of reconciling scientific investigation and mystic revelation. He states that he is beginning to appreciate that there are limits to the scientific method, and that it is impossible to observe some things without substantially changing them in the process. "I find that most of the time my line of investigation brings me in the end directly to the place where my mystic friends have been operating all along . . ."

THE CONFUSION OF LIFE WITH DEATH—THE ROMEO ERROR

The book's title comes from Shakespeare's play *Romeo and Juliet*:

> Nurse: She's dead, deceas'd, she's dead!
> Lady Capulet: She's dead, she's dead, she's dead!
> Capulet: Her blood is settled and her joints are stiff;
>   Life and these lips have long been separated.

Romeo took their word, and his life. . . but he was wrong.[1]

Or is the error ours? Lyall Watson thinks it is, and he describes our traditional view of death as an error of perception, like Romeo's tragic misunderstanding of Juliet's apparent lifelessness. Commenting on the "death" of Juliet and the actual death of Romeo, Watson writes:

> When Romeo found Juliet pale and lifeless in the tomb and assumed she was dead, she *was* dead. The fact that she later recovered and became more lifelike does not cancel out her death. When Juliet found Romeo lying lifeless with poison in his hand, he too was dead and his death would remain valid even if some

quick-witted physician had rushed in from the wings and pumped out his stomach in the nick of time . . .

The Romeo Error is a confusion of life with death and is made so often simply because there is no absolute difference between the two. They are manifestations of the same biological process and differ only in degree.[2]

LIFE AND DEATH INDISTINGUISHABLE

What we call death, then, is merely a change of state, often temporary and "sometimes 'curable.' " "That death on its own has no clinical, logical, or biological reality and exists only as a construct with validity in interpersonal relationships," as Watson writes. The evidence of biology, psychology, and anthropology points toward the conclusion that life and death exist alongside each other in a constantly changing dynamic relationship. Death, then, does not extinguish the flame of life; it merely changes its form and direction. Put another way, death is not a period but a comma in the story of life, as the writer Vern McLellan noted.

Poets, too, with immaculate perception, have seen into the indivisibility of life and death. Samuel Butler (1835–1902) wrote:

> The dead are often just as living to us
>   as the living are,
> Only we cannot get them to believe it . . .
> To be dead is to be unable to understand
>   that one is alive.

The second writing is a koan, a spiritual problem growing out of the words and actions of the Zen masters. Like every koan, it points to the nondual One-mind common to all existence. It appears in a book of koans called *The Blue Rock Record*, a treasure-house of the sayings and doings of some of the wisest of the Zen masters of old. In Zen centers and temples this koan is often assigned to students tormented by the dilemma of life and death. If grappled with, the koan can help dispel this dilemma by revealing that these are not demarcated conditions existing independent of each other but are merely two facets of one natural process, both present at any given moment.

THE KOAN "ALIVE OR DEAD?"

One day Zen master Dogo,[3] accompanied by his disciple, went to offer his condolences to a bereaved family in the neighborhood of his temple. Tapping the coffin, the disciple said to his teacher, "Alive or dead?"

Master: "I won't say alive, I won't say dead."

Disciple: "Why won't you say?"

Master: "I won't say. I won't say."

On the way back to the temple the following exchange took place:

Disciple: "Teacher, if you don't tell me I'll hit you."

Master: "Strike me if you wish, but I won't say."

Whereupon the student struck his teacher.

Later, after Dogo had passed away, the student went to Sekiso, Dogo's successor, and recounted the whole episode.

Sekiso said, "I won't say alive and I won't say dead."

Upon these words the disciple had a deep realization of the meaning of birth and death.

BUT ISN'T A CORPSE DEAD?

PSYCHOLOGIST: I would like to know why the student asks, "Is he alive or is he dead?" Isn't it obvious that the person in the coffin is dead?

To understand the deeper implications of the question, we need to know what lies behind it. Here is an individual so anguished that he ignores the mourners and doesn't even wait until he and his teacher have returned to the temple, but presses the master for a clear answer. The question of life and death obviously weighs heavily on him. He assumes, of course, that the body in front of him is clinically dead, but since he also believes that we are more than our senses and intellect, he asks, in effect, "Does the life force continue beyond death?"

Sooner or later, all of us, if we are to have true contentment, must face and resolve the same perplexity. Not philosophically but existentially: "Why am *I* on this earth? Where did *I* come from? When I physically pass away, what happens to the energy force I call 'myself'? Do I face total extinction or will I survive in some form or other? Is there a soul substance, independent of my body, that will migrate and reembody itself in a form commensurate with my thoughts and deeds in this life? Or is there perhaps some kind of afterlife, either material or bodyless, in an unknown realm? In short, do I go into nonbeing or a new being?" The query "Is he alive or is he dead?" is really a metaphor for all these questions.

Be aware that several years elapsed between the time the first teacher died and the time the student went to the second master, a period during which he unceasingly meditated and reflected on this gnawing problem. To what end? To free himself of the binding chain of birth and death, for no loftier goal or greater need exists for a human being. To be free from life and death is to be free from the dualistic *restrictions* of life and death. That is, one now lives with absolute freedom because life and death are at once no-life and no-death.[4]

Dogo replies, "I won't say alive and I won't say dead." What else *can* he say? He knows that what we call birth is merely the reverse side of death, as with a door called Entrance from the outside and Exit from the inside. He knows that life and death are mutually dependent, and that you can't desire one without inviting the other. Clutching at life, then, means denying the reality of death.

Consider a burning candle: its life is also its death; death and life constantly interact. Just as one cannot experience true joy without having suffered great pain, so life is impossible without death, for they are a single process. Death is life in another form.

To live with life *just as it is* and to die with death *just as it is* —how many can do this? Very few, we may infer, if the reasons given by Freud in an essay titled "Our Relation to Death," which he wrote in 1915, are valid.

This relation [to death] was not sincere. If one listened to us we were, of course, ready to declare that death is the necessary end of all life, that every one of us owes nature his own death and must be prepared to pay this debt—in short, that death is natural, undeniable, and unavoidable. In reality, however, we behave as if it were different. We have shown the unmistakable tendency to push death aside, to eliminate it from life. We have tried to keep a deadly silence about death . . . After all, one's own death is beyond imagining . . . At bottom no one believes in his own death. Or, and this is the same: in his unconscious every one of us is convinced of his immortality . . .

More recently Dr. Jack B. Weissman, an infectious disease specialist, is quoted in *The New York Times* to this effect:

In this country, death is such a dirty word. We all act like we're going to live forever. We don't discuss death or our desires in the event of serious illness. Yet there's one constant of life for all of us: statistically, the death rate is one per person. What strikes me about our system is that more people are afraid of how they are going to die than the fact that they are going to die. How did the medical profession get to where people are so afraid of us?[5]

Given the unconscious belief in our own immortality, one would expect that, as a corollary, a belief in the continuity of life would follow. But that does not often happen. And while it is true that a number of Americans believe in an afterlife—but not a rebirth—the notion that death, when it does come, will spell finish to our life is far more common. Without faith in the continuity of life, however, there is bound to be fear and distress when one faces the reality of approaching death.

To return to our discussion of the koan:

"Why won't you say? Don't be evasive, teacher. Give me a definite answer," the disciple is demanding. He is crying from the heart. Perhaps this is his first direct encounter with clinical death and he may be thinking, "I see what appears to be death, but where has the life that animated this corpse gone?"

"I won't say! I won't say!" the master persists. "Are you deaf? Can't you hear what I'm telling you?" He too is crying from the heart because of his helplessness to say more. Not even the Buddha could put it differently. If birth is a *temporary* point between what precedes and what follows, and so is death, then at every second there is life, and at every second, death. Which condition is life, which death?

Unable to contain himself any longer, the disciple lashes out at his teacher. "If you don't tell me I'll hit you!" The violence of his words is the measure of his desperation.

Master: "Strike me if you wish, but I won't say. Whether I'm beaten or not, there's no other way to put it."

Later, after Dogo had passed away, the student went to his successor and told him everything that had happened. And once again he hears the old refrain: "I won't say alive and I won't say dead." With that he awakens as if from a deep sleep.

COMPUTER PROGRAMMER: Why did this disciple have an awakening with the second master when he didn't with Dogo? The second master repeated exactly the same words.

The words were the same, but what lay behind them—the spirit—was newly alive and vigorous. Moreover, having continuously chewed on the bitter bone of "What is life? What is death?" after the master's passing, the disciple when he confronts the second master is a totally different person. Now he is in a state of "no-mindness,"[6] totally absorbed to the point of self-forgetfulness and needing only the master's rapierlike thrust to awaken him to the real meaning of birth and death.

THERE IS NO DEATH

PSYCHOTHERAPIST: May I say something? I have heard you say that Zen rejects the notion of absolute death. Recently I went to my grandmother's funeral and took a good look at her in her coffin. She was stiff as a board. Where was the life in her? Doesn't Zen repudiate the idea of a body separate from a soul that reincarnates?

Yes, it does.

PSYCHOTHERAPIST: So who was lying in the coffin? Was it any more than a corpse?

DANCE INSTRUCTOR: I went to my grandmother's funeral, too. Frankly, I thought she was radiating more energy lying in her coffin than all the dead people staring at her![7]

(Laughing) Alive or dead, grandmothers are remarkable people, aren't they?

THE MASTERS' REACTIONS TO DEATH

The Zen masters saw life and death as an unbroken continuum, the swinging of an eternal pendulum. Many of them met "the inevitable hour" with a smile and even laughter, often choosing to die in the lotus meditative posture ("death is the supreme liberation") or even while standing. For they saw life steadily and whole; they were unfettered by overinvolvement with any of its parts, death included. It could be said that they had already transcended the self that clings to life. And just as the Zen masters in their moment-to-moment movements are nonverbally teaching their followers how to live, so in their last hours they are teaching them how to die. Thus if they utter any last words, they are not striving for the classy exit line or seeking to express the compacted significance of their life, but are giving their students one last instruction.

ZEN MASTER TAKKAN

When Zen master Takkan (1573–1645) was dying, his disciples asked him to write a death verse.[8] He demurred at first, saying, "I have no last words." They pleaded with him, so he took up a brush, wrote the character for "dream," and passed away. With this word Takkan summed up ultimate reality, or absolute Truth, beyond all logic and reason. To realize his meaning of dream is to realize that oneself and everything else are dreamlike, that nothing in the universe is not a dream. Which is to say that all phenomena in the universe are evanescent, illusory, insubstantial. Our bodies are phantomlike, images reflected in the water. Or as a philosopher wrote, "Waking life is a dream controlled."[9]

Takkan often spoke of "Dream Zen." In one of his *One Hundred Dream Poems* he wrote that "right is a dream; wrong too is a dream." So, too, for him life is a dream and death is also a dream. Heaven and earth and all things under the sun are a dream. This is the same as saying there is no dream at all.

For Ikkyū Sōjun, a Zen master of fifteenth-century Japan, life and death were also dreams, as witness this verse of his:

> Born like a dream
> In this dream of a world
> How easy in mind I am,
> I who will fade away
> Like the morning dew.
>
> One prays for the life of tomorrow
> Ephemeral life though it be.
> This is the habit of mind
> That passed away yesterday.
>
> The Original-nature
> Means non-birth, non-distinction.
> Then know that illusion
> Is birth, death, rebirth.[10]

The perception of life as a dream is by no means confined to the Zen masters. Leo Tolstoy (1828–1910), the Russian novelist and social philosopher, has much to say about dreams and past lives in a letter published two years before his death:

> Now our whole life, from birth unto death, with all its dreams, is it not in its turn also a dream, which we take as the real life, the reality of which we do not doubt only because we do not know of the other more real life? . . . The dreams of our present life are the environment in which we work out the impressions, thoughts, feelings of a former life . . . As we live through thousands of dreams in our present life, so is our present life only one of many thousands of such lives which we enter from the other, more real life . . . and then return after death. Our life is but one of the dreams of that more real life, and so it is endlessly, until the very last one, the very real life—the life of God . . . I wish you would

understand me; I am not playing, not inventing this: I believe in it, I see it without doubt.[11]

ZEN MASTER TAJI

As Zen master Taji (1889–1953) approached death, his senior disciples assembled at his bedside. One of them, remembering the master was fond of a certain kind of cake, had spent half a day searching the pastry shops of Tokyo for this confection, which he now presented to him. With a wan smile the dying master accepted a piece of the cake and slowly began munching it. As he grew weaker, his disciples inquired whether he had any final words for them.

"Yes," the master replied.

The disciples leaned forward eagerly so as not to miss a word. "Please tell us!"

"My, but this cake is delicious!" And with that he slipped away.[12]

ZEN MASTER TUNG-SHAN LIANG-CHIEH

When Zen master Tung-shan Liang-chieh, (807–69) the first patriarch of the Sōtō Zen sect in China, was dying, a monk said to him, "Master, your four elements[13] are out of harmony, but is there anyone who is never ill?"

"There is," replied Tung-shan.

"Does that one look at you?" asked the monk.

"It is my function to look at him," answered Tung-shan.

"How about when you yourself look at him?" asked the monk.

"At that moment I see no illness," replied Tung-shan. So saying, he passed away.

The "one," of course, is our Essential-nature personified. It is not subject to birth or death. It is neither being nor nothingness, neither emptiness nor form-and-color. Nor is it something that feels pain or joy. It is beyond all sickness.

ZEN MASTER HUI-NENG

On the eighth of July, Zen master Hui-neng (638–713), the sixth Chinese patriarch of Zen, announced to his monks, "Gather around me. I have decided to leave this world in the eighth month."

When the monks heard this, many of them wept openly.

"For whom are you crying?" the master asked. "Are you worrying about me because you think I don't know where I'm going? If I didn't know, I wouldn't be able to leave you this way. What you are really crying about is that *you* don't know where I'm going. If you actually knew, you couldn't possibly cry, because True-nature is without birth or death, without going or coming . . ."[14]

How is it that the masters can regard death so lightly? Only because they know that whether we are killed or die naturally, death has no more substantiality than the antics of puppets in a film. Or that it is no more real than the cutting of air with a knife, or the bursting of bubbles, which reappear no matter how often they are broken.[15] Moreover, the masters know they will be reborn through affinity with a father and a mother when their karma relations so impel them.

MANAGEMENT CONSULTANT: If there is no notion of death in Zen, why do even Zen masters cry when somebody close to them dies? I read about a Zen master who conducted a funeral for one of his disciples and wept the whole time. After the service was over, a younger disciple said, "Master, I was amazed to see you crying. I expected a Zen master to be beyond such a display of emotion."

The master replied, "If I don't cry when a gifted disciple of mine dies at an early age, when will I?"

My question is, if there is no death, and rebirth is sure to follow, why did the master cry?

Here is your answer from a man mourning the death of his wife:

> I know that all things are impermanent,
> That everything must pass,
> And yet . . . and yet . . .

Some masters have cried, others have laughed, and still others have done neither. If one has an urge to cry, one cries. There is no prescribed way to respond to what we miscall death; attitudes vary from culture to culture and also from one century to another.[16] The following stories, and my comments on them, further illustrate the diversity of reactions of enlightened beings to the death of those close to them.

CHUANG-TZU

Chuang-tzu, the Chinese Taoist sage of the fourth century B.C., was visited after the death of his wife by his friend Hui-tzu, who came to express his condolences. The latter arrived to find the master sitting on the ground with his legs spread wide apart. The widower was singing away and whacking out a tune on the back of a wooden bowl. "You've lived all these years with your loving wife and watched your eldest boy grow to manhood. For you not to shed a tear over her remains," exclaimed Hui-tzu, "would have been bad enough. But singing and drumming away on a bowl— this is just too much!"

"Not so," the master replied. "I am a normal man and grieved when she died. But then I remembered that she had existed before this birth. At that time she was without a body. Eventually, matter was added to that spirit and, taking form, she was born. It is clear to me that the same process of change which brought my wife to birth eventually brought her to death, in a way as natural as the progression of the seasons. Winter follows autumn. Summer follows spring. To wail and groan while my wife is sleeping peacefully in the great chamber between heaven and earth would be to deny these natural laws, of which I cannot claim ignorance. So I refrain."[17]

SATSUJO

When Satsujo, a deeply enlightened woman, lost her granddaughter, she could not contain her grief. An old man from the neighborhood came and admonished her, "Why are you wailing so much? If people hear this they'll all say, 'Why does the old lady who was enlightened under the famous Zen master Hakuin mourn her granddaughter so much?' You ought to lighten up a bit." Satsujo glared at her neighbor and scolded him, "You bald-headed idiot, what do you know? My tears and weeping are better for my granddaughter than incense, flowers, and lamps!"[18]

DANCE INSTRUCTOR: What does the grandmother mean when she says that her tears and wailing are better for her granddaughter than incense and flowers?

Incense and flowers are, after all, *symbolic* offerings to the memory of her granddaughter. They are outward forms for her inward grief. Like Hamlet, who is taxed by his mother for his "inky suits of woe" upon his father's death, Satsujo could exclaim:

> But I have that within that passeth show;
> These but the trappings and the suits of woe.[19]

DANCE INSTRUCTOR: But what's the point of any kind of offering?

Offerings are a way of relating concretely to the dead through objects. But Satsujo, as a deeply enlightened woman who has seen into the nonduality of life and death, doesn't need to enlist such aids to reach her granddaughter.

DANCE INSTRUCTOR: If the grandmother had said her crying made her feel better, this I could accept. But I still don't see in what way it was better for her granddaughter.

How could it *not* be better for her granddaughter?

DANCE INSTRUCTOR: But you're still not explaining how it is better for the granddaughter.

Some things can't be explained; they need to be intuitively grasped. Let me just say this: Satsujo sees her granddaughter not as a spiritless bag of bones, but as a living being. You might ask, "Why, then, is she crying?" Her tears, which express her deep love for her granddaughter, have the power to bridge the land of the living and the land of the dead. But I'm trying to explain too much! There's an old saying, "The more I speak the less I say," so I'd better stop here.

SOCIOLOGIST: At the risk of being called a bald-headed idiot, I, too, can't help but wonder why an enlightened person would carry on so emotionally.

Being enlightened doesn't mean you have no feelings, that you are cold and unemotional like Mr. Spock of "Star Trek." On the contrary, it means that you are able to express your feelings freely and spontaneously. This point is illustrated by an old Zen story. A young novice became disenchanted with Zen when he heard his revered master scream in pain as he was being murdered by thieves. The young man contemplated leaving Zen training, feeling that if the old master screamed in the face of death, Zen itself must be a fraud. However, before he was able to leave, another teacher taught him something of what Zen is all about and removed his misconceptions.

"Fool!" exclaimed the teacher. "The object of Zen is not to kill all feelings and become numb to pain and fear.[20] The object of Zen is to free oneself to scream loudly and fully when it is time to scream."[21]

ZEN MASTER SOYEN SHAKU

Another story concerns a well-known Zen master of recent times, Soyen Shaku (1859–1919), who was the abbot of a large Zen monastery in Kamakura, Japan.[22] It was the abbot's custom to take a walk through the town early each morning with his attendant. On one such occasion he heard wailing coming from a house. Going inside to investigate, the abbot inquired, "Why is everyone crying?" He was told, "We are mourning the death of our child." Immediately the abbot took a seat among the family and began loudly weeping and wailing with them. On the way back to the temple the attendant asked the master, "Do you know those people?" "No," replied the abbot. "Then why did you cry with them?" "To share their sorrow," responded the abbot.

To many readers this story may seem bizarre. Yet a true Zen

master is nothing if not compassionate. To rejoice with those who rejoice and to cry with those who sorrow would be most natural for such a person even if the grieving family were total strangers to him.

ZEN MASTER NAN-CHUAN

A reaction to death with a twist involves Zen master Nan-chuan. When he died, one of his senior disciples stood in front of the master's coffin and gave a loud laugh. A priest, who was also a student of the late master, reproached him, saying, "Wasn't he your teacher? Why do you laugh when you should be grieving for him?"

The disciple replied, "If you can say an appropriate word that fulfills the Buddha's teaching, I will grieve." The priest stood mute. Deploring this, the disciple said, "Alas, our teacher has truly gone," and he wept loudly. The significance of this last statement is crucial to understanding the whole dialogue.

WHAT IS AN "APPROPRIATE WORD"?

MANAGEMENT CONSULTANT: What is an "appropriate word" in this situation and why couldn't the priest say it? Secondly, why did the disciple weep? Was it because the priest couldn't give the proper word? Or was it because he was sorry about his laughing and decided that crying was more appropriate?

An appropriate word is any live, spontaneous word or action charged with the force of one's whole being. The admired live word is the gut word, concrete and vibrant with feeling. The dead word is the explanatory word, dry and lifeless, issuing from the head. The first unifies, the second separates. Now, the important thing is not to wobble but to respond at once. The same idea is expressed in the folk saying "He who hesitates is lost."

The senior disciple wants to test the priest, so he deliberately laughs in front of the master's coffin to see what kind of response it will evoke. The latter fails the test by scolding the disciple for laughing instead of weeping. Whereupon the disciple baits another "trap" with the words "If you can say an appropriate word I will grieve." Unable to respond, the priest stands mute. There is a place for silence, of course, but this isn't it.

Advanced Zen disciples, to test one another's insight and awareness and express their own in all sorts of situations, constantly engage in what might be called "spiritual sparring." Obviously this priest was no match for the senior disciple, who, by the way, was a high government official and a longtime personal friend of the master.

[To the management consultant] Suppose you had been there and had been asked for a proper word. How would you have responded?

MANAGEMENT CONSULTANT: I guess I would have been just as dumb as the priest. Roshi, what would you have done if you had been there?

I don't know. I might have laughed too, or else cried, or I might have put my hands palm to palm and bowed down reverently before the master in the coffin. The idea is not to waver or vacillate but to respond unhesitatingly, wholeheartedly—yet in a manner appropriate to the situation. Also vital is strong spirit behind the words. Now savor the last, crucial line of the dialogue: "Deploring this, the disciple said, 'Alas, our teacher has truly gone,' and he wept loudly." What is he conveying by this seeming about-face? Something like "What a pity that the seeds of the Buddha's teaching transmitted by the master fell on the parched landscape of the priest's mind." That's why the disciple weeps at the end, and not because he's lamenting the master's passing, for he knows that in an absolute sense the master hasn't gone anywhere.

If you oppose life with death or death with life, you set up a duality that doesn't exist except as a mental construct. That's why a master could say, "In me there's no life or death." A student once came to see Engen, a well-known Zen adept, and told him, "I have come to you so I can train myself to solve the question of birth and death." The master drove him away, saying, "At Engen's place there is no such thing as birth and death."[23]

Do you see why the master dismissed him? What we call birth is one aspect, death another. From the perspective of original Self, however, nothing is born, nothing passes away. So an ancient sage wrote: "There is no death of anyone save only in appearance, even as there is no birth except in seeming. The change from being to becoming seems to be birth, and the change from becoming to being seems to be death; but in reality no one is ever born, nor does one ever die."[24]

"Birth" and "death," then, are simply convenient labels to which we cling because of our dualistically ensnared minds. Ultimately there is nothing but the nameless "It."

DANCE INSTRUCTOR: *I'm totally confused. Can't we believe the evidence of our senses at all?*

We are talking about an area beyond the senses and yet not apart from them—an area in which we also exist, dead or alive.

DANCE INSTRUCTOR: *You've lost me completely!*

This is not easy to understand. You must see right on the spot. As soon as you begin to ponder and reflect, you miss it. You know the old proverb "Seeing is believing?" Well, a wiser observer turned it around this way: "I'll see it when I believe it."

WHAT IS "BIRTH AND DEATH"?

DANCE INSTRUCTOR: *I'd like to ask a question on another subject. What exactly is meant by "birth and death" in this context?*

In Sanskrit it is called *saṃsāra:* the mundane phenomenal world of toil and struggle; of impermanence; of the transformation which all phenomena, including our thoughts and feelings, are ceaselessly undergoing in accordance with the law of causation. Birth and death can be compared to the waves on the ocean. The rise of a wave is one birth; the fall, one death. The size of each is conditioned in part by the force of the previous one, the force itself being generated by air currents, ground swells, rain, the moon, and perhaps other elements. This process infinitely repeated is birth-death-rebirth—the wheel of existence. The other side is that in our *Essential*-nature there is no coming or going, no birth, no change, no death. The problem, then, is how to transcend birth and death and find the place where there is no birth and no death. According to Zen master Dōgen, that place is the very realm of birth and death.

MOMENTARY BIRTH AND DEATH

We can speak of two kinds of birth and death: momentary and "regular." Momentary birth and death—that is, momentary creation and destruction—takes place every millionth of a second, or at some such phenomenal speed, as old cells die and new ones come into being. So we can say that a new self is constantly being born, and that a man of sixty is not the same as, yet not different from, the person he was at thirty or at ten. Living is thus dying, and dying living. In fact, with every inhalation we are being reborn and with each exhalation we are dying.

You can compare birth to the appearance of clouds in the sky, and death to their breaking up and scattering in all directions. Although a cloudy and a clear sky can be described as different conditions, the sky is unaffected. Or, to change the metaphor, our True-essence is like a mirror, which reflects different phenomena. These phenomena have a limited existence in time and space and in that sense are ultimately unreal. But the mirror itself is permanent and real—only in terms of this simile, of course—since it projects varying images without being marked by them. Similarly, True-mind embraces all phenomena without being affected by them.

PSYCHOTHERAPIST: But you can't deny that death does exist as an observable experience, can you?

From an objective, relative point of view, yes, we can speak of the cessation of bodily functions and the decay of the physical organs. From the absolute standpoint of true Self, no.

By training ourselves to live fully with life and to die wholly with death at *every* moment, we are able to transcend both, going beyond even the dualistic distinctions of transcendence and non-transcendence, subjective and objective. (See "Daily Dying.") Our life, as someone said, is not a mystery to be solved but a reality to be lived.

THE IDENTITY OF CONTRARIES

PSYCHOTHERAPIST: Are you saying that life and death exist objectively but not subjectively? I don't understand.

Tell me: Upon death, what happens to the force, the energy, that created and sustained the physical organs and bodily functions? Does this energy have an objective aspect? What can we *understand* about that realm where consciousness has not yet divided itself into subject and object? Nothing at all. The world we see is a reconstruction made by the limited instruments of our intellect and five senses. It follows, then, that whatever you understand intellectually is only an *aspect* of truth. What is beyond understanding—uncognizable—is the *whole* truth. From the absolute standpoint of Original-nature, then, the terms "subjective" and "objective" have no validity. That is why we can say that life is no-life and death no-death. And that is why I say your grandmother is neither dead nor alive.

PSYCHOTHERAPIST: Then what is *she?*

I won't say. I won't say.
(Laughter)
Actually, we can't say whether anything exists or doesn't exist, simply because nothing has an enduring life of its own; all forms are empty of a self-substance, and nothing is the same from moment to moment. Everything is in flux, constantly forming, dependent upon causes and conditions, disintegrating, and re-forming again. It's like a film. We get the impression that people are moving or acting in it, but it's all an illusion. The actions are real enough in terms of the film—they're not a hallucination—but otherwise they are unreal.

Speaking of the identity of contraries, the sage Chuang-tzu says, "The sage knows nothing of the distinction between subjective and objective. From the standpoint of the Way, all things are One. People guided by the criteria of their own mind see only the contradiction, the manifoldness, the difference; the sage sees the many disappearing in the One . . ."[25]

That this notion of the identity of contraries is not simply a product of the oriental mind can be seen in these words of the Greek philosopher Heraclitus: "Listen, not to me but to reason, and confess the true wisdom that 'All things are One, All is One,' the divided and undivided, the begotten and the unbegotten, the mortal and the immortal, reason and eternity, father and son, God and justice . . . The beginning and the end are one. Life and death, sleeping and waking, youth and age are identical." By seeing inaction in action and action in inaction, immobility in motion and motion in immobility, and the like, we arrive at the true state of things, their Thusness.

PSYCHOTHERAPIST: If life and death are identical, why didn't any of us detect any signs of life in my grandmother's body? And what about the doctor who pronounced her dead? He was at the funeral, too.

The doctor was interested in her body and its functions—or lack of them—merely from a clinical point of view. And so evidently were the rest of the mourners. Your intuitive perceptions were not keen enough to go beyond physical appearances.

PSYCHOTHERAPIST: I have one final question. Where is my grandmother right now?

Will you believe me if I tell you?

PSYCHOTHERAPIST: Why shouldn't I believe you if you give it to me straight?

She's right under your nose!

PSYCHOTHERAPIST: What do you mean?

Listen to this verse:

> Do not stand at my grave and weep;
> I am not there. I do not sleep.
> I am a thousand winds that blow.
> I am the diamond glints on snow.
> I am the sunlight on ripened grain.
> I am the gentle autumn's rain.
> When you awaken in the morning's hush,
> I am the swift uplifting rush
> Of quiet birds in circled flight.
> I am the soft stars that shine at night.
> Do not stand at my grave and cry;
> I am not there. I did not die.[26]

When Zen master Ikkyū was on his deathbed, he was asked by his followers to write a death verse. So he took up the brush and wrote:

> I shan't die,
> I shan't go anywhere,
> I'll be here.
> But don't ask me anything,
> I shan't answer.

Then he let go of the writing brush and passed on.

Upon clinical death, what happens to the life force, the energy that animated the being you called grandmother? The law of the conservation of energy says no energy is ever lost—it is only transformed. So where has that energy gone? Biologists have demonstrated that although cells die and bring about what we call the death of the individual, the atoms that make up the cells are not destroyed. They become parts of other cells, other individuals, and it is for this reason that we can truly speak of an essential kinship among all living creatures. The atoms that were part of your grandmother's biological makeup may one day nourish the roots of a tree and travel to its springtime leaves, which turn toward the sun. In Johann Gottfried von Herder's beautiful phrase, "Every creature is a numerator of the grand denominator Nature."[27] (See also "Rebirth" section.)

THE FORCE OF THE UNIVERSE

COMPUTER PROGRAMMER: But what is the basis *or propelling force behind the change from life to death and from death to life again?*

The power or force or energy of the universe animates all existences. It cannot be named, for to name it is to limit it and it is beyond all categories and limitations. But if we must give the nameless a name—and we need to if we want to speak about it—we may provisionally call it True- or Essential-nature. "It" also relates to the flow of cause and effect, that is, the generation and disintegration of phenomena according to causes and conditions. Simply put, all phenomena are transformations of True- or Essential-nature. In other words, everything by its very nature is subject to the process of infinite transformation—this is its True-nature.[28] Now, you may ask, what is True-nature grounded in? *Shunyata,* a Sanskrit word that is usually translated as "the Void," or "no-thing-ness." This *shunyata,* though, is not mere emptiness or a negative cipher. It is alive, dynamic, devoid of mass, beyond individuality or personality—the womb of all phenomena.

SPIRIT DOES NOT EXIST APART FROM FLESH

Now let me ask you a question. Does a worm have True-nature?

COMPUTER PROGRAMMER: I suppose so.

If you cut the worm in two, which half would possess the True-nature?

COMPUTER PROGRAMMER: Each, I suppose.

Are you saying that True-nature can be cut in two?

COMPUTER PROGRAMMER: I guess not.

Can you separate the worm's body from its True-nature?

COMPUTER PROGRAMMER: I don't know.

You can't. Neither can the spirit, or Essential-nature, of the psychotherapist's dead grandmother be separated from her body. An early sage sang:

> The corpse is here,
> Where is the man?
> Truly, I know
> The spirit is not in this bag of skin.

However, Ta-hui, a great Zen adept, refuted the heretical notion that spirit exists apart from flesh:

> This corpse as it is is the man [woman]
> The spirit is the bag of skin.
> The bag of skin is the spirit.

The implications of this latter are far-reaching. We cannot repudiate the material world of form in favor of an opposing world of spirit or soul—or vice versa—without setting up a duality that inherently does not exist. The basis of the material world is the spiritual, and the world of form in turn influences and is inseparable from the spiritual realm. Or to put it another way, since the spiritual is the power or force that pervades and underlies everything material, what happens in the physical world depends primarily on spirit—that is, Mind.

In his book *Modern Man in Search of a Soul,* Carl Jung confirms the identity of spirit and body:

> But if we can reconcile ourselves with the mysterious truth that spirit is the living body seen from within, and the body the outer manifestation of the living spirit—the two being really one—then we can understand why it is that the attempt to transcend the present level of consciousness must give its due to the body. We shall also see that belief in the body cannot tolerate an outlook that denies the body in the name of the spirit.[29]

We see evidence of the role of the body in the attitude of those American families who, in the Vietnam War, lost sons or brothers or husbands or fathers whose remains were never found or who in one way or another were never accounted for by the military authorities. As you know, our government has been under pressure over the years from many American families to get Vietnam to repatriate the remains of their loved ones in spite of a long lapse of time. Equally significant is an agreement signed recently by Vietnam and France in which the former agreed to exhume and repatriate the remains of French soldiers who died in Vietnam after 1939.[30] Why all this concern for remains? My perception is that, at some level of their being, the American and French families feel that the remains embody the *substance* of the missing loved ones.

SOCIOLOGIST: But couldn't this also spring from a desire to know for sure that their relatives are really dead? The uncertainty can be very disturbing. When you know *somebody is dead, you manage to reconcile yourself to it. There could also be legal problems—you know, the estate or an insurance claim could be at stake. And, of course, a lot of people want to bury their dead in the family plot or a cemetery close to home so they can visit the grave from time to time.*

There's a lot of truth in what you say, of course. I believe, though, that in many states, after five or seven years a missing person is declared legally dead, so you don't need physical evidence of death to legally establish that fact. What is involved here, I feel, is something deeper: the need for families to come to grips with unresolved emotions that have smoldered for a long time. For this purpose you need a body, or at least some portion of it. Because the destruction of the loved one took place in a remote country under chaotic wartime conditions, and with much suffering, the need to repossess the remains, and honor them in a formal ceremony becomes compelling. In reverencing the remains as relics, the family reaffirms its link with the departed and reassures its members of their love for and fidelity to the memory of the departed. The intuitions of the families must tell them that spirit cannot be abstracted from body.

Why Do We Fear Death?

HOMEMAKER: Why do we fear death?

Not all cultures fear death and therefore deny it, as ours does. Lyall Watson insists there is absolutely no evidence to suggest that fear is a natural and inevitable part of our dying behavior. "On the contrary," he writes, "in cultures where death is dealt with more openly and seen as part of the living process there is no fear of death . . ." He also says that he does not know of a single organism "that manifests a natural fear of death itself . . . When terminal patients have had enough time, or have been given enough of the right kind of help to conquer their fears and accept the inevitability of dying, they often experience feelings of peace and contentment . . ."[31]

Socrates in a striking passage implies that fear of death is *unnatural* because it is grounded in the egoistic notion that one knows what one does not know: "To fear death, gentlemen, is nothing other than to think oneself wise when one is not; for it is to think one knows what one does not know. No man knows whether death may not even turn out to be the greatest of blessings for a human being; and yet people fear it as if they knew for certain that it is the greatest of evils."[32]

Why, then, in the developed Western nations is the fear of death so widespread? What are the causes and how can they be overcome? Some have their genesis in the unprecedented violence of our time and its explosions into intermittent warfare; others can be traced to the ongoing threat of nuclear annihilation and the destruction of all life as we now know it. Generally, the fear of death can be broken down into the specific fears of pain, loneliness, abandonment, mutilation, and loss of self, however self is defined. No doubt it also has a nonrational dimension, like the fear of the dark and the fear of the unknown. But it has deep psychological roots as well. These are set forth by the French psychotherapist Ignace Lepp in his book *Death and Its Mysteries*.[33] Since his observations are perceptive, I will try to summarize them and also indicate what I believe to be the root cause of the fear of death from a Buddhist perspective.

Lepp feels that the fear of death, which he distinguishes from a paralyzing anxiety about death, is normal and actually increases our joy in living. (Lepp also distinguishes the fear of death from the fear of *dying*.) He observes that if human existence obeyed the laws of logic, we could expect to find that those who live most intensely and love life most passionately would fear death the most, and that those who find life a painful burden would welcome death. But his research shows that the opposite is usually true. He cites examples of people in France during World War II who "vegetated more than they lived"; these people were the most afraid and the first to run for the shelters during air raids.

Lepp then goes on to point out that there are human beings who aren't afraid of their own death but of the death of others, particularly those they love or depend on. Furthermore, he makes the pertinent observation that sometimes we experience an agonizing fear of another's death because we see in that person's death a harbinger or reminder of our own mortality.

An aspect of our fear of death which is relatively recent in origin, and which Lepp treats in his book, is a fear of collective death. Since the fifties, with the onset of the insane race for nuclear superiority, the fear of collective death has become pervasive. Lepp finds it psychologically significant that the fear of death by thermonuclear war or accident is greatest in those countries that have the largest number of these frightful weapons. Today, the stronger and richer a nation is, the greater is its insecurity. Lepp feels this is a partial explanation of the disarray of our time, which is expressed in crime, vandalism, and eroticism, and in the accelerated pace of life. Even modern music and dance seem to express the despair of a humanity that no longer believes in its own future.

Ultimately, Lepp argues, the neurotic fear of death is closely related to a person's sense of individuality; the more one is conscious of oneself as an individual rather than as a member of a group, the greater is the fear of death. For Lepp the principal cause of the fear of death, at least in the civilized countries of the West, seems to be the excessive individualism of modern people. In the older civilizations of the East, relatively little importance is given to individual destiny. In the prosperous countries of the West we live more exclusively for ourselves, and our sense of self-identity is more developed.

What is Lepp's prescription for overcoming the fear of death? After identifying alcohol, narcotics, and the frenzied pursuit of pleasure in today's society as so many efforts to dispel this fear, he surveys the various philosophic approaches of the West and finds them all sadly lacking. Finally he concludes, "It is my conviction that an intense love of life is the best and perhaps only effective antidote against the fear of death."[34]

With his emphasis on individuality, Lepp, I feel, hints at the cause of the dread of death without directly pinpointing its roots. This fear, to put it more precisely, seems to me to be *grounded* in a strong sense of the "I"—an attachment to a finite self—and the feeling that death may bring about its dissolution. Death is feared because it is seen as the end of our existence; it precipitates us into oblivion.

This became clear from a series of clinical interviews conducted by Charles Garfield among different American subcultures. The objective of the interviews was to find out as precisely as possible the actual extent and nature of the subjects' thoughts and emotional reactions to death. There was a clear aversion to loss-of-control experience:

> As long as I am the decision-maker, I can handle the image, but when I think of death as a "Grim Reaper" snatching me from life, or when I think of letting go and losing control, I get very upset. In fact, I have to physically shake my head very hard to get rid of the thoughts and images. It seems like, in theory, I can picture my death as a slow, controlled process, but I can't tolerate thoughts of a rapid decline into nothingness.

And there was a fear of dying:

> I'm slowly realizing as I answer these questions that I am afraid of dying. Death itself and being dead are not threatening to me at all. Why should they be? I can't experience the no-experience of death, but I can extrapolate my experiences to something like

what dying would be like for me, and that space is very threatening.

And then:

> I suppose dying terrifies me the most since it means the well-
> functioning "me" isn't operating anymore. The thought of my
> brain deteriorating in a stroke and the loss of my ability to think
> about myself and the world is the worst fate.[35]

Yet fear is not an unmitigated evil; a certain amount of it is
healthy because it may help eliminate excessive risk taking.

Let us get back to my comments about Lepp's statement that
"an intense love of life is the best and perhaps only effective
antidote against the fear of death." How, it may be asked, can
an intense love of life develop when one's "fiery energies" are
constantly focused on the assertion of the ego-I—a stance our
individualistic society actively encourages? In those cultures
which equate human perfection with the loss of ego, death is not
the tragedy it is felt to be in societies such as our own which
worship at the altar of the finite self. So long as we associate
Mind with brain and see the brain only as part of the body, we
will be terrified at the thought that one day we will disintegrate
and become a nothing—a zero.

Speaking of the fear of death, the philosopher Horace Kallen
writes, "There are persons who shape their lives by the fear of
death, and persons who shape their lives by the joy of life. The
former live dying, the latter die living. Whenever I die, I intend
to die living."[36] As a way of life, Kallen's philosophy is admirable.
But like Lepp, he doesn't tell us how our puffed-up egos, the bar
to the cultivation of that joy, can be deflated.

Understandably, Lepp, as a psychotherapist, employs the
methods of his profession in dealing with the death anxiety,
which he feels is neurotic (although the *fear* of death, he says,
is not). He goes on to say that "a neurotic fear of death
is most often the expression of a general anxiety whose real
causes are unconscious and originate with the trauma of adolescence, childhood, or birth." However, a serious illness or

the death of a loved one can cause the fear to blossom into consciousness. Coping with this neurotic fear may require isolating childhood or adolescent traumas that have crystallized into repressions, obsessions, depressions, phobias, or other psychological conflicts, all of which are a bar to a healthy, joyous rapport with life.

Moreover, straightening out a convoluted psyche can be a long and laborious process requiring many years' treatment, with results not always favorable. It can also be expensive. If the root cause of the fear or anxiety about death, namely a full-blown sense of I, is not dealt with, such apprehensions, I believe, cannot truly be dispelled. Still, if the fear of death can be saddled to an aspiration for awakening, it can spur one toward enlightenment.

The ultimate aim of the psychotherapist, presumably, is to adjust a patient to the norms of society so that he or she can function freely within them. But since those norms themselves reflect a neurotic state—one that views reality from the false standpoint of self and other instead of as a nondual whole—the patient's inner vision, even when freed of neurotic restraints, is still myopic. And so while psychologically well-adjusted individuals may want to cultivate an intense love of life, they are unable to do so for the reasons indicated; inevitably they end up chasing shadows—shadows of hope as well as of fear.

How to Dispel the Fear of Death

HOMEMAKER: So what do you do about ego to get rid of the fear of death?

We loosen the fetters of ego every time we forgo indulging our own desires but rather support the group effort, whether that group be our own family, fellow workers, friends, neighbors, or even one's country. But equally important, we must stop despising or adoring our personal self, neither retreating from life nor pushing at it. Every horizontalizing of the mast of I is a step in the direction of whittling down ego and thus the fear of death.

THE STRANGE AGONY OF SUCCESS

NURSE: I don't want to contradict you, but the successful people that I have known weren't laid back; they were people who had to push and fight to get where they are and to hold on to what they feel is theirs.

Is anything really ours? Even life itself, which we cling to so tenaciously, is not ours. If it were, we would be able to postpone or even prevent our death, wouldn't we?

The crucial question is, how happy or contented are these people you are talking about? My perception is that they lead stressful, restless lives. If their overriding ambitions do not send them to an early grave following a heart attack or a stroke, they gravitate from one ulcer specialist to another and from one psychiatrist to the next.

This is confirmed by a feature article in *The New York Times* for August 24, 1986, titled "The Strange Agony of Success," by Daniel Goleman. "Tens of thousands of young people," says the writer, "are finding that in achieving business success today, they have distorted their lives and fallen into emotional turmoil . . . Many tell their therapists that they have lost all sense of themselves, that they consider themselves frauds in their very success, and that money has become the main symbol of their human worth."

The truly contented are not self-seeking but modest and self-effacing persons who, if anything, tend to play down their accomplishments. Do you remember Socrates' famous words? "I know one thing, that I know nothing."

NURSE: Yes, and look what happened to him!

Who remembers the names of the judges who condemned him to death? Not one in a million! But nearly every educated person has been stirred by the life of Socrates and esteems him.

SOCIOLOGIST: Is any great man truly modest?

There are degrees of modesty just as there are degrees of greatness.

SHALL THE MEEK INHERIT THE EARTH?

Tell me, what do you suppose Christ meant when he said, "The meek shall inherit the earth"?

NURSE: I don't know. I've sometimes wondered about it.

He wasn't referring to the spineless and the obsequious, but to those with forbearance and humility, those not overly proud or self-assertive. Meekness does not translate as weakness. In the original sense of the word, meekness means self-surrender—giving up all self-seeking. In the words of the philosopher Moses Maimonides, "No crown carries such royalty with it as doeth humility."[37] But as we know, modesty can also be the worst form of vanity: "You can have no greater sign of a confirmed pride than when you think you are humble enough."[38]

To effect a complete and authentic transformation, we need to sidestep the twin evils of a mock, prideful humility on the one hand and compulsive self-assertion on the other. It is only from this purified state that it is possible to awaken to the realization of who and what we are.

Mahatma Gandhi in a letter to a friend tells why he believes the meek will inherit the earth: "The truth that moral force is a higher power than brute force will be proved by the people who are unarmed . . . The day is sure to come when the frail man of spirit, completely unhampered by air fleets and dreadnoughts, will prove that the meek are to inherit the earth."[39]

The compelling need to sever the attachment to an ego-self is forcibly articulated by the Buddha himself: "I say that a [saint] is fully emancipated because he has completely and entirely abandoned all imaginations, agitations, and false notions about an ego and anything pertaining to an ego."[40]

HOMEMAKER: Don't you think it's true that a lot of people fear death because they've heard that when you're dying all the evil things you've ever done come up to consciousness? And they think that somehow they will have to atone for that evil in a future lifetime?

Possibly, and that is why repentance at this crucial time can ease the burden. (See "Dying" section.) However, there are other cogent reasons, as we have seen—chief among them the fear of collective annihilation—why many people, especially the young, fear death more strongly nowadays than did older generations. They're not sure they're going to be able to make it to old age.

HOMEMAKER: I agree with the psychotherapist you quoted who thinks it is natural to fear the unknown, death. He makes the distinction between fear of death, which he feels is natural, and anxiety about death, which is neurotic. As he points out, the fear of death has survival value.

Are we really strangers to death and dying? As the masters and deepest thinkers of all spiritual traditions and cultures remind us, each of us has lived, died, and been reborn through innumerable lifetimes.

Thoreau, who apparently had the ability to recall past lives, wrote to his friend Emerson: "And Hawthorne, too, I remember as one with whom I sauntered in old heroic times along the banks of the Scamander amid the ruins of chariots and heroes."[41] (For further examples see "Rebirth" section.)

All life is life after death, or life within death. It is phoenixlike, re-creating itself again and again from its own ashes.

EGO

PSYCHOLOGIST: Earlier you spoke of the illusory nature of ego. How would you define it more precisely?

The ego-I can be defined as the sense of oneself as an isolated being set apart from other selves—in other words, the unshakable belief that "*I* am here and the world stands outside me." But this notion of oneself as a discrete individual is a fiction produced by our senses and bifurcating intellect. Modern psychology, I understand, views ego somewhat differently. It attaches importance to the ego because it sees it as relatinq to our self-image, that is, to understanding ourselves as a particular organism that experiences the external world through our senses. In this view, consciousness is inconceivable without an ego. If there is no ego, there is nobody to be conscious of anything. And so the ego is said to be indispensable to the consciousness process with which it is identified.

We are talking here about what may be called the individual empirical consciousness, a level of awareness tied to the five senses and the discriminating intellect. Buddhist psychology, however, holds that there are deeper aspects of consciousness. (See Diagram 1: The Nine Levels of Consciousness.)

THE ROLE OF EGO IN LIFE

The image of ourselves that grows out of our time-and-sense-bound consciousness is, in an ultimate sense, unreal. In fact, all of our self-limiting activities grow out of this false picture of ourselves. As a result of this false picture, we postulate a dualistic world of self and other, of things separated and isolated, of pain and struggle, birth and death, killing and being killed. This picture is untrue because it barely scratches the surface. It is like looking at the one eighth of an iceberg above the water and refusing to acknowledqe the seven eighths underneath. For if we could see beyond the ever-changing forms into the underlying reality, we would realize that fundamentally there is nothing but harmony and unity and that this perfection is no different from the phenomenal world of incessant change and transformation. But our vision is limited and our intuitions, weak.

Now ego, that shadowy, phantomlike figure with insatiable desires and a lust for dominance, sits astride the senses like some oriental potentate. Or, to change the metaphor, ego is like a magician carrying up his sleeve the deadly tricks of greed, anger, and wrong thinking. Worse, he is quite capable of rationalizing his actions with an air of sweet reasonableness. This wily and slippery conjurer deludes us into believing we can enjoy the delights of the senses without pain only by delivering ourselves into his hands.

Of the many devices employed by ego to keep us in his power, none is more effective than language. The English language is so structured that it demands the repeated use of the personal pronoun "I" for grammatical nicety and presumed clarity. Actually this "I" is no more than a figure of speech, a convenient convention, but we talk and act as though it were real and true. Listen to any conversation and see how the stress invariably falls on the "I"—"*I* said . . . ," "*I* did . . . ," "*I* like . . . ," "*I* hate . . ." All this plays into the hands of ego, strengthening our servitude and enlarging our sufferings, for the more we postulate this I the more we are exposed to ego's never-ending demands.

Our relative mind of ego, aided by language, deceives us in other ways. It constantly tempts us into distinctions, comparisons, and judgments which take us further and further from the concrete and the real into the realm of the speculative and the abstract. Take the case of an individual walking along who suddenly hears the sound of a bell. Immediately his discriminating mind evaluates it as beautiful or jarring, or distinguishes it as a church bell or some other kind. Ideas associated with a similar sound heard in the past may also intrude, and these are analyzed and compared. With each such judgment the experience of pure hearing becomes fainter and fainter, until one no longer hears the sound but hears only his *thoughts* about it.

THE EVOLUTION OF EGO

NURSE: Where does ego come from, anyway?

It has surely been around as long as the human mind. The evolution of ego will be clearer, I think, if we consider it from the standpoint of the aggregates (*skandhas* in Sanskrit) that make up psychophysical existence, and from the nine levels of consciousness. The five aggregates consist of form, sensations, perceptions, mental formations, and consciousness. Form comprises past elements of consciousness that have formed the body and are represented by the body. These include sense organs, sense objects, and their mutual relationship. Here we have the beginning of individuality and the division of experience into subject and object.

In the second cluster are the feelings—that is, the self reacting to its surroundings. These feelings comprise pleasure and pain, joy and sorrow, disquiet and equanimity.

In the third group are the perceptions of discriminating awareness, which comprise the reflective or discursive as well as the intuitive faculty of discrimination.

In the fourth group are the mental formations—the forces or tendencies of the will. These represent the active principle of consciousness. That is, these mental constructs are the consequences of past karma and the progenitors of future karma. They are produced by conscious volition and are what put things together and build up the patterns of personality and karma.

The last component is consciousness, which combines and coordinates all the sensory perceptions.

Thus the egocentric self creates its own world instead of perceiving the world as it really is. The aim of spiritual training is to see into the ultimate unreality of the ego-I and to transform these five aggregates of the confused and unenlightened mind into enlightenment, or a selfless-I.[42]

THE NINE LEVELS OF CONSCIOUSNESS

Let us now examine the source of ego from the standpoint of the nine consciousnesses of Buddhist psychology. The first five are the root-consciousnesses of seeing, hearing, tasting, touching, and smelling. The sixth consciousness is the conceptual faculty that distinguishes and classifies the data of the senses and is what we call the intellect. The seventh root-consciousness is the seat of the persistent I-awareness and is the source of our value judgments, egoistic opinions, self-centeredness, and illusory notions, all of which give rise to actions that accord with them. The eighth is the repository, or storehouse, consciousness, where the seeds of all mental activity and sense experiences are recorded moment after moment. This consciousness, which persists even after death, retains vestiges of awareness of previous existences and the seeds of new karmic causes. Also to be found on this eighth level are certain memories of the prebirth condition—feelings of floating or flying, of freedom, of an oceanic oneness with all things. These sensations often occur in dreams and are usually accompanied by a sense of tremendous well-being. To those sensitively attuned to them, such vestigial memories of the prebirth period can give a hint of the freedom of the state we miscall death.

The ninth level is the pure, formless Self-consciousness—our True-nature. It is related to the eighth level so intimately that there is almost no difference between the two. It can be compared to a limitless ocean, in which each individual life is a wave on the surface. (See diagram 1.)

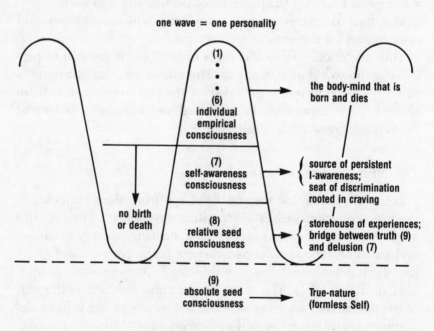

Diagram 1: The Nine Levels of Consciousness

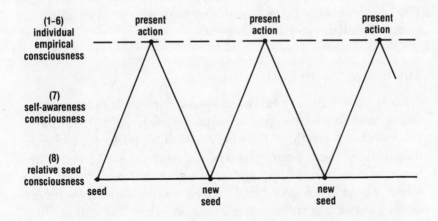

Diagram 2: Cause and Effect and the Levels of Consciousness

In a sense, the eighth level is the basis of personality and character since it continuously seeds new actions, giving rise to different thoughts and varying behavior. (See also Diagram 2.) These thoughts and behavior patterns in turn change the quality of the repository consciousness as they are instantaneously impressed upon it to become new seeds of action. Karma (which will be discussed in detail later) develops as the ever accumulating seed experiences, in response to causes and conditions, blossom forth as new actions—which are not only effects but also causes of seeds. This process, even while it is fragmented, is continuous and endless.[43]

Strictly speaking, ego itself cannot be said to survive death. However, the seventh level of consciousness, the former abode of the I-awareness, does persist. It can be likened to a blank sheet of paper—flypaper—lying in wait for the ego's return. In fact, it is the ego-serving desire for a body, and all that that implies, that is the propelling force behind rebirth. Or, stated another way, rebirth is the inevitable consequence of our not having attained total liberation in the preceding life. (See "Rebirth" section.) Thus the unending cycle of birth-living-dying-death-rebirth continues unbroken, driven by the volition, instincts, and habit patterns born of craving, anger, and delusion—driven by, in a word, ego. The physical body is, as it were, a composite or crystallization of our deluded, ego-based thoughts.

THE EGO-SELF AND REALITY

Let us now consider ego from the standpoint of epistemology. Our knowledge of the phenomenal world is gained through a subject-object relation. That is, we as subjects look at objects, discriminate them from ourselves and from other objects, assign them names, properties, and characteristics, and make judgments about them. We tacitly agree among ourselves, for example, to call a certain object a tree. We then forget that "tree" is an arbitrary concept that in no way reveals the true identity of this object. What, then, is a tree? A philosopher might call it ultimate truth; a botanist, a living organism; a physicist, a mass of electrons swirling around nuclei; an artist, a unique shape with distinctive coloring; a carpenter, a potential table. To a dog, however, it is a urinal. All descriptions or analyses are but a looking from one side at that which has infinite dimensions. The essential quality of the tree is more than anything that can be said about it.

Similarly, we tinker with time by dividing it into past, present, and future, and into years, months, days, and so forth. This is convenient, but we need to remember that this "slicing" is artificial and arbitrary—the product of our discriminating mind, which discerns only the surface of things. Timelessness is unaccounted for. Thus we conceive a world that is conceptual, limited, and far removed from the actual. Because we view objects as from a distance, we do not have an all-embracing, direct, intuitive awareness of them. And since we have not penetrated them to their core, our knowledge of them is limited and one-sided.

At the center of this process is the ego-self. Because it stands apart from all other selves, it considers itself the unique center of things. In reality it is merely an objectified self and not the true, living, unconditioned Self, which underlies and unifies all existence. This latter cannot be objectified or be known through reason or conceptualization, for it is inconceivable and unimaginable. It is the elusive, unnameable actor always behind the scenes. Thus all attempts to know our original Self through intellection and imagination are doomed to failure.

Actually there is no personal self: the entire universe is the Self. Not knowing we are this majestic Self, we imagine ourselves to be no more than this puny body, just a speck in the universe. Thus we mistakenly postulate an other, imagine a gulf between self and other where none exists, and then exalt ourselves and put down others. This is the basic delusion of sentient beings.

THE ESTRANGEMENT FROM SELF

Our estrangement from the real Self is reflected in the unsatisfactory quality of our life—the pain, the existential anxiety, the unfulfillment. This human predicament can be compared to a wheel not running true on its axle and thus grinding. Fragmented and frustrated, we long for wholeness and freedom.

We are split off from our true Self in yet another way. Even as we exist in time and space, in a world that is finite, impermanent, and material, *simultaneously* we inhabit a world that is infinite, eternal, and formless. Owing to our bifurcating intellect, which divides and separates, we are alienated from our Essential-mind. This Mind cannot be perceived until we are in an awakened state. Thus we are the flawed children of Mother Earth and Father Spirit. Living in our temporary home, the biosphere, with its pain, its beauty, its joy, we are estranged from our permanent abode, the viable Void.

NURSE: How are we flawed? Can you explain that more precisely? And what splits us off? I thought you said earlier that we are whole and complete.

The estrangement from our true Self is brought about by this same discriminating intellect, so that we see our self as both actor and observer. This is the root source of our imperfection.

We therefore oscillate between the pleasures of the senses and the longing for the eternal. It is like a man who has a wife whom he loves and a mistress to whom he is irresistibly attracted. What splits us off, again, is ego, functioning as the lackey of the discriminating intellect. Fundamentally we are whole and complete, endowed with virtue, wisdom, and compassion, but since we are victimized by our ego, which fancies itself the true master of our being, we become polarized.

Nor is this all. Living an uneasy coexistence within us are our older emotional nature, dating back to the origin of our species, and our cognitive or rational nature with its relatively new neocortex (only about five hundred thousand years old, some neurologists say). Our unfinished business, then, is to reconcile and harmonize our emotional and intellectual sides.

Arthur Koestler relates a telling anecdote which he feels is a perfect paradigm of man's split mind—a mind in which belief and disbelief, emotion and rationality, lead an agonized coexistence: "A woman who had lately lost her daughter was questioned as to what she supposed had become of her soul. The mother replied: 'Oh, well, I suppose she is enjoying eternal bliss, but I wish you wouldn't talk about such unpleasant subjects.'"[44]

Philosophy, art, literature, and science are attempts, conscious or unconscious, to heal the basic rupture. To the degree that the split persists, we lead restless, discontented lives; we are condemned forever to seek and never to find, for all seeking implies a subject that seeks and an object to be found, once again dividing into two what is inherently One. We cannot seek entrance to a place we have never left. Nor is there anything to attain, for we basically lack nothing. A master of old put it this way:

> Before the foot is lifted,
> The journey is over.
> Before the tongue has moved,
> The teaching is finished.[45]

Since we are there already, where is there to go? Since we embrace all time, how can our journey have a beginning or an end? Since all wisdom and virtue are our birthright, what is there to say, what is there to learn? With awakening to this our True-nature, deluded thoughts and actions drop away, allowing the free flow of our innate wisdom and compassion.

The Holy Grail legend, the Gilgamesh epic, the travail of the Wandering Jew—all these allegories vividly portray man's alienation from his True-nature and his quest for wholeness and eternal life—what some call God.

Speaking of the role of the Janus-faced ego,[46] Professor Masao Abe perceptively pinpoints the human predicament:

> Self-estrangement and anxiety are *not* something accidental to the ego-self, but are inherent to its structure. To be human is to be a problem to one's self regardless of one's culture, class, sex, nationality, or the era in which one lives. To be human means to be an ego-self; to be an ego-self means to be cut off from both one's Self and one's world, which means to be in constant anxiety. This is the human predicament. The ego-self, split at the root into subject and object, is forever dangling from a bottomless abyss, unable to gain any footing.[47]

The split can be healed, all religions teach, through symbolic death (of the ego) and rebirth to a higher life which can truly be called religious.

INTELLECT AND EGO

This brings us to a consideration of intellect and its relation to ego. It should be remembered that the illusion of ego—of one's own separate existence as an enduring reality, set off against the rest of the universe—may be seen as the root cause of the problems of life and death: fearful clinging to life and terror of a death which appears to be the annihilation of one's life. The discriminating intellect is perhaps the foremost instrument of the ego in perpetuating this illusion. In Western psychology, I understand, intellect is usually considered the last faculty to develop in a child. Actually, intellect exists in a rudimentary state even in the embryo. With intellect's further unfolding, our perception of the world as it really is becomes distorted. I touched on this earlier. Now let me expand on it. Conditioned as we are to filter all perceptions through the intellect, which in turn conveys them to the seventh level of consciousness (where the sense of an ego-I takes hold), we find irresistible the belief that each of us is a discrete and separate entity. As the persistent ego-I awareness develops and strengthens over time, it becomes more and more solidified through the intellect, affecting in turn our perception of the world.

The net result is that we begin to think and act as though we were separated entities confronted by a world external to us. In the unconscious, the idea of I, or selfhood, becomes fixed, and from this arise such thought patterns as "I hate this, I love that; I need this, I don't want that; this is mine, that's yours." Nourished by this fodder, the ego-I comes to dominate the personality, attacking whatever threatens its position and grasping at anything which will enlarge its power. Antagonism, greed, and alienation, culminating in suffering, are the inevitable consequences of this circular process. The ego-I, or small self, can be compared to a tumor: in one sense it is foreign to the body; in another, it was produced by it. Or, to change the metaphor: "Far from being a door to the abundant life, the ego is a strangulated hernia. The more it swells, the tighter it shuts off that circulation of compassion with the rest of life on which man's health depends absolutely, [and] the more pain is bound to rise."[48]

THE VALUE OF EGO

In spite of what you have just heard about ego, this wily creature is not to be despised; for when his machinations become unbearably painful, there arises within us an irresistible longing for freedom from the restriction and pain, and a desire to transcend these sufferings so as to attain inward peace and wisdom.

Ego performs yet another valuable function. Behind all creative endeavors—whether it be designing a spacecraft, creating a work of art, or uncovering an unknown law of nature—lies the desire, conscious or unconscious, for Self-knowledge. And the propelling force behind this desire is ego—the wish of the self to undertake these activities. We can also say with Ernest Becker that ego represents a natural urge by the life force itself toward an expansion of experience, toward more life.

* * *

For those of the highest spiritual attainment the ego is transmuted into a selfless-I. Because the body still exists, however, the pull toward the reinvigoration of an ego-I continues. For this reason even spiritual masters must be on guard against falling into habit patterns that favor the reassertion of ego. Only one who is free from the slightest thought of self can be said to be truly egoless and therefore Buddhalike. For such a one no thoughts of the body remain. In this state it is possible to go to one's death without the slightest trace of sorrow, rancor, or fear. Dying, for such an individual, is no different from living, living is another form of dying, and both at base are seen as unreal.

BANISHING EGO

NURSE: But can an ordinary person ever hope to reach even a semblance of this state?

It is possible because Buddhahood is latent in each of us. After all, the Buddha himself was once no different from you and me. But we do need to strive to get out of ourselves, to "get lost," to immerse ourselves totally in whatever confronts us. In losing ourselves we gain a relationship to something greater than the self:

> Bravely let go your hold
> On the edge of the precipice
> And die to the small self.
> Then what is naturally revealed
> Is the True-nature in which
> There is neither life nor death.

This vivid image of a precipice is a metaphor for the varied circumstances, more painful on the whole than joyous, of our life. Most of us are, metaphorically speaking, hanging by the skin of our teeth from a precipice. At any moment we may fall and be dashed to bits on the jagged rocks below. Dying to the I means freeing oneself from attachments, from *clinging*—to people, to wants, to hopes, to fantasies, even to ideals ("poisoning the real with the ideal," in D. H. Lawrence's seminal phrase), and, above all, to one's sufferings. We need to stop clutching at the momentary aspects of life and let go of our preconceived notions of how things should or should not be. Only then can we be reawakened to a wholly new world—greater, freer, and more beautiful than the old, ego-dominated one. Kierkegaard sums it up superbly:

> To let go is to lose your foothold temporarily.
> Not to let go is to lose your foothold forever.

While Kierkegaard may overdramatize, he nevertheless captures a profound truth. The process of dying is as important for life as the process of being born. It is only because we identify the process of dying with the dissolution of the body that we arrive at our one-sided and negative conception of death.

THE GREAT DEATH AND THE GREAT RENEWAL

A death-dealing blow to the I is at the same time a life-giving action. In Zen this is called the Great Death and the Great Renewal. To die the Great Death is to transcend life and death and achieve utter freedom. It makes the prospect of physical death secondary and unimportant. Zen master Bunan put it this way:

> Die while alive
> And be thoroughly dead.
> Then do what you will,
> All is good.

When a master was told by a prospective student, "I would like to learn Zen from you," the master asked, "Are you prepared to die?" The student replied, "I came here to learn Zen, not to die." "If you can't die you will never learn Zen," responded the master.

The true spiritual heroes in all the religious traditions have been those who did not hesitate to leap, hands high in the air, into the abyss of fire confronting them, into the ever burning flames of their own primordial nature.[49] With this leap of faith, all delusive feelings and perceptions perish with the ego-root and one is reborn into a luminous world of true freedom. Only such a revived one can sing:

> He who dies
> Before he dies
> Does not die
> When he dies.[50]

CAN EGO BE DESTROYED?

MANAGEMENT CONSULTANT: With all due respect, it is easy to say, "Die to the I!" "Let go your hold on the precipice!" But as a practical matter, how do you do that? In Zen and other spiritual traditions, aren't there techniques or methods for destroying the ego?

You can't set out to destroy ego and not end up inflating it, any more than you can try to empty your mind of thoughts without filling it with the thought of getting rid of thoughts. As to the particular question of techniques, while one initially seeks to master and apply them, they must at some point be abandoned if one is not to be trapped by them. The most fundamental way I know of to transcend ego (not destroy it) is by selfless meditation and total absorption in the task at hand, by living *in the moment* rather than *for the moment*. The latter is the hedonist's self-indulgent pursuit of pleasure as a way of life. Self-forgetting in whatever activity one faces is actually the manifestation of a love of life, for there is no awareness of a self, an I, that blocks full involvement with life.

This raptness, which is a loss of the part and a gain of the whole, can be seen most acutely in animals. Have you ever watched a cat stalking a bird? With its full being it involves itself in the drama of the encounter. Or try holding up a bone to a hungry dog. At that moment the size and color of the dog's world is personified by that bone. So concentrated is the dog, so complete its identification with the *one thing* in front of it, that it becomes the bone itself. This is more than concentration as we ordinarily understand it: the mind focused on a particular object or thought. It is a self-forgetting in which an altered state of consciousness emerges.

PSYCHOTHERAPIST: I can accept most of what you have just said, but it bothers me that you seem to be implying a condemnation of intellect. What I mean is, you have implied that ego is the source of our personality and that it dominates the discriminative faculty, which is a function of intellect. In putting down ego, aren't you also putting down intellect?

Not at all. All I have been implying is that intellect is a limited instrument for realizing ultimate Truth. This is because intellect can see Truth, which has infinite dimensions, only from one angle. As an ally of ego, the bifurcating intellect (aided by the senses) slices reality, which is fundamentally whole, into self and other, thereby creating an illusory world of good and bad, wise and stupid, and the like. Thus the world we perceive is intellectually reconstructed and is not the real world. Listen to Zen master Hakuun Yasutani on this point: "In the case of the ordinary person, intellect promotes discrimination and delusion, but if it is employed with a knowledge of its limitations by one who has awakened, it can directly illumine the Way itself and act as a vital means of showing the Way to others."[51]

SECOND PSYCHOTHERAPIST: Are you saying that intellect serves a dual purpose: it fosters ego, creating the irritant that leads eventually to a spiritual quest, and then helps to illumine that Way?

Intellect may or may not lead one to embark on a spiritual path; everything depends on how far one's karma has matured in that direction.

HEALTHY PEOPLE EXALT LIFE, NOT DEATH

SOCIOLOGIST: I'd like to get something off my chest. In this workshop you've spoken of death as "the great liberation," as "the bow that shoots life's arrow," and used similar phrases. What bothers me is that you seem to be converting death into some kind of ideal. You and all those other "death and dying" people are practically elevating it into a religion. What's so great about death? Spiritually healthy people celebrate life, not death. After all, life is full of promise and hope. Death is an unknown. No one can speak of death, or of a hereafter, with any degree of authority. We belong to the earth, not to heaven or hell or any other worlds.

I've brought with me some quotations that reinforce what I've been saying. The first is from the Bible: "God said, 'I have set before thee life and death, the blessing and the curse; therefore choose life, that thou mayest live, thou and thy seed.' "[52]

The next is from an article on AIDS that appeared in Newsweek *magazine:*

> *Chaco was the worst—the angriest, meanest, most mulish patient [Dr.] Friedlander [the head of the AIDS unit] had ever seen. He yelled, cursed, refused his food, rejected his medicines and regularly sent nurses and technicians fleeing in terror from his room. But Friedlander came to like him precisely for his anger—for the way he shook his fist at AIDS and refused to let it run his life even when it was killing him. He* scared *the disease, Friedlander thought. It was the passive ones who gave up too soon, and when they quit fighting they died.*[53]

I personally find these attitudes more natural and admirable than the attitude of surrendering passively to death. When death is glorified as the fulfillment of life, as the supreme liberation, it's easy to slip into a mind state that welcomes euthanasia or suicide when you develop a serious illness or are terribly frustrated with life. Why shouldn't we resist death and promote life? Our dominant instinct is for life, not death, although I know that Freud and certain philosophers feel there is also a death instinct. Why should death be a triumph and life merely a preparation for it? By fighting death we affirm life. If you don't struggle against death you negate life. And you die quickly. What have you gained except extinction? There's more I'd like to say—may I continue?

Yes, go on.

WHY SACRIFICE LIFE TO DEATH?

SOCIOLOGIST: Even if we accept your contention that death is a stepping-off point, who knows what that next life will be like?

And why is it assumed that the intermediate stage after decease, as you call it, brings with it spiritual regeneration? Doesn't painful karma have to be expiated in this or another existence? I've read that the after-death state can be a terrifying experience, so why idealize it? (See "Rebirth" section.) I believe we should do everything in our power to prolong this life even when its quality is impaired. Life—all life—is unique and precious, the greatest of all miracles, as you yourself have said. So why sacrifice it to death any sooner than we have to? Furthermore, I don't believe in tiptoeing through life just so you can make it safely to death, as someone said. The human body has formidable recuperative powers, and we know there have been remarkable remissions in so-called terminal cases where there's been a strong will to live. I don't believe in a passive attitude toward death any more than a passive attitude to life. We should live all the days of our life and not give up on it. Let's not forget the trite but true saying, "While there's life there's hope."

Your impassioned speech—and this is not said sarcastically—takes me by surprise. I must have stated things pretty badly. It never occurred to me that I sounded like a samurai crying, "Long live death!" Quite the contrary. I've been trying to strip death of the tragic solemnity, the denial and fear with which we surround it so that when our time to slip off comes, we won't tremble with fear or "struggle like a crab with its seven arms and eight legs in boiling water."[54] Our stubborn denial of death, as I said earlier, betrays a deep-seated fear of life. Life, let me emphasize, is our main concern, not death. To the awakened, our world is enchanting, filled with wonder and awe. It teems with endless diversity. The marvels of nature are a delight to the eye, the ear, the nose. Human and other creatures, plants, trees, rivers, rocks, insects, anthills—all palpitate with life. Every single thing shines with its own light. Every single thing sings out the glory of creation. Existence is a marvelous thing.

> We are all flowers
> blossoming
> in a blooming universe.[55]

Ultimately, our aim is to transcend both birth and death and attain to the state of no-birth and no-death.

As to your contention that painful karma has to be expiated in this or another lifetime, I will go into that subject in some detail later.

You mentioned the intermediate stage after decease, also known as the *bardo*. Be aware that this not only is the state between physical death and physical rebirth but also refers to every moment of our life. Like a traveler putting up for a night's lodging, we pass from one husk into another. The ordinary unaware person spends a good part of his life suspended between two worlds—one dead, the other powerless to be born, as the saying goes—like a sleepwalker. He lives in a perpetual dream.

FACING DEATH FEARLESSLY

There hasn't been a culture or civilization in history, I think it is fair to say—whether it be that of aborigine tribes in Australia or the Greek culture at its zenith—that has not bestowed its highest accolades on those men and women who faced death unflinchingly, with courage and dignity. When they knew they had to die, these heroes didn't rage against it. They conquered death by their supreme indifference to it or—and this amounts to the same thing—their total concurrence in it, robbing it of its power to sting and thus gaining true immortality. Think of Christ and Socrates, of Thomas More and Joan of Arc, and of the Zen masters and the Buddha—how inspiring their lives and deaths! And how equally inspiring the lives of innumerable ordinary men and women who calmly looked death in the face. The last tribute we owe life is a dignified death.

WHAT IS A DIGNIFIED DEATH?

HOMEMAKER: What do you call a dignified death?

A dignified, or "good," death is one in which there is no railing or struggling against imminent death—above all, a death without sadness, without regret, without apprehension, without bitterness, without terror. It is dying freely, naturally, like falling asleep, not clinging to or clutching at life, just "going with the flow"—not "flow" or "letting go" in a psychological sense, but in the transcendent sense of the "eternal yea," of yielding to an inner, mysterious force that takes over when all self-striving ceases. This can be seen in the following example:

When Zen master Tung-shan felt it was time for him to go, he had his head shaved, took a bath, put on his robe, rang the bell to bid farewell to the community, and sat up till he breathed no more. To all appearances he had died. Thereupon the whole community burst out crying grievously as little children do at the death of their mother. Suddenly the master opened his eyes and said to the weeping monks, "We monks are supposed to be detached from all things transitory. In this consists true spiritual life. To live is to work, to die is to rest. What is the use of groaning and moaning?" He then ordered a "stupidity-purifying" meal for the whole community. After the meal he said to them, "Please make no fuss over me! Be calm as befits a family of monks! Generally speaking, when anyone is at the point of going, he has no use for noise and commotion." Thereupon he returned to the Abbot's room, where he sat up as in meditation till he passed away.[56]

HOMEMAKER: Of course that man could die like that—he was a Zen master. And it doesn't sound as though he were even in pain. What about ordinary people like myself? What about people who are dying in agony as a result of a fire or an automobile accident or a terribly painful disease? How can someone in that condition be expected to die with equanimity?

Zen masters aside, not all ordinary people die in pain. But it is possible to go with the flow even if one is in deep pain. Let me illustrate this with another story. As a Zen master lay dying he cried out in pain. Upset by his cries, one of his students said, "Master! Why are you calling out like that?" The master responded, "My crying in pain is no different from my laughing in joy."

HOMEMAKER: But again you're quoting a Zen master! One would expect someone like that to be able to go with the flow while dying. I want to know how I can meet death that way.

Like these masters, if you train yourself to become one with your daily life, you will be able to go with the flow whatever the circumstances of your death—or life.

DID CHRIST DIE A DIGNIFIED DEATH?

COMPUTER PROGRAMMER: Earlier you implied that Christ died a heroic and dignified death. If he was going with the flow, why, when he was crucified, did he cry out, "My God! My God! Why hast Thou forsaken me?"

As I see it, that cry has two aspects. On the one hand it was a lament; on the other, a hosanna. For Jesus, as for the earliest Christians, death severed the vital and personal bond with God the Creator; death was said to be repayment for the sin of rebelling against God. Since life came from God, life belonged to Him and only He could end it.[57] Now Jesus, as the Son of God, is more deeply linked to Him than any other person, and therefore his distress and agony at his imminent death was all the greater. However, his very last words—after he cried out, "My God, My God! Why hast Thou forsaken me?"—were "It is finished" (sometimes translated as "It is accomplished" or otherwise narrated as "Father, into your hands I commend my spirit"[58]). These final words were followed, according to the apostles Mark and Matthew, by a loud cry, thus demonstrating that his Great Doubt was dissolved, that his bond with God was reforged, and that he and the Father were truly one; Jesus had transcended body and mind and with it his pain and agony.

SEDATION AND DYING

PSYCHOLOGIST: I'd like to add to what you said about dying appropriately. If you die in a hospital—and these days 80 percent

*of all people do [in the United States]—you may be so sedated that
you're practically unconscious. How is it possible to die properly
when you're so out of it that you don't know what's happening to
you?*

You're right, it isn't possible. One can only hope that with the
growing hospice movement, which provides nursing care to terminal patients in their homes, more people may be able to die
free of the pall of sedation, with consciousness relatively unimpaired. That would be wonderful. (See pp. xix–xx of Introduction;
also Supplement 2: "The Hospice Movement.")

ANGER AND DYING

Let's get back to Dr. Friedlander. His admiration of Chaco's
fight, the rage, is understandable in the context of the awful AIDS
disease and the toll it is taking on the young. As with many in
Chaco's condition, anger can temporarily give the dying a sense
of being in charge of their life and death. Anger is also a means
of staving off the fear of the isolation of dying, and a means of
feeling, however briefly, powerful again. Under the best of circumstances it is not easy to have one's life snatched away before one
has really begun to live. One feels terribly cheated or terribly
guilty, and undoubtedly this explains, in part at least, Chaco's
violent reaction to his impending death. But it would be a mistake
to take Chaco's behavior as a model for action in a life-threatening situation.

In this connection, let me point out that the notion of researchers at Johns Hopkins that angry defiance on the part of
cancer patients helps extend their lives has not held up. A new,
seven-year study reported in *The New York Times* tells a different
story:

> After researchers at Johns Hopkins reported that cancer pa-
> tients who showed angry defiance, a "fighting spirit," tended to
> live longer than did those who were passive and "good," Dr. Levy
> [Dr. Sandra M. Levy, associate professor of psychiatry and med-
> icine at the University of Pittsburgh School of Medicine] began

to follow a group of 36 women who had been diagnosed as having advanced breast cancer. After seven years, 24 of the 36 women had died. To her surprise, Dr. Levy found that, after the first year, anger made no difference in survival. The only psychological factor that mattered for survival within seven years seemed to be a sense of joy with life.[59]

Clearly, then, violent assertions of ego are ultimately self-defeating. At best they may add a few months of life to the critically ill; a serene, joyous mind state, on the other hand, may result in *years* of added life. Such angry outbursts are crippling in another significant way: they contribute to the continuation of the painful chain of cause and effect—of birth, death, and rebirth.

CHOOSING LIFE IS ALSO CHOOSING DEATH

You are quite right in saying, though, that we should live *all* the days of our life. *Live*—that's the word! Most people merely exist. That's why it's been said, "Death is more universal than life: everyone dies but not everyone lives." As for your quote from the Bible, my interpretation of it is that life is too precious to be squandered or frittered away or destroyed through suicide or other ways. But you can't choose life without at the same time choosing death, for dying is part of the drama of living; death is the price we pay for the gift of a body. Death, we know, cannot be avoided; it's the one constant in life for all of us, so we must make room for this final moment. Why then should we recoil from the outstretched arms of approaching death when our whole life is nothing but a journey toward it? "All days," says Montaigne (1533–92), "travel toward death; the last one reaches it."

RESISTING DEATH WITH DIGNITY AND HONOR

Nonetheless, there are times when dignity and honor are better served by resistance and struggle than by submission. Let us say you have a fatal illness and wish to visit a part of the world you have always been eager to see before you die. Or that you are determined to see a child graduated from college or married before you pass on. In those circumstances you will fight to prolong your life so that you may achieve your goal. Or one may be motivated to live by something more soul-stirring. Take the case of Lise Lesevre, an eighty-six-year-old French woman who was the main witness against Klaus Barbie—the Gestapo chief in Lyons, France, who was put on trial by the French government for crimes against humanity. Her will to live had been nourished, she reported in an interview, by the hope of facing her torturer in a courtroom one day.[60]

Consider, too, the story of the Jews of the Warsaw ghetto, who rose up against the German aggressors that sought to destroy them during World War II. These Jews believed they had a right to survive, and so they did not feel hopeless. Though vastly outnumbered and with nothing more than small weapons to defend themselves, they nevertheless fought off the attacking German tanks for twenty-seven days before dying with honor and gallantry.

For the Jews of the Warsaw ghetto, who were facing such a death-vision as that of Nazism, there was no choice but to resist, to fight to the death. For *them*, fighting to the death was an act of affirming life. The same can be said, but with some differences, of those who died in the anti-Communist uprisings in Hungary and Czechoslovakia, which were brutally crushed by Soviet forces.

A GROUP OF HASIDIM FACES DEATH[61]

Another powerful example of unsurpassed courage also comes from the Holocaust. One hesitates to encroach upon painful memories of those who survived those horrors. But if the Holocaust is a prime example of the depths of evil to which the human animal can sink, it also reveals the heights of courage and heroism to which the human spirit can ascend. Here is an eyewitness account of what happened in the Polish town of Dąbrowa Górnicza when the Germans found Rabbi Isaac (the ghetto's chief rabbi) and his Hasidic disciples hiding in an underground shelter:

The Nazis drove them to the local Jewish cemetery . . . the Hasidim were dressed in their praying shawls and had a bottle of vodka which they managed to bring to the cemetery. There, facing their executioners, as the account goes, 'they drank *lechayim* [to life] to each other, held hands and began to dance, and were shot down as they danced.'[62]

While the Warsaw ghetto fighters affirmed the basic human right to life and freedom by resisting, the Hasidim, in *not* fighting, affirmed something deeper: the indestructible life of the human spirit.

THE CONCEPT OF HEROISM IN ORTHODOX JUDAISM

How do we account for the extraordinary behavior of these Hasidim in the face of death? Philip Friedman, a Jewish historian who was active in the anti-Nazi underground in Poland, explains the nature of the main form of resistance carried on by the Orthodox Jews:

> Whereas most other nations have legacies of heroism in which heroism means physical and military prowess, in the case of Orthodox Jewry the concept of heroism is interwoven with the idea of spiritual courage, of sacrifice for the sake of religion, that is, sanctification of God's name. It was a resistance stemming from religious inspiration and it contained a deeply rooted ancestral heritage epitomized by the saying, "Not by force but by the strength of the spirit" . . . Its essence is epitomized in the idea that the evil of the world should not be fought and cannot be defeated by physical force, because the struggle between good and evil will be decided elsewhere, by Divine Providence; it will by no means be decided by physical warfare. In accordance with this view, the true weapon is the weapon of conscience, prayer, religious meditation and devotion, and not armed resistance. The Orthodox Jews did not believe that it was possible or even desirable to resist the Nazis in any other way. They believed that the recital of a chapter of the Psalms would do more to affect the course of events than the killing of a German—not necessarily immediately but in the infinite course of mutual relations between the Creator and His creatures.[63]

THE CONCEPT OF HEROISM IN SOVIET LABOR CAMPS

This notion is echoed in the writings of Russians like Solzhenitsyn, Panin, Shifirin, Terz, who were imprisoned in labor
camps in the Soviet Union for political crimes. Solzhenitsyn, for
example, is quoted by Mihajlo Mihajlov as saying that the struggle
which is occurring today in totalitarian countries is not in essence
political but spiritual. In a real sense it is the truly spiritual who
undermine the very essence of totalitarian rule—that essence
being the belief in the unlimited power of external circumstances
which supposedly direct man's inner world. By following the
mysterious callings of his internal voice—and by doing so, re-
deeming his soul—man recognizes that as long as the soul is not
forfeited, the fundamental part is not lost; this belief rests on the
basis of faith in the immortality of the human soul. To follow
the calling of one's internal voice means to act with the knowledge
that all of our deeds are grounded in eternity.[64]

Mihajlov goes on to make another vital point:

> It is important to understand that sooner or later *every human
> being* will find himself in a prison, in a detention camp, or under
> the unlimited arbitrary rule of the mighty physical forces of this
> world. Then it is impossible to avoid the choice between submis-
> sion before death—total destruction not only physically but also
> spiritually—or to follow in a daring way the calling of the spiritual
> voice. Sickness, different catastrophes, various misfortunes,
> death—all of these are the very same as arrest, inquisitions,
> prison, detention camp. And it is not given to anyone to avoid
> them . . . At any unexpected moment for every human being the
> world of freedom appears as in the cell of a prisoner condemned
> to death. "Our whole world is a prison cell of those condemned
> to death," writes Solzhenitsyn. Panin affirms that "the whole world
> is only a point of departure"; while Terz likens death to an "exiting
> into freedom."[65]

2. MEDITATIONS ON DEATH

> A good death
> does honor to a whole life.
> —PETRARCH

WHY MEDITATIONS ON DEATH?

Meditations on death are a means of purifying the mind in order to gain a crucial revelation of the meaning and significance of life and death. As such, death meditations have been regarded as an indispensable element of a wide array of cultures: the Egyptian and Indian, the Chinese and Japanese, the Hellenic and Roman, the Hebrew and Islamic, in both their ancient and modern forms. Because of death's general unfathomableness and the dread and terror it inspires in most people, the conquest of death, or deathlessness, has a central place in the teachings of all religions. Unless this fear and terror is replaced by comfort and hope, a tranquil mind state is impossible. The unwillingness to think of death is itself a kind of death, for the poignancy of life is inseparable from the knowledge of its inevitable decay.

IS MEDITATION ON DEATH MORBID?

Death meditations may strike some as a morbid preoccupation, a falling in love with death rather than with life. Yet the deep acceptance of death as the teacher of life divests these reflections of any macabre quality. The purpose of death meditations is to instill in the meditator the confidence to walk unafraid with the ever-present prospect of death, for one never knows when it may come and take us. The denial of death, so common in our culture, inevitably strengthens the fear of it and underscores what Socrates said about the unexamined life not being worth living. Actually, pondering and meditating on death is part of the religious practices of every major tradition. There are some orders of Christian monks and nuns, for example, who live with their simple coffins always in sight and who even turn a spadeful of earth daily from the place that is to eventually serve as their grave. By contrast, some people strongly feel that thinking about their demise will only hasten it—a not uncommon form of denial.

Those who are strongly repelled by the thought of confronting their own demise even in a symbolic way—as well as those who have suffered from mental illness, particularly depressive disorders, and those who are psychologically fragile—are cautioned to avoid the more intense type of death meditations described here. To undertake them under these circumstances could result in an increase in fear and anxiety rather than a lessening of them. Children, too, should not attempt these exercises.

In his book *Inventing the American Way of Death*, the historian James Farrell (1830–1920) makes a vital point about the denial of death in American society:

> Keeping death out of mind cuts people off from an important fact of their physical, mental, and spiritual existence. If knowing that we will die is part of what makes us human, then forgetting that we will die threatens our humanity. In the same way, the denial of death in American society also cuts people off from our common humanity, keeping them at such a distance from the deaths of others that they cannot grieve or mourn except in the culturally prescribed "way" . . .[66]

PLATO AND BUDDHA ON DEATH MEDITATIONS

Plato in his *Phaidon* insists that "they are the true votaries of knowledge who practice nothing else but how to die or to meet death."[67] Masao Abe elaborates on this: "For Plato . . . to philosophize is nothing other than precisely to practice dying while living. It is to live through dying, to practice dying while living.

Herein is the way of the philosopher for Plato—the way in which death is overcome."[68]

The Buddha was equally emphatic about the value of such meditation: "Of all footprints, that of the elephant is supreme. Similarly, of all mindfulness meditations, that on death is supreme."

As well, Marcus Aurelius (A.D. 121-180), the Roman emperor and Stoic philosopher, wrote, "The constant recollection of death is the test of human conduct."[69]

Meditation that totally involves body and mind takes us beyond the senses, beyond our thoughts and feelings, into a transcendent state. But death meditations are valuable not only for that reason. When they are fueled by the primal terror of death, they can break through the psychological armor encasing us and evoke what may be called the "questioning mind," the prerequisite for genuine transformation.

Understandably the various religions have cultivated forms of death meditation appropriate to their basic spiritual aims. The methods of these religions have been preserved in both the written and oral traditions of the different cultures. *The Egyptian Book of the Dead*, *The Tibetan Book of the Dead*, and the medieval text *The Art of Dying* are perhaps the best known.

MEDITATION IN GENERAL

The material that follows is drawn partly from these writings, but also from the various Buddhist traditions, with which I am most familiar. These meditations on death are intended to help the student confront the reality of his own finitude in a concrete way and thereby gain an intense awareness of his own eventual death, and with it a greater appreciation of life.

Generally, meditations on death can be divided into philosophic reflections and experiential aspects. The philosophic portions, consisting of ancient writings by prominent masters, are still taught in many monasteries and spiritual centers in both the West and the East as a theoretical basis for the practices themselves. For the so-called practical, I have drawn upon the oral teachings handed down by masters in the various traditions. Also included are specific methods of meditation transmitted to me by my own teachers during my fifteen years of training in Asia, thirteen of them in Japanese Zen monasteries and temples. In addition, I have added methods of practice congenial to Western students. Where any of the practices are inextricably entwined with their native cultures, I have sought to put them in the context of our own Western culture.

REFLECTIONS ON DEATH: EIGHT POINTS OF VIEW

These death meditations are abstracted from the *Visuddhimaqqa*, by Buddhaghosa (fifth century A.D.), a highly respected Buddhist monk-teacher. I have consulted two English translations of this writing: one by the well-known Buddhist scholar Edward Conze, the other by Professor George Bond.

To enable the meditator to come to grips with the reality of his own death, the text instructs him to reflect on death from the following eight points of view: (1) death as having the appearance of an executioner, that is, as though a murderer were standing in front of one ready to strike one down; (2) death as the ruin of all success; (3) death as the inevitable end for all persons: just as it strikes down the great and mighty, so will it strike us down also; (4) death as the result of "sharing the body with many": a reflection on the infinite number of factors, both internal and external, that can cause death; (5) death as lying near at hand; (6) death as "signless" that is, nothing about it can be predicted or known in advance; (7) death as the certain end of a lifespan that is short at best; and (8) death as a constant phenomenon, occurring at every moment.[70]

I will elaborate on only one of these eight points, the third, and will briefly touch on some of the others, leaving it to the reader to supply his own examples illustrating the substance of each of the other points. Reflecting on these points is indispensable preparation for meditation on the word "death," the core of the practice. We all know intellectually that we cannot escape death; only an idiot would deny it. But intellectual recognition is one thing, experiential awareness another. Herein, then, lies the value of the symbolic confrontation with death through these meditations.

THE THIRD POINT

The third point concerns death as the end for everyone. In this practice one is instructed to reflect on the deaths of about seven accomplished individuals who have had worldly success, fame, and power and yet could not avert death. They might be past figures or contemporary. For example, one might think of Julius Caesar in this line from *Hamlet*:

> Imperious Caesar dead and turn'd to clay
> Might stop a hole to keep the wind away.

One can reflect, "Caesar was the most powerful man of his day, his armies had conquered most of the known world, his wealth was enormous—yet death eventually struck him down and returned him to dust. How can *I* hope to escape the same end?" One should remind oneself that the powerful and the weak, the sage and the fool, the generous and the stingy, the most honored of men (an Einstein, for example) and the most miserable beggar—the same fate awaits them all, and us too: death. In the grave we are all equal. Similarly, one can reflect on the violent deaths of tyrants such as Hitler and Mussolini. Both dictators had absolute power over the lives of millions of people, yet their ultimate fate, too, was death.

PONDERING THE EIGHT POINTS

One may ponder these eight views while sitting, standing, lying down, or walking, or when one is riding in a car, a bus, a plane, or a train. It is helpful to memorize them or to write them on a small card to keep for reference. They can be elaborated or modified as one sees fit. That is, one may supply more personally meaningful metaphors or may relate these eight points to one's own life experiences. Their value, however, lies in retaining their essential formulations as reference points and reflecting on them.

In connection with these reflections, and as an adjunct to them, one needs to remind oneself again and again of how fortunate one is to have the rare privilege—the good karma—of being born a human being in this lifetime, and that the deepest purpose of human life is to awaken to the meaning of birth and death.

It is inadvisable to perform these exercises at random. Rather, begin with one exercise and continue to meditate on it until it has sunk deeply into your consciousness, after which you can go on to the next practice, working with it in the same manner.

MEDITATING ON THE WORD "DEATH"

The *Visuddhimaqqa* defines death as "the cutting off of the life force for the length of one existence." The meditator is instructed to retire to a quiet, solitary place and focus his mind on the thought "Death will take place, the life force will be cut off," or simply to meditate on the word "death." The practice seems outwardly simple, yet to develop an ongoing mindfulness of death is actually quite difficult. This is due to what Freud in his essay on death called "our relation to death"—that while we airily proclaim that death is the fate of all of us, actually we act as though an exception will be made in our case.[71] Implicit in Buddhaghosa's treatise is his conviction that only constant mindfulness of death and frequent meditation on it will dislodge this deepseated belief.

If early in life one works at dispelling this subconscious belief that "Somehow death will spare *me*," and reflects on the everpresent possibility of death, life takes on new meaning and direction. The uncertainty of when death may come makes us value each moment and frees us from the illusion, common to the young, that we have an infinite amount of time to accomplish things. The conviction that death may strike at any time enables us to focus on what is meaningful and to discard the nonessentials on which we expend so much precious time. The realization that the grave is our common destiny arouses compassion for the least among us; this is not unlike people's experiences in European bomb shelters during World War II, where strangers, made intimate by sharing the possibility of immediate death, gave of themselves to help others in ways rarely seen in more ordinary times. And not the least, it encourages us to live each day as though it were the last.

This is attested to by many people, among them the distinguished psychologist Abraham Maslow, who suffered a near-fatal heart attack and afterward wrote a letter about it to a friend: "The confrontation with death—and the reprieve from it—makes everything look so precious, so sacred, so beautiful, that I feel more strongly than ever the impulse to love it, to embrace it, and to let myself be overwhelmed by it. My river has never looked so beautiful . . ."[72]

Let us now focus on the meditation itself. Masters of old advise, "Stick the word 'death' on your forehead and keep it there." In the beginning it is effective to harmonize the inhalations and exhalations with the soft vocalization of the word "death." Later the word may be uttered only on the exhalation. One need not visualize the word itself, unless picturing it helps keep it in mind. The mind should be fully concentrated on the meaning of the word "death"; care should be taken to avoid a mechanical repetition of it.

MEDITATION ON A DEATH KOAN

Let us now reflect on what a famous Zen master has to say about the value of meditating on a death koan:

> If you should have the desire to see into your own nature, you should first investigate the word "death." If you want to know how to investigate the word death, then at all times while walking, standing, sitting, or reclining, without despising activity, without being caught up in quietude, merely investigate the koan: "After I am dead and cremated, where has the 'true person of no rank' gone?" [Or, in other words, "After I'm dead, where am I?"]
>
> Among all the teachings and instructions, the word *death* has the most unpleasant and disgusting connotations. Yet if you once suddenly penetrate this "death" koan, [you will find that] there is no more felicitous teaching than this instruction that serves as the key to the realm in which birth and death are transcended, where the place in which you stand is the Diamond indestructible, and where you have become a divine immortal, unaging and un-

dying. The word *death* is the vital essential that you must first determine for yourself.[73]

The Transitory Nature of Life

In all earnestness tell yourself, "The most important task facing me as a human being is to transcend the ceaseless cycle of births, deaths, and rebirths, to awaken to the true meaning of my life and death." To arouse this determination, one must be deeply aware of the evanescent nature of life: that we are born in the morning and die in the evening; that the friend we saw yesterday is no longer with us today. Most of us see impermanence in the life of another but do not relate it to our own body. Seriously tell yourself, "Even though I live to be seventy or eighty, death will surely catch up with *me*." But even this is putting it too mildly. Think of what might happen to you tonight or tomorrow. You might be killed in a plane or car crash, or be caught in an avalanche, flood, or earthquake. Or you could be tortured or shot by terrorists. Or, closer to home, you might discover that you have a life-threatening disease.

A Meditation Using Beads

Many years ago in Burma I stayed at the home of a business-man with a spiritual outlook on life. He meditated every day, and to judge from his serene, radiant countenance and deep contentment (he was sixty-five at the time), his meditations, though informal, were most effective. This is how he performed them: Every morning he rose at five and seated himself, with his feet firmly on the ground, on a park bench overlooking a brook that flowed through his property. He told me he made it a point not to slouch or lean back, but to sit erect. In his right hand he held a long string of smooth beads, which he rubbed one at a time while he visualized each member of his family, then his friends, and lastly those about whom he had harbored unkind thoughts. All these people he then embraced mentally, directing thoughts of loving kindness toward them. This exercise over, he began concentrating on the word "death," more or less in the manner outlined above, fingering each bead as he focused on the word. All told, these meditations consumed about an hour and a half each morning.

This type of meditation has much to commend it. It is easily performed, and because it makes no inordinate demands on the body or mind, it is suitable for beginners and advanced students alike. Instead of ordinary meditation beads, one could use a skull rosary. In Japan, where such skull-shaped beads are available, many people use them for this purpose.

THE DAY OF THE DEAD IN MEXICO

The skull, which survives the disintegration of the flesh and sinews, is a symbol of both the impermanence of the body and the indestructibility of our Essential-nature. This seeming disparity has parallel religious and social significance. It can be seen most vividly on the Day of the Dead in Mexico. Throughout the country on November 2, *calaveras* ("living" skeletons) rise up from their sepulchral abodes, magically called back to life for a brief day in a symbolic mingling of life and death. These whimsical memento mori can be seen merrily playing musical instruments, engaging in trades they practiced in their earthly existence, or taking part in such social activities as weddings and dances. They are striking reminders of the fleeting nature of earthly existence and the vanity of human desires. Calaveras are actually another form of meditation on death and, as such, are more personal and real since they are objectifications of departed parents or grandparents or children. They forge a link between animate and inanimate existence, thus helping to preserve the chain of continuity of the family.

On the days leading up to the Day of the Dead, families welcome back the departed with food and drink, song and merriment. If Grandfather José was fond of tamales during his earthly existence, a plate of them is placed in front of his photograph on an altar set up for the occasion in his family's house. And on homemade altars in other homes, families place special cakes inscribed with the names of their departed, yellow flowers (associated with the dead), and candles—offerings made not to death but to the "returning dead." On the final night of the festival, José's family joins other families in a candlelight vigil at the local cemetery to "light his way (and that of the other 'returning dead') back" to the grave.

These rites are a symbolic way of bringing "alive," if only for a few days, the loved one who is gone. As Antonio Rodriguez has written, "So great is the faith of the Indian in this magical rite that he does not have to see the absent loved one on that day of communion between two forms of life that are so disparate in order to feel his presence. The father, mother, child, brother or sister are there in spirit, almost physically, and it is they who are being celebrated."[74]

Death is teased and made to dance and merrily cavort in these calaveras. The Grim Reaper is unmasked and revealed to be a jolly fellow underneath his macabre exterior. Death is thus seen for what it is, a temporary point between what has been and what will be, and not as the black hole of oblivion. As an old' Mexican refrain sings:

> Get used to dying
> before death arrives,
> for the dead can only live
> and the living can only die.[75]

Mexicans from all walks of life participate in Day of the Dead festivities to one degree or another, but in certain small towns and villages, the celebrations seem to be more widespread. It must not be supposed that Mexicans are enamored of death, or view with joy, for example, the demise of a loved one, simply because they surround themselves during these days with the symbols of death in their dance, costumes, music, and folk art. Quite the contrary. Death is given its due—as in other countries, the death of a loved one is a sad, tearful event—but death is not denied or glossed over or hidden away. In fact, the very presence of such elaborate festivities proclaims that the living still love the ever-present dead.

THE DAY OF THE DEAD ELSEWHERE

Other cultures have similar celebrations, though perhaps not so vivid as the Mexican. In Japan, for example, on the Buddhist holiday of O-bon, when the spirits of the dead are said to return to their ancestral homes, similar scenes take place, usually in the villages. In Europe in the medieval period the Dance of Death served the same function, and perhaps still does in certain countries. But in the United States and Canada, Halloween, a children's festival peopled by goblins and ghosts and shorn of all religious significance, has largely supplanted All Souls' Day, the Christian equivalent of the Day of the Dead. Many churches, however, still perform services and prayers for the dead, and many people place commemorative messages and verses in the newspapers.

MATTERS OF WORLDLY ANXIETIES . . .

Lastly, this advice from a Zen master is worth heeding:

Matters of worldly anxieties are like the links of a chain joined together continuously without a break . . . If you don't exert yourself to struggle with them, then as time goes on, with you unknowing and unawares, they will have entered deeply into you. Finally, on the last day of your life, you won't be able to do anything about them.

If you want to avoid going wrong when you face the end of your life, from now on whenever you do anything, don't let yourself slip. If you go wrong in your present doings, it will be impossible not to go wrong when you are facing death.[76]

3. FACING DEATH

Death never takes the wise man
by surprise.
He is always ready to go.
—JOHN DE LA FONTAINE

Most of the following accounts sum up the lives and deaths of
people in history who have faced death with lofty serenity. These
people include the Greek philosopher Socrates, a monk of old,
the Indian sage Ramana Maharshi, and the Buddha himself. Also
included are two contemporary people who died of cancer—one
unperturbed, the other terror-stricken. Except for this last account, all these passings exemplify a theme of this book: that a
calm, accepting death, so desirable and yet so rare, is the outcome
of a life artfully lived—"the actualization of the fierce energies
of the life processes," a life characterized by enlightened awareness and a resolute acceptance of death whether as a natural
process or as an event imposed from the outside.

Notwithstanding, we know that in every culture and civilization throughout history, ordinary, heroic individuals, many of
whom lacked a spiritual orientation—a practiced belief in either
God, karma, rebirth, or the life of the spirit—have faced their
own death without a qualm. A number have bravely died as
martyrs, condemned to death for their convictions, for their actions in defending religious, political, or social freedoms in the
face of brutal repression and injustice, or simply because they
belonged to a certain ethnic group. More commonly, countless
soldiers in wartime have courageously faced death. The same is

true of civilians. And of course there have been those admirable women and men who, though suffering from a fatal illness or disability, have uncringingly looked death in the face.

In the history of America one thinks of Nathan Hale and the words he uttered as he was about to be hanged by the British as an American spy: "I only regret that I have but one life to give for my country." If he actually did speak these words, can we infer from them that he faced death with utter equanimity? In World War II, members of Japanese kamikaze squads often wrote home, "As I go into my last battle, how happy am I to be able to sacrifice myself until my seventh lifetime[77] for the glory of the emperor and the honor of Japan!" Were these lofty sentiments inspired by a heroic patriotism or did they conceal a deep fear or neurosis?

Stated more concretely, did all these courageous individuals somehow manage to overcome their fears, or were they fearless? And if the latter, was it perhaps because of an inability to imagine their own death? In other words, how consummate was their seemingly composed acceptance of death? We can't say, for we know so little of their lives. We do, though, know much more about the life and the manner of death of those whose brief biographies follow.

SOCRATES

Socrates (470?–399 B.C.), the Greek philosopher of Athens, is one of the best-known models in the West of a solitary hero who moved as freely into death as he walked through life, with utter serenity and fearlessness. From Plato's dialogues we learn that this "wisest of men" was completely unintimidated by death, and where one would expect despair and anxiety in his last hours, he is full of peace and loving wisdom. His only concerns are to comfort those who have come to comfort him, and to set an example of how to die a laudable death.[78] From what source came the wisdom that inspired such serenity? To get an answer to this question, let us briefly examine some significant milestones in Socrates' life: that of soldier and philosopher; his trial, sentencing, and imprisonment; the extraordinary scene preceding his drinking the hemlock poison decreed by his captors, and its fatal aftermath.

Very little is known of Socrates' early life, since Plato—our principal source of information about Socrates—was with him for only the last ten years of his life. We do know that Socrates was an Athenian soldier distinguished by his courage, endurance, and presence of mind in battle. When nominated for military honors, he demurred, giving the honors instead to his superior, whose life he had saved. Once, while on campaign, Socrates amazed his fellow soldiers by standing rapt and intent for twenty-four straight hours; Plato implies that such "rapts" were not an uncommon occurrence. In later life Socrates showed conspicuous courage in defending the constitutional rights of an accused group against an angry and confused assembly, and on another occasion he defied a murderous group of tyrants at the risk of his life.

Socrates trained himself so that all his needs were satisfied with the smallest means, but he was no ascetic in his youth. Plato says that Socrates "knew how to want and how to abound." His temperament was a happy one, marked by a peaceful outlook, a gentleness toward his interlocutors, and a sense of ironic humor that was famous even in his day. At the same time he spared no one from his candid observations and piercing logic, and this quality, along with his Olympian detachment, unsettled and probably angered many people in Athens.

Socrates felt a divine mission to seek truth and to uncover all pretensions to wisdom, a mission given him by the oracle at Delphi. Although a private man in the sense that he never sought public office, he identified strongly with his fellow Athenians and cared deeply for their spiritual welfare. He urged people to discover and live by fundamental values, and he likened himself to a gadfly to the state, a *true* statesman because he attended to what was really best for the people rather than what was merely popular.

The formal indictment against Socrates was made on charges of heresy and of corrupting the youth of Athens. For these charges the prosecution urged the death penalty. In his defense Socrates turned the tables on his accusers and, without attacking them, put all Athens on trial. He was convicted by a narrow margin and asked to name an alternate penalty—exile might have been a possibility. Instead, he suggested that he ought to be supported by the state in return for his services. The judges, used to more humble supplication, angrily sentenced Socrates to death by an even greater margin.

During the time between the sentencing and the execution, Crito, who was one of Socrates' oldest friends, urged Socrates to escape and provided the means to do so. Socrates refused, saying that, among other reasons, while the decision was wrong, the court was a duly constituted one and should be obeyed. In this, as at the trial, he showed himself to be a true citizen, more upright and discerning than his accusers, the court, or his friends. The trial, the prison scene with Crito, and the manner of Socrates' death—quoted later from Plato's *Phaedo*—have stirred the hearts and minds of people for twenty-four centuries with their dignity, calm, and clarity of insight.

How could Socrates face death so courageously? The simplest answer is that he was used to dying. He had died to his personal interests in battle, as he states in the *Apology*; he had died in his "rapts," when he would forget his body in contemplation; he had died to pleasure often in his search for wisdom, a search conducted in poverty and simplicity; and he had died emotionally and intellectually to his old self many times in his process of spiritual growth, both in discourse and in silence. In a very real sense, then, he was in the habit of dying every day, and the manner of his death was the proof of his sincerity in all that had come before. In the *Phaedo* Socrates is quoted as saying, "Then in fact, Simmias, those who rightly love wisdom are practicing dying, and death to them is the least terrible thing in the world."

Obviously, then, Socrates felt in his bones that death was no punishment or evil. A good man can never be harmed by a bad, he said; virtue transcended temporal power completely. After death, Socrates believed, life continues; the *true* judgment then occurs, with judges unblinded by any mortal veils and thus able to apprehend, penetrate, and intimately know the soul of the newly dead. The reward of the truly virtuous and undistracted votary of wisdom is to go where he can converse with and test the gods and the ancient heroes and worthies. This was Socrates' unshaken faith.

At the same time, reason told him that death was an unknown, and since unknown, a possible good. To debase himself prior to death was a known evil, one that could impair his spiritual progress after death. He saw no reason to desire a known evil, possibly a great one, instead of a possible good. For other men, this kind of thinking does not penetrate very deeply into the mind and heart. For Socrates, his intellect, emotions, and spiritual life were all of a piece; he had trained himself to live by the highest lights he was aware of, and thus he narrowed the gap between knowing, doing, and being.

While Socrates was unable to turn the tide of Athenian decline, his words and actions have been of immense influence in forming what is valuable in Western civilization. And in this sense Socrates still lives today. He is always waiting to test us, and his trial is going on right now, as all of us choose between the good, as much as we may know it, and the expedient—between the genuine search for value and the hollow conventionalities that are all around us.

THE LAST HOURS OF SOCRATES*

Crito made a sign to the servant, who was standing by; he went out and returned with the jailer, who was carrying the cup of poison. Socrates said, "You, my good friend, who are experienced in these matters, shall give me directions how I am to proceed."

The jailer answered, "You have only to walk about until your legs are heavy, and then to lie down, and the poison will act." At the same time he handed the cup to Socrates, who in the easiest and gentlest manner, without the least fear or change of color or feature, looking directly at the jailer, took the cup and said: "What do you say about making a libation out of this cup to any god? May I or not?"

*(as adapted from Benjamin Jowett's translation of Plato's *Phaedo*)

The man answered, "We only prepare, Socrates, just so much as we deem enough."

"I understand," Socrates said, "but I may and must ask the gods to prosper my journey from this to the other world—and so be it according to my prayer."

Then raising the cup to his lips, quite readily and cheerfully he drank off the poison. And hitherto most of us had been able to control our sorrow, but now when we saw him drinking and saw too that he had finished the draught, we could no longer forbear, and in spite of myself my own tears were flowing fast; so that I covered my face and wept, not for him but at the thought of my own calamity in having to part from such a friend. Nor was I the first; for Crito, when he found himself unable to restrain his tears, had got up, and I [Plato] followed; and at that moment Apollodorus, who had been weeping all the time, broke out in a loud and passionate cry which made cowards of us all.

Socrates alone retained his calmness. "What is this strange outcry?" he asked. "I sent away the women mainly in order that they might not misbehave in this way, for I have been told that a man should die in peace. Be quiet, then, and have patience."

When we heard his words we were ashamed and refrained our tears. Socrates walked about until his legs began to fail, and then he lay on his back, according to directions. The man who gave him the poison looked at Socrates' feet and legs now and then. After a while he pressed Socrates' foot hard and asked him if he could feel anything. Socrates said, "No." Then he pressed higher and higher on Socrates' legs and showed us that they were cold and stiff. Socrates felt them himself and said, "When the poison reaches the heart, that will be the end."

He was beginning to grow cold about the groin when he uncovered his face, for he had covered himself up, and said—they were his last words—"Crito, I owe a cock to Asclepius; will you remember to pay the debt?"

"The debt shall be paid," said Crito. "Is there anything else?"

There was no answer to this question, but in a minute or two a movement was heard, and the attendants uncovered him. His eyes were set, and Crito closed his eyes and mouth.

Duncan Phyfe (1895–1985)

The hero of the previous biography was a charismatic figure, a stalwart individual who challenged the political, social, and religious ideologies of his time and as a consequence suffered execution at the hands of the state. Duncan Phyfe, the subject of the present biography, was no such mover and shaker—he was Everyman. He merits a place in this book by reason of his having lived an ordinary life extraordinarily well, thus preparing the way for a beautiful death, with no regrets. At a time when so many of his contemporaries, overcome by fears of a painful death, prefer to die by their own hand and not by God's, so to say, Duncan Phyfe's death stands out in marked contrast. Neither death nor life held terrors for him, for he was in love with life and accepting of death. Until he died, in his own bed at the age of ninety, he wavered not the slightest in his conviction that death was not the end but the springboard to yet another life.

The circumstances of Duncan Phyfe's outer life give scarcely a hint of the rich spirituality that developed within him in his later years. Born in 1895 in Cold Spring, New York, the nephew of the famous furniture maker Duncan Phyfe, he served in World War I in France as an ambulance driver and was decorated by the French. Later he became a sound engineer. After installing sound systems in South Africa, he returned to the United States to work for RCA, where he invented the speaker that attaches to cars in drive-in theaters.

He married twice and had two children, a daughter and a son. After he retired in the early sixties, he and his wife traveled all over the United States in an Airstream trailer, finally settling in San Diego, California. A Christian but not a churchgoer, in San Diego he became interested in a sect of Christianity that believed the Kingdom of God is here on earth. He had been born and baptized in the Methodist church, but he left it when he became an adult because, in his own words, "I did not find in it the basic truths I was looking for."

Upon his wife's passing he went to live in a trailer in Santa Fe, New Mexico. His zest for adventure and joy in living led him, in his eighties, to buy a motor scooter on which he zipped around Santa Fe. About this time he was "discovered" by a group of idealistic New Age artists and writers who had been drawn to this Shangri-la of the Southwest by its promise of greater personal freedom and the chance to make a name for themselves in the arts. But artistic and personal success was slow in coming; meanwhile they had to struggle to eke out a living. They were sheep who needed a shepherd, and in Duncan Phyfe they found one. He became their benefactor, father confessor, and spiritual mentor; at the same time he was nourished by their freewheeling spirits and youthful enthusiasms. He had always gravitated toward younger people rather than people of his own age because of his youthful outlook on life. "I never felt I was getting old," he said. "I love people, and my greatest joy was giving them joy."

With characteristic energy and thoroughness, Duncan devoted himself to helping his newfound friends become acclimated to the rarefied atmosphere of Santa Fe. But he did not confuse his priorities. When they lacked groceries, he did not give them the pap of heaven but edible kitchen stuff; he knew that the rumblings of an empty stomach will drown out the sounds of the most eloquently spoken spiritual truths. Similarly, when their roofs leaked and the wiring in their run-down quarters wouldn't work, he didn't pray to God to help his young friends acquire the wherewithal to make the necessary repairs; instead, he made them himself at his own expense. Mechanically talented, he constantly made his skills available to them. Despite his advanced age, he was ever ready to chauffeur a young friend around town or to baby-sit for those with small children.

My first meeting with this remarkable man took place at the home of his son and daughter-in-law. He was in bed with cancer of the gallbladder and liver. Earlier he had been operated on and was told his cancer was terminal. His cheerfulness and lucidity —he was ninety at the time—belied the fatal character of his illness.

As we talked, he sat propped up in a double bed in a comfortable room containing a large stereo set that he himself had built. In addition to Duncan, in the room were his writer friend who had introduced me to him; my assistant, who was taping our talk; and I. Duncan seemed entirely at ease, making no effort to sound profound or holy.

"Duncan, what do you feel the purpose of your life to be?"

"To prepare myself for the doors beyond."

His friend interrupted to ask, "Might not part of your purpose here also be to give light and joy to other people?"

"That is so. A great desire of mine has been to give light to those who are seeking it—to give it to them to the best of my ability and the best of my understanding—that is, to give them fundamental truths. There are so many dimensions of consciousness besides this three-dimensional time set we are boxed into."

"I understand that death might come to you at any time. How do you feel about that?" I asked. His reply startled me:

"I think that's wonderful."

"You really aren't afraid?" I pressed him.

"No, I have no trauma about it whatsoever. I am at peace with the world and with my Creator. What more could I ask?"

To determine the source of his serenity and confidence, I asked him what he thought would happen to him after he died. Unhesitatingly he replied, "All the most wonderful things one could conceive of. Death is nothing but an ongoing expansion of life, to which there is no limit."

Again I asked, "No doubt in your mind that you will be reborn in one form or another according to your karma?"

"Not the slightest."

"Has this belief or awareness given you great peace of mind?"

"Yes, it has." There was no mistaking the sincerity of his words or the peace of soul he radiated.

At one point I asked whether he was having physical or mental pain. "No, not really. It is just that I hate to part from dear friends. But I know I will go beyond what you might call this present 'vale of tears.' " Questioned whether this life had really been a vale of tears for him, he said he had used the term merely as a figure of speech—that after all, there was so much pain in the world today: wars and other violence. "But if you look around, you can also see some beautiful spots of love in this world," he added. Earlier, in fact, he had insisted that everything boils down to one word—love. "It holds the world together and is the source of divine Mind." That could have sounded trite but for the radiance that shone in his face as he uttered that one word "love." He looked positively beatific.

Another time I asked him why he thought most people were afraid to die.

"I suppose it's a revulsion against what they take to be eternal oblivion. Most people want to continue on—not necessarily in this life but to go on and on and not feel that this is all there is; and if it is all there is, why did it ever start? Most people who are afraid of dying," he continued, "feel that death is the end, a closed thing."

"Duncan, can you honestly say that you face the prospect of death without fear or dread—willingly?" Raising himself higher in the bed and looking me straight in the eye, he answered— "Willingly." No one could doubt the conviction behind his words.

Duncan Phyfe died August 12, 1985, some three weeks after our interview. His son and daughter-in-law, who were with him, said that during the last few days of his life he was semiconscious, responding mainly with smiling eyes. Strongly evident was his love for everyone and his eagerness for the unknown ahead. Said his son, "It was almost a euphoria. He wanted to go." In fact, about a week before he died he had asked, somewhat impatiently, "Why doesn't God come and take me?"

For the last six hours he was calm and unconscious. He died curled up in the fetal position.

He was loved by many.

LEAH (1933–87)

The following narrative by a psychotherapist describes how his friend and colleague Leah (not her real name) died. It has been included here to illustrate a painful, panic-stricken death—a classic example of someone who, by her own admission, had not prepared herself for dying.

Leah was diagnosed with ovarian cancer at age fifty-two. Her initial reaction to the doctor's report was brief: "I don't have a good feeling about this." She quickly made up her mind to fight the cancer on all levels. But despite chemotherapy and radiation, with their usual side effects, the cancer kept spreading and she was in pain more often. Doctors were running out of alternative treatments.

We talked about how the mind worked to deny things. She would say, "When I'm in pain, all I want to do is accept that I'm dying and be prepared for it . . . But then the pain subsides and I find myself looking through the newspaper to see if there's a sale on dresses."

A month before she died, Leah was hospitalized for the last time. She had deteriorated fairly rapidly, and death became an any-day-now proposition. She lost more and more of her physical functioning and there were fewer and fewer choices about what to do with her time. The simplest act required her complete attention, if not someone's assistance.

On the last evening, I was at her bedside, as was her daughter, Gail, along with a friend of Gail's. I had met Gail only once, the previous night, and she now told me that the doctor had said, "Tonight will probably be the night." Leah was wearing an oxygen mask. She was very weak, barely talking.

Leah had said before that she liked hearing others talk even if she couldn't participate directly. So Gail and her friend reminisced about their childhood. At one point Gail mentioned that her mother had always liked the sound of her friend's laughter, and her friend asked Leah, "Want to hear a joke?" In her clearest, most energetic act of the evening, Leah took off the oxygen mask and said, "What is it?" Gail's friend told the joke and we all laughed, with Leah smiling a little-girl smile. She became a little more animated, complaining about the incompetent nurses, praising the good ones, and joking about "the crazy one who was only interested in [her] bowel movements." She knew she was being entertaining, and we laughed quite a lot.

* * *

After a little while Gail's friend left. Then Leah said she wanted a priest to come and give her the last rites. Although Leah was actually Jewish, she grew up in Europe during the Second World War, and her mother, unable to take care of her, put her in a nunnery at age five. She often said that the nuns were her real mothers.

I went to call the priest. When I returned there was a noticeable change. Leah was quieter. I held her hand and was quiet with her. Gail sat on the other side of the bed and held her other hand. The priest came. Leah had her eyes closed and didn't appear to notice him. Her daughter asked, "Do you want to see the priest?" Leah opened her eyes and looked. She said, "Not yet," and pulled her body back as much as she could. She began to look agitated. The priest asked her if she was Catholic, and she explained a little about her background, saying she wanted the blessings of both the Catholic and Jewish faiths. She told the priest that in her most desperate moments of pain and despair, she saw Jesus and called on him for help.

The priest began to administer the last rites. His voice was so low while he was saying the prayers that we couldn't really hear him. Gail and I stepped out into the hall while he heard Leah's final confession. We both were dismayed that in this critical moment his ability to transmit any kind of spiritual inspiration seemed nonexistent. He called us back in, completed the ritual, and left. Gail asked her mother if she felt any better for having seen him, but she didn't answer.

Leah was quiet now for longer periods, but with a growing sense of mental agitation. I could feel it very clearly. Not knowing what to say or do, I held her hand and began to focus my own mind as I had learned to do in meditation. I could feel her mind very clearly, feel the fright starting to build. The more I was able to let go of anything arising in my mind, the more I could "touch" her, and her agitation subsided.

This period of relative quiet was interrupted after thirty or forty minutes by a tremendous upsurge of terror. Leah was starting to panic. She said, "I'm frightened!" and began to shake. I focused my own mind more intensely, and from time to time I could feel it having an effect, but more and more she was on her own. She started to call to God with great intensity, over and over. For days she had barely been able to talk above a whisper; now she cried out to God, and to us she begged, "Help me! Help me! I want to get back to the peace I was feeling!" The terror began to come in waves over her, and her whole body shook. She began hallucinating, talking in a fragmented, disconnected way about images she alone saw. She would speak for long periods in French, her native language, and would call out, *"Peur! Peur!"* (Fear! Fear!)

She asked us to help her sit up, and without real help she sat up herself for the first time in a week. I have never seen such terror.

Gail said to me from the other side of the bed, "You really die alone . . . She had a hard life and she's having a hard death." How much of our lives is spent in the illusion that we can avoid the results of our actions; we believe this until the hour of our death, when there's no escape from the fruits of what we've sown in our life. Helplessly I watched Leah as she was swept along by a stark and relentless river of everything that was unresolved in her life. She took off her oxygen mask and said to me, "You've been so impressed with me. You thought I was dealing with my death, but I did nothing to prepare for this!" She put the mask back on, still very agitated, and withdrew into herself. Suddenly, almost violently, she took the mask off again and said in desperation, "I want to die but I can't get out!" She pointed to her chest and made a motion with her hands as if to tear it open. Gail and I took turns fanning her to keep her cool. She became weaker and quieter, and what she said was not lucid.

Leah had been quiet and seemingly far away for at least half an hour when, at 2 A.M., I decided to go home. Gail, too, went to lie down in the lounge for some much needed rest, and she asked a nurse to wake her if anything happened. Leah had once said she wanted to be alone at the moment of death because she felt it would be easier for her—that she would find it less painful to let go if others weren't present.

Leah died, alone, sometime within the next hour.

SENG-CHAO

An example of remarkable composure in the face of death is that of the Buddhist monk Seng-chao (384–414). An exceptionally talented writer and a religious genius, he wrote many philosophical treatises and religious tracts. The emperor, hearing of his abilities, ordered him to leave the monastery and return to lay life to serve as the imperial secretary. Seng-chao refused, and as a result he was condemned to die by decapitation. He was only thirty. He appealed to the emperor for a week's reprieve in order to complete a book on metaphysics titled *Treatise on the Jewel Treasure*. It was granted. When the work was finished, he calmly submitted to the execution. At the point of death he composed the following verse:

> The four elements[79] essentially have no master.
> The five *skandhas*[80] are fundamentally void.
> When the naked sword cuts off my head
> It will be like cutting a spring breeze.

Admirable as Seng-chao's sublime indifference to death is, one cannot but speculate that in a previous existence he had killed someone and was therefore expiating that karma in this life. For the moral law of cause and effect decrees that violence to another never goes unpunished. As a Buddhist, Seng-chao must have known this. He may even have considered his untimely death atonement for a past capital offense.

SRI RAMANA MAHARSHI

The manner of dying of Sri Ramana Maharshi (1879–1950), one of modern India's most revered religious figures, is reminiscent of that of the Zen masters, whose teachings his own closely resembled. He was honored as much for his wisdom as for the exemplary character of his life. When asked where he would go upon his death, he replied, "They say that I am dying, but I am not going away. Where could I go? I am here . . ."[81]

Here follows a fuller account of the death scene of this re-markable sage:

> On Thursday, April 13, a doctor brought Sri Bhagavan [Ma-harshi] a palliative to relieve the congestion in the lungs, but he refused it. "It is not necessary, everything will come right within two days," [insisted the Maharshi, who was dying of cancer.] . . .
>
> At about sunset Sri Bhagavan told his attendants to sit him up. They knew already that every movement, every touch, was painful, but he told them not to worry about that. He sat with one of the attendants supporting his head. A doctor began to give him ox-ygen, but with a wave of his right hand he motioned him away . . .
>
> Unexpectedly a group of devotees sitting on the veranda outside the hall began singing "Arunachala-Siva."[82] On hearing it, Sri Bha-gavan's eyes opened and shone. He gave a brief smile of inde-scribable tenderness. From the outer edges of his eyes tears of bliss rolled down. One more deep breath, and no more. There was no struggle, no spasm, no other sign of death: only that the next breath did not come.[83]

GAUTAMA THE BUDDHA

Lastly, as an example of a quintessential approach to death among the masters, let us now consider the *parinirvāna* of Gau-tama the Buddha (563–483 B.C.). The Sanskrit word *nirvāna* lit-erally means extinction: the unconditioned state beyond birth and death that is reached after all ignorance and craving have been extinguished and all karma, which is the cause of rebirth, has been dissolved. The term *parinirvāna*, used only in reference to the Buddha, means complete extinction, the state of perfect freedom from bondage reached by Gautama Buddha at the time of his utter passing away.

To set the stage for the final act of the drama of Gautama's earthly life, let us trace the significant events of his final days. A good starting point is his last preaching tour. Tradition tells us that when he came to the town of Pava, in northern India, he halted at the mango grove of Chunda, a pious follower and worker in metal, who invited the Master and his monks to dine at his house the following day. The meal consisted of sweet rice, cake, and mushrooms. Stricken with grievous pains as a result of eating the mushrooms—which, it turned out, were poisonous—the Buddha, mindful and self-possessed, nonetheless bore the pains without complaint. When they abated somewhat, he said to Ānanda, his faithful attendant, "Let us go on to Kushinagara." They had not gone far when the Master turned aside from the path to the foot of a tree and said, "Ānanda, fold my robe in four and spread it out for me. I am weary and must rest awhile."

And then he spoke to Ānanda concerning Chunda the smith, saying that none should impute the least blame to Chunda because the Master died after receiving the last meal at his hands. "On the contrary," said the Buddha, "there are two offerings of food which are supremely precious: that which is given before the Tathagata[84] attains to Perfect Insight, and the other before his utter passing away. Good karma has redounded to Chunda the smith; therefore let him not feel any remorse."

"Come, Ānanda, let us continue our journey to the sala grove of the Mallas."

When they got there he said, "Spread out for me the couch, with its head to the north, between the twin sala trees. I am weary, Ānanda, and would like to lie down." He laid himself down on his right side, with one leg resting on the other. Then he told Ānanda that his utter passing away would take place at the third watch of that night.

The texts tell us that the Buddha first passed through the four stages of rapture. Rising from the fourth stage, he entered the successive stages of the infinity of space; the infinity of thought; emptiness; the realm between consciousness and unconsciousness; and the realm where the consciousness of both sensations and ideas has wholly passed away.

Now it seemed to Ānanda that the Master *had* passed away; but he entered again into every stage in *reverse* order until he reached the second stage of rapture, and then he passed into the third and fourth stages of rapture. And passing out of the last stage of rapture he immediately expired.

Earlier, when many of the Buddha's followers were weeping at his announcement that he would soon pass away, he reprimanded them for grieving when they should be rejoicing:

> In this hour of joy it is not proper to grieve. Your despair is quite inappropriate, and you should regain your composure. The goal, so hard to win, which for many aeons I have wished for, now at last is no longer far away. When that is won, no earth or water, fire, wind or ether is present; unchanging bliss beyond all objects of the senses, a peace which none can take away, the highest thing there is; and when you hear of that and know that no becoming mars it and nothing ever there can pass away—how, then, is there room for grief in your minds? At Gaya,[85] at the time when I won enlightenment, I got rid of the causes of becoming, which are nothing but a gang of harmful vipers; now the hour comes near when I get rid also of this body, the dwelling place of the acts accumulated in the past. Now that at last this body, which harbors so much ill, is on its way out; now that at last the frightful dangers of becoming are about to be extinct; now that at last I emerge from the vast and endless suffering—is this the time for you to grieve? . . .[86]

By ordinary reckoning the Buddha lived to the venerable age of eighty; he had been teaching and preaching for forty-five years since his supreme enlightenment at the age of thirty-five.

Two: DYING

You have to learn to do everything,
even to die.

—GERTRUDE STEIN

Learn to die and thou shalt live,
for there shall none learn to live
that hath not learned to die.

—THE BOOK OF THE CRAFT OF DYING

Since dying has become fashionable,
no one's life is safe anymore.

—JEWISH PROVERB

1. THE DYING PERSON
AND DEATH

THE PROCESS OF DYING

In a box in a corner, a very dark corner of the mind of each of us, is a voice. The voice says, "I am going to die. One day I am going to die."

We tend not to venture near that corner. We rarely listen to that voice. Sometimes it speaks to us so clearly and emphatically that we have to listen. When we're sick, when we narrowly escape harm, when someone we know dies, we hear it speaking to us. We hear it more frequently as we age, as our bodies fail, as our cumulative experience of death increases. Sometimes the voice emits a powerful, powerful scream that shakes us mercilessly. When someone we love dies, the voice tells us that our life is forever altered, that there is no going back.

The voice reminds us that we are, like everyone else who ever lived, mortal, expendable. How we react to this voice, how we try to block it out, determines how we live our lives.[1]

If we are to die with a measure of peace, we must have some understanding of who or what it is that dies. Most people believe they are a body and a mind, an I, an ego, a self, a soul, identified by the name Tom or Mary. But "body" is only a name for a combination of changing elements, and "mind" a name for a succession of thoughts. Without thinking too much about it, we believe that the psychophysical combination called Tom or Mary is the real person. But this is true only in a conventional sense. Actually:

> There is no doer but the deed
> There is no experience but the experiencer
> Constituent parts alone roll on.[2]

Everything mental or physical is in a state of change; nothing is stable or static. If we reflect on this carefully, we will see that there is no person who dies, only a *process* of dying. Just as moving is a process and walking is a process, so dying is a process. By refusing to identify our True-self with our actions, we are able to grasp the fact that all life is just a process.

How "Not to Be There" When Dying

Some of you may have read these lines of Woody Allen's:

> I don't mind dying.
> I just don't want to be there
> when it happens.

These words are more than just funny: a deep truth is concealed in them. If you "don't want to be there" when dying, learn how to merge with dying, so that *you* "disappear," transcending body and mind. Rid yourself of the thinking that distinguishes death from dying, self from other, and similar antagonistic opposites. Who remains then to say or think, "I'm dying"? In this highly desirable condition there can be no clinging to life, no railing against death.

Becoming One with Dying

HOMEMAKER: What exactly do you mean by "merge with dying"?

Perhaps this example will make clear what I mean. Let us say you are at an art gallery where a number of first-class paintings are being exhibited. You look around and suddenly you are "grabbed" by one of them. You take in the entire picture in one fell swoop. Irresistibly it draws you into itself. Your reflective mind now begins to analyze the painting. "The colors are rich, the forms pleasing, the relationships intimate"—all this is the functioning of your analytical mind. But you have not yet merged with the painting. You gaze and gaze at it, going deeper and deeper, losing yourself in it. The picture engulfs you. Time and space disappear. You are no longer you, a subject separate from the painting as object; your mind and body have merged with the painting—you have entered its heart. This state defies description. Tears begin to well up, yet you aren't aware of them. You are one with the painting.

What Is Samadhi?

NURSE: How could a dying person possibly get into such a state?

There are, of course, degrees of *samadhi* (oneness), to use a technical term. Absolute, or complete, samadhi is a state of total immersion in which one is no longer aware of oneself as a subject separate from a person, thing, or activity as an object. It is a state of intense yet effortless concentration, of heightened and expanded awareness. Limited, or positive, samadhi is partial unity with an object or action.

Let us say you are absorbed in watching a gorgeous sunset. That is positive samadhi. You start with an object and then transcend it. Absolute samadhi, on the other hand, is objectless. Since there is no subject-object awareness to begin with, this state is not entered into in relation to anything. The concentrative power developed through certain kinds of objectless meditation makes it possible for one to reach the uncommon state of absolute samadhi. But upon entering that condition, one has no self-conscious awareness of being in it. States of absolute samadhi are of much longer and deeper duration than those of positive samadhi. In positive samadhi one often experiences blissful feelings. In absolute samadhi, on the other hand, no thoughts or feelings arise. This "no-thoughting" is not an insensibility or trancelike condition in the negative sense. Human thought is awareness in motion; samadhi is awareness at rest. Samadhi and enlightenment can be said to be identical from the view of our intrinsic wisdom mind. But seen from the developing stages leading to awakening, absolute samadhi and enlightenment are different.

All the senses—and the intellect as well—can be a vehicle for positive samadhi. Hearing music, looking at a painting, engaging in a sport, pondering a subject, even engaging in sex—all these can be the means of attaining the *temporary* state of positive samadhi. "Temporary" is an important distinction, for one enters and leaves positive samadhi with relative ease. The more you cultivate oneness in your life, the easier it becomes to achieve positive samadhi.

Let us turn now to the matter of everyday dying, for it's central to our subject.

DAILY DYING

Tell me, were you ever rejected by someone you deeply loved?

HOMEMAKER: Yes, and it was terribly painful. I still think about him sometimes even though it was more than five years ago.

At the time, didn't you feel as though you had died? And how did you feel when someone very close to you passed away? Didn't part of you die with him or her? There are so many little dyings every day, aren't there? These daily dyings are the price we pay for a commitment to any relationship.

Disruptions of human relationships occur regularly throughout life. They include loss of parents, death of a mate, divorce, death of family members, death of close friends. Because we attach ourselves to forms, letting go is not easy. The more we cling to people and things, the more we experience pain at our loss of them. We meet change with resistance and fear and therefore try to avoid it. Change produces the greatest stress for most people. The standard rating scale for stress shows that virtually all major stress grows out of recent transitions, such as sickness, moving from one city to another, divorce, change of job, change in health, change in economic status. But at the top of the list is death. Death alone is the only change over which we have no control. All seasons of life—infancy, adolescence, middle age, old age—inevitably involve human loss. But these "deaths" are also precursors to a new life, for if we merge with the sorrow—not standing outside it—suddenly the pain, the suffering, disappears; and it is followed by a heightened awareness, a liberating joy. From such dyings emerges the unshakable knowledge that loss and gain, good and bad, cannot reach our innermost being. These daily deaths, then, are resurrections. No one need wonder what it means to die, for everyone at one time or another has had intimations of his or her own mortality. But because the picture of death painted by our culture is tinted in such gloomy colors, we shrink from it, often in terror, and pretend it can't happen to us. As Robert Samuelson wittily observed, "We Americans are great optimists. No one has yet devised a preventive for death, but we keep looking."

To be reborn hourly and daily in this life, we need to die—to give of ourselves wholly to the demands of the moment, so that we utterly "disappear." Thoughts of past, present, or future, of life and death, of this world and the next, are transcended in the superabundance of the now. Time and timelessness coalesce: this is the moment of eternity. Thus our every act is a matter either of giving life or taking it away. If we perform each act with total absorption, we give life to our life. If we do things half-heartedly, we kill that life.

Jacques Lusseyran, a blind French Resistance leader who survived a Nazi death camp, pinpoints how to achieve such a transcendent relation to life and death:

> Memories are too tender, too close to fear. They consume energy. We had to live in the present; each moment had to be absorbed for all that was in it to satisfy the hunger for life . . . Don't hoard. Eat the food right away, greedily, mouthful after mouthful, as if each crumb were all the food in the world. When a ray of sunshine comes, open out, absorb it to the depths of your being. Never think that an hour earlier you were cold and that an hour later you will be cold again. Just enjoy.
>
> Latch on to the passing minute. Shut off the workings of memory and hope. The amazing thing is that no anguish held out against this treatment for very long. Take away from suffering its double drumbeat of resonance, memory, and fear. Suffering may

persist, but already it is relieved by half. Throw yourself into each moment as if it were the only one that really existed. Work and work hard.[3]

We die because we are alive. Living means birth and death. Creating and destroying signify life. The evidence of our having lived is the fact that we die.[4] Dying to (that is, total immersion in) the task at hand—whether one is working on an assembly line, engaging in a sport, dancing, playing chess, mountain climbing, or singing—paradoxically leads to a heightened sense of awareness, a peak state in which there is a feeling of invigoration and relaxed awareness coupled with a rapturous joy.[5]

We are not, of course, speaking here of those who are understandably fearful of a long and painful illness and the great financial burden it will impose on their family. And yet essentially the problem is the same for all: how to live fully with life while alive and die serenely with death when dying, free from anxiety and other worrisome emotions. In the end the quality of our death, like the quality of our life, is a matter of an unbridled (pain-producing) ego or a restrained (peaceful) one.

DANCE INSTRUCTOR: I've heard that at the moment of death your whole life passes vividly in front of you. How do you tie up all the emotional loose ends of your life—the severed relationships, the broken promises, the neglects, the regrets—so that you can die a peaceful death?

You have to start *now*. The first step is to begin a spiritual practice—Zen, if you like. Beware of substituting reading for actual practice, for it is easy to be enticed away from practice by the sirens of literature, psychology, philosophy, and the like. The reading of certain books can provide a compass and a map, but they are no substitute for personal experience. The good book, to paraphrase Emerson, is the one that gets you onto the meditation mat (or chair).

Painful memories, bothersome feelings, and other "incomplete business" once lodged in your unconscious will surface to consciousness as your mind becomes quieted and deeper levels are attained. As you continue to meditate regularly and are aware and alert in your daily doings, the disruptive elements in your life will lose their hold over you and eventually disappear. Too, you will experience greater clarity in your life as a whole, and this will reflect itself in peace and tranquillity when your dying hour is at hand.

In this connection a middle-aged woman wrote me recently, "If on my deathbed I can look at my life knowing I struggled with my [spiritual] practice but had not reached full awakening, I would still have more peace of mind than if I never tried anything at all."

WE DIE AS WE HAVE LIVED

For the way we die reflects the way we have lived. A good death puts the stamp on a good life. "Just as a well spent day brings happy sleep, so a life well used brings happy death."[6] But if we have lived a life of emotional turmoil and conflict, or a selfish and inane existence, our dying will be troubled and painful. Instead of seeking ways to prolong our lives through medical technology, we would better serve ourselves and society by dedicating ourselves to improving the spiritual and moral quality of what life we have.

The mental agony of facing death for one who has lived a troubled and alienated life is vividly portrayed by Tolstoy in his moving story "The Death of Ivan Ilyich." In the story, Tolstoy describes the unbearable spiritual suffering of the dying Ilyich, who in a moment of truth understands that in itself death is not frightening. Rather, what evokes the greatest pain is the type of life he has led—the knowledge that his life has been sinful, not in the commonly accepted moral sense but in relation to the inner voice, what we might call conscience. Put simply, he feels that his life was useless and ill spent. And as he approaches death, the only real relief comes to him in those rare moments when he follows the promptings of his inner voice and not popularly accepted opinions and customs.

Significantly, many who survived cruel oppression and the utmost loss of freedom in slave-labor and concentration camps affirm that it was not imprisonment itself, and all that that implied, that was frightening; rather, it was recollection of the life they had led prior to arrest. In his well-known book *The Gulag Archipelago*, Solzhenitsyn more than once attests that mental suffering was greatest when he and his fellow prisoners reflected on the unwholesome aspects of their life prior to prison, "about sinning with respect to one's own soul—which meant sinning with respect to other people as well."[7]

SURVIVAL AND THE INNER VOICE

To these cases may be added another group of men and women who did not die passively but survived life-threatening circumstances because they listened to and followed a mysterious inner voice. Among them is Jacques Lusseyran, mentioned earlier. When only nineteen he was seized by the Gestapo, along with five of his coworkers in the Resistance movement, and condemned to death "for subversive acts against the German occupation authorities." During the 180 days he was incarcerated, he was ceaselessly interrogated. Then, instead of executing him, the Gestapo inexplicably shipped him and his companions to the notorious Buchenwald death camp in central Germany. In his book *And There Was Light* Lusseyran writes that of the two thousand Frenchmen who were shipped off with him in cattle cars to Buchenwald at the end of January 1944, about thirty survived, he among them.

What enabled Lusseyran, blind and virtually defenseless, to survive? Chiefly it was his refusal to submit to fear and despair—a refusal buttressed by a strong faith in God that neither hunger, constant cold, oppressive labor, nor sickness could diminish:

> Have I said that death was already there? . . . Sickness and pain,
> yes, but not death. Quite the opposite—life, and that was the
> unbelievable thing that had taken possession of me. I had never
> lived so fully before. There were names which I mumbled from
> the depths of my astonishment. No, my lips did not speak them,
> but they had their own song: Providence, the Guardian Angel,
> Jesus Christ, God . . . There was one thing left which I could do,

not refuse God's help, the breath He was blowing upon me. There was the one battle I had to fight, hard and wonderful all at once: not to let my body be taken by fear. For fear kills and joy maintains life. Also I could try to show other people how to go about holding on to life. I could turn toward them the flow of light and joy which had grown so abundant in me . . . From that time on they stopped stealing my bread or my soup . . . Hundreds of people confided in me. The men were determined to talk. They spoke to me in French, in Russian, in German, in Polish. I did the best I could to understand them all. That is how I lived, how I survived . . .[8]

Lusseyran's response to his imprisonment coincides with those of Solzhenitsyn and other sensitive Russian writers who were imprisoned in labor camps in the Soviet Union and who have written books about their experiences. Some of these books are analyzed and commented on by Mihajlo Mihajlov in his article "Mystical Experiences of the Labor Camps":

All the authors agree that arrest, prison, and camp—simply to say the loss of freedom—have formed the most profound and significant experiences of their lives . . . Athough they underwent the most extreme spiritual and physical suffering during their imprisonment, they also experienced a fulfilling happiness undreamed of by people outside the prison walls . . . Those having gone through the most adverse circumstances, which threatened both soul and body, unanimously affirmed that those who have sacrificed their souls to save their body have lost both; while for those who were prepared to sacrifice their body to save their soul, some kind of strange and mysterious law, eluding understanding, preserved both . . . Life experience has revealed to us that deep in the human soul is an unfamiliar force which is stronger than all the external forces of enslavement and death . . .[9]

SHOULD ONE STRUGGLE AGAINST DEATH?

NURSE: I work in a hospital ward where there are a lot of terminal patients. Many of them don't really know whether to fight their disease or to give up and die, and they seem to be in agony with the problem. I have to admit that in watching them I grapple with this question as well: should one fight against death?

From what I have seen, read, and been told by doctors and nurses, that problem is eventually resolved by the patients themselves in a natural manner. It is true that in the beginning, patients are confused and often distraught. Their minds are filled with conflicting thoughts and emotions. On the one hand, there are feelings of denial, guilt, fear, depression, loneliness, apathy, and despair; on the other hand, there is the desire, often desperate, to prolong their life. And always there is the pain to cope with—physical and mental. Some terminally ill patients I have been with feel they are letting their family down if they don't struggle against their illness. Others in chronic pain often oscillate between fight and flight, especially when the pain is associated with symptoms of deterioration, such as loss of appetite and weight and increasing physical dependence. The message from the body is clear: "Unless a miracle occurs, you can't survive for long." The patient knows she is on a collision course with death. Still, if she becomes convinced that what we miscall death is not the black void of extinction but merely a transitional stage, it is unlikely she will clutch at life or surrender to death out of deep despair. In the end "a dying man needs to die, as a sleepy man needs to sleep, and there comes a time when it is wrong, as well as useless, to resist."[10]

Dying Well

How individuals respond to a fatal illness—in other words, how they die—depends of course on their personality and their values, but mostly on the quality of their faith and spiritual awareness. And these latter qualities can be developed through training, as the seventh Dalai Lama points out: "In order to die well, with the joy and confidence of being within the white rays of spiritual awareness, it is essential to begin readying yourself now. Familiarize yourself with the profundities of the scriptures." Few in our culture, though, whether priests or scientists, seem willing to believe that dying well can be an achievement. Many magazine articles and books tell us how to live, but few tell us how to die. Most focus on the loss, the tragedy, the pain.

HOMEMAKER: What do you mean by "dying well"? Dying without pain? Or do you mean dying without fear? Or are you equating an artful death with a spiritual one—that is, dying with calm acceptance, without struggle—because you're certain that the destruction of the body is not the end of existence?

The writer Nikos Kazantzakis expressed it this way:

Thinking of death, he [Nikos Kazantzakis] wrote to a friend in 1947: "To conquer illusion and hope, without being overcome by terror: this has been the whole endeavor of my life these past twenty years; to look straight into the abyss without bursting into tears, without begging or threatening, calmly, serenely preserving the dignity of man; to see the abyss and work as though I were immortal . . ."[11]

To die artfully is to die thinking of nothing, wishing for nothing, wanting to understand nothing, clinging to nothing—just fading away like clouds in the sky. That is the acme of artful dying; such an accomplishment, though, presupposes considerable spiritual insight. To be able to die thinking of nothing implies that, through meditation and other spiritual practices, you have gained control over your wayward thoughts and a high degree of mastery over your emotions. To die wishing for nothing assumes you have realized that fundamentally you are whole and complete and therefore lack nothing. To die wanting to understand nothing means you have perceived that all things, including your thoughts, feelings, and perceptions, are impermanent, arising when certain causes and conditions bring them into being and passing away with the emergence of new causal factors. To die clinging to nothing means you have realized that nothing is really ours, neither body nor mind nor life itself—and that therefore death is a letting go of that which we never really owned in the first place. As he lay dying, the mystical philosopher Plotinus (A.D. 205?–270) spoke cryptically of the "that":

I am making my last effort to return
that which is divine in me
to that which is divine in the universe.

Two Different Ways of Dying

NURSE: I think I'm beginning to get the idea, but could you clarify it a bit more?

Let me tell you about two people with whom I was acquainted who died in totally different ways; you may draw your own conclusions as to their relative merits.

Peter (not his real name) was a man in his late thirties with a lovely wife and two young children. He led an active life, traveled extensively, engaged in many sports, and had friends in all walks of life. Then he suddenly, or so it seemed, came down with a particularly malignant form of bone cancer. Chemotherapy was prescribed. At first he responded to it, but then he grew worse as the disease entrenched itself in his bones. He took to his bed and began to lose weight rapidly as his appetite evaporated. At this point a new experimental drug was tried. If it worked, Peter's doctor told him, he might go into remission and add six months or more to his life. At first the new drug did seem to help, for with the aid of a walker Peter could get out of bed to go to the bathroom. Soon, however, the excruciating pain returned, a pain so severe that stronger and stronger pain-suppressing drugs had to be prescribed along with more powerful sleeping pills.

Peter was a fighter and he fought his disease with both fists. He would not accept the judgment that his cancer had marked him for an early death. He had much to live for: two young children whom he adored and who needed him as much as he needed them. The new drug, unfortunately, neither alleviated the pain nor gave him added vitality. At this point several cancer specialists were consulted. They recommended yet another experimental drug. When this new drug failed to produce any lasting improvement, Peter fell into a deep depression. More than once he lamented, "Have I led such an evil life that I deserve this terrible pain and suffering?" Still Peter fought on. There were additional drugs, and with each new one his hope again soared. However, his wife and friends, moved by his continuing pain and mental agony, urged, "Let go! . . . let go! . . . it's all right. Why prolong your suffering?" It was as though they understood what Peter did not understand, that "there was wisdom in knowing when to die with the least inconvenience to others and distress to oneself, and that much medical progress only prolonged life for a few uncomfortable months to the greater glory of the patient's doctor."[12]

But Peter wouldn't give up. "If I can get six months more through these drugs," he insisted, "I'll have that much more time with my kids." So he battled his cancer even as it was literally killing him. His condition steadily worsened. A priest was called and Peter was given last rites. Miraculously, he again rallied and pulled himself out of death's grasp, to everyone's amazement.

At this point, at his wife's urging, I visited Peter, whom I knew. I spoke to him about what he might expect in the intermediate state after decease, and I gave him several simple mantras for later use. Since Peter was still conscious, I recited the mantras slowly to him and he repeated them after me. Although he rehearsed these procedures with me, I felt that his heart was not in them: not because he didn't believe in the continuity of life—he did and had read much about it—but because of his unwillingness to come to grips with his own death. One week after I saw him he died in his wife's arms, heavily sedated and semiconscious. Some eight months had elapsed from the time he had been stricken with his fatal illness to the time of his death.

What did Peter gain from his fierce struggle with his cancer? He may have added several months to his life. If so, he paid a high price for it. He shriveled to a mere husk of a man; he suffered such excruciating and unremitting pain that he was unable to handle a visit from his children. Moreover, the effect of his pain and struggle on his wife and parents was such that it left them exhausted and depressed. Was the trade-off worth it? Granted that it is a tricky business for a doctor to predict how long a patient with a life-threatening illness may live, was the doctor justified in feeding Peter's hopes by holding out to him the possibility of added months of life with each new drug? "Many new therapies have severe side effects—some even shorten life," says Dr. Robert J. Temple, director of the Food and Drug Administration's Office of Drug Research and Review.[13] When none of the drugs proved to be the "magic bullet" Peter hoped for, he suffered a relapse and his anguish and depression deepened. Perhaps even worse, since his focus was on extending his life and not confronting his imminent death, he made little effort to prepare himself psychologically. When the moment came for him to exit from what had become for him and his family a vale of tears, he could not, as we have seen, do so with consciousness unimpaired.

Now let me tell you about another kind of dying.

Grace (not her real name) was a middle-aged woman with grown children. She was diagnosed as having a large, malignant tumor that required surgery. While in the hospital she became aware of how strong was the fear of death and dying among the other patients. Seeing and hearing of these fears of others, she thought, "How can I help people who are afraid of death? I have met death already in a car accident in which I came close to being killed, and I lost my fear of death with that experience. I know that in helping other people I will be helping myself."

Although her surgeon removed the large tumor, it came back, having metastasized. Eight months later she had further surgery. Shortly after that I made her acquaintance via a videotape in which she was interviewed at her home by the director of the Life Center for Attitudinal Healing[14] in Santa Fe, New Mexico, of which she had become a member. Asked whether she was having any pain, she told the interviewer that while she had some, only occasionally did she take painkillers; she had found that doing hatha yoga, which made her mind peaceful, enabled her to dispense with painkillers most of the time.

Told by her oncologist that her particular cancer was resistant to radiation and chemotherapy, she chose alternative therapies. One was diet. Another was acupuncture treatments, which, she said, "seems to do something for the endorphins, which are that part of the brain which helps to combat or reduce pain and heightens energy levels." Even with acupuncture, the pain she did experience was real enough, and in mentioning it to her doctor she quoted this amusing though pertinent limerick:

> There was a young fellow of Deale
>   Who said, "Although pain isn't real,
> When I sit on a pin and it punctures my skin,
>   I dislike what I think that I feel."

To cope with her cancer and the pain it generated, Grace also resorted to meditation and visualization. The methods of visualization were detailed in a series of tapes she had obtained from Dr. O. Carl Simonton's Cancer Counseling and Research Center in Texas. The procedure was to visualize the immune system and then to imagine white blood cells searching through the body to attack the cancer cells. Another method she used, also recommended on the tapes, was to visualize white dogs consuming the cancer cells. Sometimes she did the first, sometimes the second. She felt that through these techniques the tumor had reduced somewhat. And by using guided imagery— imagining a burning sensation, for example, to be the tingle of a cool shower on a hot day—she was able to distract herself from the pain.

Unfortunately, at this time her mother died and Grace began going downhill. It wasn't just the grief occasioned by her mother's death, she explained, but also the fact of knowing she had a fatal illness. "When people learn for the first time that they have a life-threatening illness, it often comes as a shock and there's a lot of anger connected with it. Some feel this anger more than others, and they ask, 'Why should this happen to me?' "

Grace went on to make clear that she herself never felt this anger. Still, she did say that it was a mystery why one person would contract a serious illness and not another, or why one person in a bad car accident might become a quadriplegic while another in the same accident emerged unhurt. "We don't know why these things happen," she told the interviewer, "so I did think, 'Why me?' Nevertheless it is a challenge to learn how to cope with an affliction. Having worked in the medical field for many years, I took an interest in my illness as if it were something out of a book."

Grace felt that an enthusiastic rapport with all aspects of life helped alleviate illness, because it took one's thoughts off oneself. She also spoke of the value of music. In her room in the hospital, she often sang with the occupant of the bed next to hers. Grace also felt strongly that with a sense of humor and a lively attitude, one could do much to help lessen the pain of one's illness. In this connection she spoke of the value of laughter—citing the book *The Anatomy of an Illness* by Norman Cousins, in which Cousins described his experience of curing himself of a serious illness by using laughter, among other methods. Laughter, according to Cousins, actually changes body chemistry.

When asked whether she herself was using laughter, she replied, "Oh, definitely." When her daughters visited her in the hospital, she said, "We all just cracked up and laughed our heads off about all sorts of things. You go on being you no matter what is happening to your body. The illness may be attached to you somewhere, but it is not you. Even though you can't have a hike up the mountains, you can go on having fun in many ways."

She went on to say, "You know, there is really no security in good health, because at any point you may become ill. We [the seriously ill] are in a way no different from a healthy person in that our security should be in a spiritual life. We need to deal with the bad things as a way of learning and growing, and find a way to turn them around, to sort of leap over or grow out of them."

When asked whether she and others in her support group at the Life Center for Attitudinal Healing ever talked about death, she replied, "Yes, we talk about death a lot, and some people are very frightened about that experience. Of course, when you have a malignancy, there is always the question of death and you have to face it. And so I asked myself, 'What is good preparation for death?' and I came to the conclusion that it was the same as good preparation for life.

"Many people seem to feel that death will be the end of them totally, the end of everything, the end of seeing their loved ones. They think it is just a huge, blank abyss. A lot of us don't believe that at all."

In response to the question "What do you believe?" she answered, "I believe in life after life. I think that death is going through another door. I am sure of it. The times when I have been faced with death there has been a sort of prerecognition of what I was going through, and it was something wonderful. There was the feeling of 'This is it. This is it, and it's going to be just wonderful.'"

Grace died in the summer of 1984.

Two to three weeks before her death she wasn't taking anything but liquids. The evening before she died one of her daughters sat with her and held her hand. She reported that her mother lay there peacefully and then said, "You know, I'm ready to go into a dark room and close the door."

Later that evening Grace's daughters had a delightful conversation with their mother, after which she said, "I'm going to take a nap now." She never awoke from it. The next morning, around eight, one of her daughters, who was sitting beside her bed knitting, reported hearing the death rattle.

Grace's attitude toward her life-threatening illness was admirable. Many people with a belief only in life after death find that this alone can guide them well through dying to death. However—and this was the case with Grace—ignorance of the nature and significance of karma produced painful questioning. Had she understood the relation of karma to sickness, she would never have asked, "Why me?" when she learned she had a malignant tumor.

STAGES OF DYING

PSYCHOLOGIST: Can we regress a bit? You are probably aware of Elisabeth Kübler-Ross's classifications of the stages the dying person goes through, the last being acceptance. I have had some contact with dying patients, and most of them meet their end unre-

sistingly. That's been my own experience and that of colleagues of mine.

NURSE: I have worked with quite a few dying patients, and my experience has been that people don't always die according to Kü-bler-Ross's formulations. Not all patients go through all of her stages, and acceptance doesn't always come at the end either.

One hospice nurse I interviewed, a woman who has worked in hospitals and homes for some twenty years, criticized what she called the Kübler-Ross philosophy—the notion that the dying go through five sequential stages, namely denial and isolation, anger, bargaining, depression, and acceptance. According to my informant, at first it was felt that these stages were the universal mode of behavior of the dying person. Then the experience of professionals with dying patients taught them that not everyone went through those sequential steps. So while the professionals respect Kübler-Ross as a pioneer in understanding and improving the lot of the dying, they no longer expect each dying person to progress through all these phases, for they have found that some stay in one stage and never go through any of the others; that some die quite apart from these five stages; and that a few, because of their determination to live, get another three or perhaps six months longer than anticipated. This same hospice nurse said she once had a patient, a man, who spoke no word to anyone the last six months of his life, evidently because of feelings of denial or anger.

Having told you the foregoing, I would like to add a personal note about Dr. Kübler-Ross. A number of years ago, the University of Rochester (located in Rochester, New York) and the Strong Memorial Hospital in that city sponsored a conference on death and dying. A number of psychiatrists and other health professionals were invited to speak, among them Kübler-Ross. I was in the audience. The quality of Kübler-Ross's presentation—its caring warmth, its sympathy and compassion—was in such marked contrast to the detached, clinical attitude of most of the other speakers that when she finished talking, the audience gave her a rousing ovation.

So while her formulations of the stages the dying go through have not held up completely, her extensive work with these people has brought their plight to public attention. As a result, there is a strong movement to provide the dying with compassionate care and attention instead of abandoning them to die alone.

2. THE DILEMMA OF PAIN

Oh, it is real. It is the only real thing.
Pain. So let us name the truth, like men.
We are born to joy that joy may become pain.
We are born to hope that hope may become pain.
We are born to love that love may become pain.
We are born to pain that pain may become more
Pain, and from that inexhaustible superflux
We may give others pain as our prime definition.

—ROBERT PENN WARREN

No dialogue on dying would be complete without a discussion of the dilemma of pain. We will consider two manifestations of pain: first, the pain inherent in the life process—in birth, "minor" sickness, old age, death, and other incidents of life; and second, pain arising from an injury, a serious sickness, or a life-threatening illness—cancer, let us say. In the course of this discussion we will also consider pain and suffering not as an abstract fact but as the teacher of life. Thus, we will discuss how we can learn from pain as well as how we can bring it to an end, or at least minimize it. Here I am using the terms "pain" and "suffering" interchangeably, though, strictly speaking, they are not quite the same; suffering, it has been said, is the "psychic component of pain endured."

In the first part of our subject I will rely mainly on the Buddha's teaching of the Four Noble Truths of Suffering and his Noble Eightfold Path on how to dispel suffering. Every religion gives suffering a central place of importance only because suffering is so universal an experience. The reason I am confining myself to what the Buddha had to teach about suffering is that, as John Bowker has pointed out, "Of all religions, Buddhism is the one that concentrates most immediately and directly on suffering."[15]

Before we continue, let us savor those lines of Robert Penn Warren. Do they strike some of you as a deification of pain, an unusually pessimistic appraisal of the human condition? The poet, please observe, is not simply saying that life is pain—a statement any thoughtful person would agree with—but is going much further: he is saying that *pain is life*. Considering the extent to which the universality of suffering is affirmed by thinkers, humanitarians, and poets of different ideologies—those sensitively attuned to the human spirit—can we doubt that life, despite some pleasant, "rainbow-hued" facets, is on the whole grim? Anatole France (1844–1924), in what may be called a one-sentence history of humanity, wrote, "They were born, they suffered, they died." Even Albert Schweitzer (1875–1965), who often accused the East of pessimism, could write, "Only at quite rare moments have I felt really glad to be alive. I could not but feel with a sympathy full of regret all the pain that I saw around me, not only that of men but of the whole creation." And Sir Edwin Arnold (1832–1904), in his book *The Light of Asia*, summed up the human condition in these vivid words:

> Lo! as the wind is, so is mortal life:
> A moan, a sigh, a sob, a storm.

The Buddha, too, never doubted the agonies of existence. It is not surprising, therefore, that the relief of suffering, and not philosophic speculation, lay at the core of his teaching. This can be seen in his oft-repeated statement

> One thing only do I teach,
> Suffering—its causes and the way to
> overcome them.

The term the Buddha used for "suffering" was *dukkha*, a word of greater depth and complexity than is implied by the bald translation "suffering." We get a sense of the deep meaning of dukkha when we understand that the word was used to describe a wheel not running true on its axle, or a bone slipped out of its socket. Because life is out of joint, there is friction and pain. Dukkha, then, implies pain, grief, affliction, distress, or frustration. It also refers to impermanence, to a lack of wholeness or perfection.

EXISTENTIAL PAIN

THE FOUR NOBLE TRUTHS OF SUFFERING

Having a rational mind of the highest order,[16] the Buddha analyzed the specific life dislocations that give rise to pain, and like a good physician—he was in fact called the Great Physician—he prescribed the remedy. This diagnosis he called the Four Noble Truths—convictions about life which came to him in the course of his six-year quest for enlightenment. (They are called noble because adherence to them exalts life.) His teaching, then, went beyond the simple observation of facts. He penetrated the causes of suffering and showed how they could be overcome.

The first of these truths affirms the fact of the universality of suffering—not suffering as a theoretical problem but suffering as a part of what it means to be alive: "The [First] Noble Truth of Suffering is this: Birth is suffering; aging is suffering; sickness is suffering; death is suffering; sorrow and lamentation, pain, grief, and despair are suffering; association with the unpleasant is suffering; disassociation from the pleasant is suffering; not to get what one wants is suffering—in brief, the five aggregates[17] of attachment are suffering."[18]

To this may be added the afflictions and mental woes to which children are subject and which are as hard or often harder to bear than the catastrophes awaiting them later in life. Sensible men and women know that illness may strike them at any time, while the middle-aged often look forward to old age with the fear of protracted illness, the fear of being unloved and unwanted, and the fear of "the final agony"—death. Moreover, for countless numbers of people there is the suffering caused by cold, hunger, or near starvation. Nor can we ignore the painful struggles of so many to survive earthquakes, typhoons, floods, fires, pestilences,

THE DILEMMA OF PAIN

and epidemics, not to mention wars, slavery, and terrorism. With good reason the Chinese describe life as "a bitter sea of suffering."

Although the Buddha's message has been called pessimistic and life-denying by some, actually it is neither. "That Buddha gave his life to demonstrating how well-being might be attained," writes Huston Smith, "is . . . proof that his basic optimism was maintained in the face of the most unromantic recognition that the affairs of men and society are in the most imperfect state imaginable, a state of misery bordering on complete chaos."[19] Buddha, for example, recognized that there are great joys in family life, in pleasures of the senses, in mental well-being, and in many other ordinary human experiences. In a well-known Buddhist scripture, the *Dhammapada*, there is a section on happiness which includes the following: "Let us live happily, then, we who possess Nothing.[20] Let us dwell feeding on happiness like the shining gods . . . Health is the greatest of gifts, contentment is the greatest wealth; trust is the best of relationships. Awakening[21] is the highest happiness."[22]

And yet when we feel happy and at the same time know that happiness doesn't last forever—that in itself is a source of grief. The fleeting nature of happiness only emphasizes the ubiquity of suffering.

"The [Second] Noble Truth of the Origin of Suffering is this: It is this thirst [craving] which produces re-existence and re-becoming, bound up with passionate greed. It finds fresh delight now here and now there, namely, thirst for existence and becoming; and thirst for nonexistence [self-annihilation]."[23]

The term Buddha used to describe the origin of life's pain or dislocation was *tanha*, a word usually translated as "craving," "thirst for," or, more commonly, "desire." He did not condemn all desires, for he knew there are those that are life-enhancing and those that lead to suffering. The desire to improve oneself mentally, physically, and morally, for example, is surely worthwhile. The desire to help others without thought of personal gain is likewise commendable. Even more meritorious is the desire for spiritual liberation, or awakening.

It is the desires that arise from ego, strengthen it, and cause pain that are harmful. In the words of the scholar John Blofeld:

The cause of all our sufferings and rebirths is—if we are compelled to state it rather inadequately in one word—desire, which, like many other Buddhist terms, is a word used to connote both itself and its own opposite, in this case aversion. It is because, in our ignorance, we cling to some things and abhor others that we have to revolve endlessly in samsara's round; for desire and aversion lead us to think in such dualistic categories as self and other, existence and non-existence, good and bad, desirable and repulsive, and all the rest. We fail to see that this vast universe, with its beauty and its horror, is a creation of our own minds—existing in that Mind with which our minds are in truth identical. However, if we are willing to accept this as at least a working hypothesis; if we begin training ourselves to refrain from desire and aversion and from every other kind of dualistic thought and behavior; if we withdraw from the realm of appearances into the secret place of the heart and surrender our so-called and previously cherished "selves" to its stillness, then mental creations will gradually lose their power to afflict or disturb us. Whereat our minds will become like polished mirrors, reflecting every detail of the passing show and yet remaining unstained, perfectly unaltered by reflections of things, whether beautiful or hideous.[24]

What lies at the root of all sorrow, then, is the delusory notion of an ego-I—that "I am here, and what is not me is out there"—and the concomitant dualism of self and other. These in turn lead to craving for things to satisfy the imperious demands of the ego-I, and clinging to those things as though they were substantial and enduring instead of in a state of change and decay. We build the house of our life on sand, the grains fall apart and the house crumbles.

"The [Third] Noble Truth of the Cessation of Suffering is this: It is the complete cessation of that very thirst, giving it up, renouncing it, emancipating oneself from it, detaching oneself from it."[25] This truth logically follows from the second one. If the cause of life's pain is exalting the ego-I and thirsting for the objects that sustain it, the cure lies in getting rid of this craving. If we can get out of our cocoon of personal wants and desires and shift our focus to the greater expanse of life outside us (yet of which we are a part), our conflicts and frustrations, and the pain arising from them, will subside. The way to accomplish this, says Buddha, is through the Noble Eightfold Path: "The [Fourth] Noble Truth of the Path Leading to the Cessation of Suffering is this: It is simply the Noble Eightfold Path, namely right view; right thought; right speech; right action; right livelihood; right effort; right mindfulness; right concentration."[26]

THE CESSATION OF SUFFERING

What Buddha's treatment amounts to is a therapy, a practice, a training for life itself. This intentional way of living he called a path. A path, we must not forget, needs to be walked, not talked about. What the Buddha is proposing here is a rigorous system designed to release the individual from the repressions imposed by blind impulse, ignorance of self, and craving. An entire course from starting line to winning post is mapped . . . By long and patient discipline the Eightfold Path intends nothing less than to remake the total man and leave him a different being, a person cured of life's crippling disabilities.[27] As Buddha tells us, "Happiness he who seeks may win if he practices."

This practice involves more than just sitting on a mat or in a chair and trying to calm and concentrate the mind. Among other things, it means becoming *completely* absorbed in *whatever* you do, whether it be meditating, eating, sleeping, walking your dog, or doing your income tax. It also means learning to be mindful and self-possessed in every situation. Training, then, in the widest sense means being aware and alert at all times and cultivating a mind state free from gratuitous judgments, discriminations, preconceptions, and emotional colorations. When we are full of things to do, places to go, wants to be satisfied, how can we become absorbed in each moment? "Simplify, simplify, simplify!" urges Thoreau.

THE ESSENCE OF LIFE IS CHANGE

Craving or clinging to things or people inevitably leads to suffering. Why? Because impermanence is a law of life, so sooner or later we must part from what we try to hold onto, and this parting is painful. The nature and consequences of this clinging are well stated by the German master Lama Anagarika Govinda:

The very essence of life is change, while the essence of clinging is to retain, to stabilize, to prevent change. That is why change appears to us as suffering. If we did not regard objects or states of existence from the standpoint of possession or selfish enjoyment, we should not feel in the least troubled by their change or even by their disappearance; on the contrary we enjoy change in many cases, either because disagreeable states or objects are removed or because it provides us with new experiences or reveals to us a deeper insight in the nature of things and greater possibilities of emancipation . . . It is therefore not the "world" or its transitions which is the cause of suffering but our attitude towards it, our clinging to it, our thirst, our ignorance.[28]

THE IMPLICATIONS OF THE EIGHTFOLD PATH

The import of the Noble Eightfold Path is this: to overcome pain and suffering and find deep contentment and joy in life, there must be an awakening. The precondition of an awakening is a life of ethical behavior, meditation, and nonattachment. To this must be added a seeing into one's True-nature and with it the True-nature of everything. Because one cannot progress on the road to enlightenment unless his mind is free of the inner disturbance which thoughtless and wanton behavior produces, a lifestyle based on decent behavior is the foundation of spiritual realization.

DEGREES OF AWAKENING

There are, of course, degrees of awakening. One may perceive dimly or may see with great clarity; the gradations are many and subtle. When we truly perceive that the Essential-nature of the phenomenal world is void of any enduring substance, we cease clinging to that world, for it becomes clear that it is illusory— as illusory as the antics of puppets on a stage. And death, too, is seen as having no more substantiality than the movements of these puppets.

Buddha's awakening was so profound that people often asked him "*Who* are you?" implying "To what order of being do you belong?"

"Are you a god?" they asked.

"No."

"An angel?"

"No."

"A saint?"

"No."

"Then what are you?"

"I am awake," answered the Buddha, and that in fact is the meaning of the word *buddha* (from the Sanskrit root *budh*, meaning "to wake up," "to know").

The following example conveys to some extent the mind state that awakening evokes. Take a person blind from birth who gradually begins to recover his sight. At first he can see very vaguely and darkly and only objects close to him. As his sight improves, he is able to distinguish things at a yard or so, then at ten yards, then at a hundred yards, then even at a thousand yards. At each of these stages the phenomenal world he has been seeing is the same, but the differences in the clarity and accuracy of his views of that world are as great as the difference between cheese and chalk. The world hasn't changed—only his vision of it has. This *seeing* has been called "the hazy moon of enlightenment."

Here's another example. Let us say you are rummaging around in a flea market. A small, seemingly nondescript painting catches your eye. Though it's dingy and its surface is scratched, you like it, so you buy it and take it home. Looking more closely at the picture, you decide you may have a fine painting underneath the grime, and you invite a friend who is an art restorer to take a look at it. He examines it carefully and then suddenly exclaims, "You know, I think you may have something here, but it badly needs cleaning and some restoration to remove this cracked finish. I'll take it back to the shop, if you like, and do that for you." "Sure," you tell him, and off he goes with the painting. A couple of weeks later he calls you and tells you your artwork is ready. When you go to pick it up, you are struck with wonder: the colors are radiant; the whole canvas palpitates with life. It's just as you had suspected: the brilliance of the painting had been obscured by the surface dust and the cracked, discolored finish. Now that all this has been wiped away, the artwork dances and sparkles.

With awakening you realize, as in the second example, that up to now you've been looking at the world as though "through a glass darkly." Now, for the first time, you see things as they really are: you find the world awash with beauty and delights of the senses that you never imagined existed. Of course, the quality of the seeing depends on whether your awakening was shallow or deep. But surprise and wonder are evident even in a relatively mild awakening.

COMPUTER PROGRAMMER: I have a question. Earlier in the workshop you told us that life was pretty wonderful, and you used an image I liked—something to the effect that we are all flowers blossoming in a blooming universe, if I've got it right. Then you said that life is one big pain. How do you reconcile those two statements?

What I said earlier was that *to the awakened* the world is filled with wonder and awe. As for the unawakened, only in rare moments do they experience great joy or feel gratitude for the presence of so much beauty in the world.

DO THE AWAKENED FEEL PAIN OR SADNESS?

COMPUTER PROGRAMMER: Are you saying that the enlightened never feel pain or sadness?

No, I am not saying that. They do feel pain and sadness, and feel them deeply, but they don't cling to these emotions. The unawakened, the deluded, go through life "in a daze and a doze." Being on the whole discontented with their lot, they are unhappy most of the time. Random, irrelevant thoughts carom through their minds all day long. So when they look they don't really see; when they listen they don't really hear. What does come through is mostly the rustle of their own thoughts, not the rhythms and melodies of life.

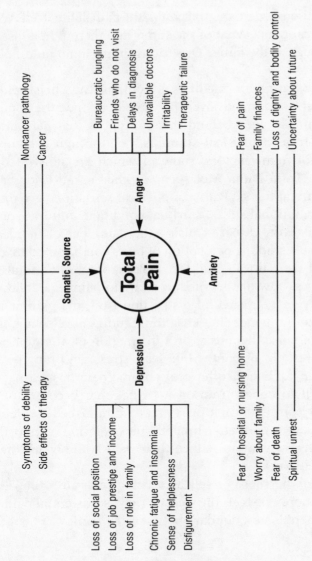

Symptoms of debility

Side effects of therapy

Noncancer pathology

Cancer

Somatic Source

Bureaucratic bungling

Friends who do not visit

Delays in diagnosis

Unavailable doctors

Irritability

Therapeutic failure

Anger

Total Pain

Loss of social position

Loss of job prestige and income

Loss of role in family

Chronic fatigue and insomnia

Sense of helplessness

Disfigurement

Depression

Fear of pain

Family finances

Loss of dignity and bodily control

Uncertainty about future

Fear of hospital or nursing home

Worry about family

Fear of death

Spiritual unrest

Anxiety

Diagram 3: Total Pain*

*From Robert G. Twycross and Sylvia A. Lack, *Symptom Control in Far Advanced Cancer: Pain Relief*

PHYSICAL PAIN

We have discussed existential pain—the pain of life itself. What about physical pain? What of the suffering inherent in a disease such as cancer of the bone? Or serious injury in an automobile accident?

Dr. Cicely Saunders, medical director of St. Christopher's Hospice near London, has over the years developed the concept of total pain. The idea behind this concept is that pain arises not simply from a physical stimulus, but through a complex interaction of many factors, some of which are illustrated in Diagram 3: "Total Pain." Most people, when asked to describe their pain, are at a loss. Pain is a physical sensation very much colored by emotional states, spiritual condition, cultural conditioning, fear of the disease causing the pain, fear of the death that may result, and the perception of one's condition relative to the cause of the pain. In addition, perception of one's total life circumstances, how one learned to relate to pain as a child, fatigue, and even the degree of distraction from the pain at any given moment influence the sensation. Studies have shown that music, white noise, hypnosis, or a distraction of attention will raise the threshold of pain, while fear, stress, and fatigue will greatly lower it. "Every sufferer of chronic pain has learned to force himself to concentrate on activities that become so absorbing that pain is not felt or is greatly diminished . . . People who suffer severe pain after brachial plexus lesions report that the most effective way to reduce their pain is to absorb themselves in their work."[29]

The tighter the sense of self as a being separate from other beings, the more one feels physical as well as existential pain. In this sense there is no boundary between the two.

ACUTE PAIN AND CHRONIC PAIN

Acute pain has the advantage of being finite—that is, one knows that, terrible though it may be, it will not continue forever. Chronic pain, on the other hand, can go on and on and on, even to the end of life—and many who suffer from it do wish the end of life were just around the corner. According to Dr. Robert Twycross, a British expert on pain, chronic pain is often due to an incomplete understanding of the source or sources of the patient's pain by his or her doctor; for physical pain can arise from much more than the specific tumor, incision, lacerations, or illness of the patient. Bedsores, constipation, anxiety, exhaustion, changes in posture or in the use of limbs in response to pain, and more will cause pain. Friends, family, doctors, and nurses interacting with the patient can, by their attitudes and responses to the patient alone, help alleviate pain. Sir David Smithers, director of the department of radiotherapy of a British hospital, made it a rule that his resident physician should visit terminally ill patients each day. However brilliant a doctor may be at clinical pharmacology, "if he has no time for chat, he knows nothing about terminal care. In this context, chat means 'patient chat' while the doctor listens. Although demanding of both time and emotion, the benefits are considerable."[30]

PAIN CONTROL

The value of pain control in raising the consciousness of the dying patient and making him or her comfortable is emphasized in a tape made under the auspices of St. Christopher's Hospice:

The last few weeks before death . . . there are so many things which need to be said, practical arrangements to be made. If during this period the patient is distracted by chronic pain, dulled by heavy sedation, or uncomfortable because of dry mouth, bedsores or constipation, then a vital opportunity is going to be missed. The doctor caring for the dying patient is no longer looking for a cure or even a means of keeping the disease in check. His medical skill is directed towards controlling a constantly changing kaleidoscope of symptoms. But if the doctor can raise the level of a person's consciousness above the immediate preoccupation with their own body, this will give them the opportunity to end their lives in comfort, at one with themselves and their family.[31]

There are many paths available for control of pain that allow the patient to remain clearheaded. It is not within the scope of this book to study them in depth, but they include (besides thoughtfully prescribed drugs) hypnosis, behavior modification techniques, acupuncture, relaxation techniques, psychiatric counseling, and meditation. Each person's pain is individual, based on his or her life experience and expectations as well as on all the other factors mentioned earlier, and so no universal prescription can be made to end or mitigate it.

It can be said, however, that relieving existential pain will also significantly relieve physical pain. And physical pain can have the great benefit of pushing a person beyond complacency to search for ultimate Truth.

One's Attitude Toward Pain

Pain can be life's greatest teacher. Some kinds of pain are so all-consuming that one's sense of separation, one's ideas of who one is, one's clinging to all manner of things, disappear into that primordial fire of pain; nothing else exists. During that eternal moment, something imperceptible happens, and when the pain retreats or disappears, one is not the same person anymore. This is possible only if there is no separation from the pain—no fighting, no resisting, no hating, just "Owwwwwwwwwwwww!"

But if one thinks, "Oh, my God! This horrible pain! It's terrible! I've never been in such pain!" one remains an isolated, small self, whipped around by one's own desire to be something other than what one is at that moment.

NURSE: You sound as if you're saying that a person in pain should just stick it out, grin and bear it. But I've seen people in such extreme pain they couldn't even speak—people who were out of their senses with pain. Surely you don't mean there should be no attempt at relief, do you?

While there is truly an opportunity to go beyond our normal, small confines when we are in pain—and I might add that many people can bear much more pain than they think they can—still, there is a point beyond which pain is not helpful. Some dying patients have such tremendous and constant pain that it can block out all other experience; such pain isolates the patient from every contact, effectively destroys the patient's personality, and prevents any sort of reflection or spiritual growth during this life's final stage. It would be foolhardy for a person with that kind of pain to stick it out. Whatever course of action is available for relieving one's pain, it should be pursued, especially if the action will result in alleviation of pain without a concurrent fogging of the mind.

On the subject of pain, let me relate to you some observations made by Americans who, like me, were living in occupied Japan following World War II. In 1953, when I returned to Japan, I was no longer connected with the American occupation. Accordingly, when I and other Americans in my situation became ill, we were obliged to go to Japanese medical clinics for treatment, since all American medical facilities at that time were restricted to military-related personnel and their dependents. The complaint of those Americans not connected with the military was nearly universal: "Japanese doctors don't have any feelings at all—or else they're awful sadists! They won't give you any drug for pain unless you're practically dead!" However, when I brought up this complaint with several Japanese doctors with whom I had become acquainted, this was what they told me:

We Japanese have a different philosophy about pain than you Americans. You Americans are accustomed to taking a pill to make the slightest pain go away. But we believe that life itself is full of pain, and unless you learn to accept a certain amount of it and cope with it, you exist only at the edge of life, not fully living. In our poetry, for example, you can read such statements as

> Without undergoing a winter that bites
> into the bones,
> How can the plum blossoms regale you with their
> piercing fragrance?

In choosing the easy way out, we are depriving ourselves of chances for growth and development that cannot come in any other way. The great sadness is that, in their fear of pain, many people are avoiding *living*.

DANCE INSTRUCTOR: I have a friend who was very selfish and conceited until he came down with an extremely painful illness— I forget the name of it, but it had the doctors stymied for a while. Jim was in agony for weeks before the disease ran its course and he began to get better. Ever since then he's been a changed man: much more sensitive to other people. And he's also lost his conceit. In Jim's case, suffering was really valuable in helping him to develop into a more loving human being.

HOMEMAKER: Back to the point about Americans' being into a pill for every pain, I'd like to relate my own experience. I was in the hospital not long ago after major surgery and had a certain amount of pain. On the first day after the operation, the nurse gave me a potent painkiller. It was quite effective, but when it wore off I felt much worse than I had before I'd taken it. So the next day I decided to do without. When the nurse came in to give me the medication again, I politely refused. She said I had to take it. I replied that it made me feel worse. So she left the room and came back with my doctor, who asked why I wouldn't take the medicine. I repeated to him that it made me feel awful.

They both left, then came back shortly with yet another doctor. Again I was asked why I wouldn't take the medicine. Once more I repeated my answer. They stood in the doorway and said in no uncertain terms, "Take your pain medicine; it's important to your recovery! You must take it!"

"No, it's not necessary," I said.

Then my doctor looked me right in the eye and, his voice dripping with contempt, said, "You must be a masochist!" With that salvo they all turned on their heels and left.

So it's not just advertising on TV and in magazines that influences people to pop pills for every pain. Doctors, too, bear responsibility for encouraging patients to do so. To be fair to the doctors, though, I know that in many cases it's the patient who keeps asking for the painkiller, not the doctors who insist on giving it to him.

Yes, our whole culture is saturated with the notion that to endure pain of any kind is masochism. Many years ago, when I was living in meditation centers in Asia, I often heard the dictum "No pain, no gain." In America, on the other hand, it's such a bizarre idea that cartoonists are caricaturing it. Not long ago the Sunday comics featured the following: Two men, lost and desperate for water, are crawling through the Sahara under the blazing sun. One says to the other, "If I hear you say 'no pain, no gain' once more, I'll strangle you!"

MEDITATION TO REDUCE PAIN

COMPUTER PROGRAMMER: You mentioned meditation in your list of ways pain could be relieved. How would you meditate to relieve pain?

Although it is true that absorbing yourself in anything that takes your mind off your own body will make you less aware of pain, meditation is especially effective for this purpose. There are, of course, many kinds of meditation. Strictly speaking, meditation involves putting something into the mind—either an image or a sacred word that is visualized, or a concept that is thought about or reflected on, or both. To the degree that one approaches a condition of samadhi (see "What Is Samadhi?")— that is, absorption to the point of self-forgetfulness—one loses awareness even of one's body, let alone of pain.

A very effective practice for attaining samadhi is meditation on a fundamental problem that grips one, such as "Where did I come from when I was born, and where will I go when I die?" or "The great spiritual masters say that each of us, that all existence, is inherently flawless. Why, then, am I in pain now, and why is there so much pain and suffering in the world?" To resolve the contradiction between the truth of the statement of the masters and what appears to our senses to be just the opposite, one must struggle with this spiritual problem. And of course there must also be present the conviction that one can find answers.

Meditation to relieve pain can be carried on whether one is bedridden or not, but if one is not forced to lie in bed, sitting upright is the most effective way to meditate. (See Supplement 5: "Basics of Meditation.")

3. SUICIDE AND EUTHANASIA

Suicide and euthanasia are the biting sides of death and dying. The former, it seems, has become more prevalent, especially among teenagers and the elderly; the latter has become more and more a topic of serious inquiry as technical advances allow people who once would have died to remain "alive" in conditions where they are hardly living. The newspapers and newsmagazines are full of stories of elderly people who—finding themselves with painful terminal illness, frightened of the specter of being completely incapacitated and having to be cared for by others, or just plain fed up with trying to live a restricted life in a deteriorating body with a fading mind—decide to "leave it all behind," sometimes with the help of friends. There are the Karen Quinlans and Paul Brophys,[32] along with countless "DNRs"—hospital lingo for "do not resuscitate"—and those terminal patients whose physicians choose to ignore a last infection. "By whom, how, and when can the decision be made that the marvelous machines, medicines and methods are no longer prolonging a life but are instead prolonging a death?"[33]

Those of you who followed the Vietnam War are no doubt aware of another kind of suicide: that of monks' and nuns' immolating themselves. They did this in an attempt to halt the terrible killing and destruction in Vietnam by bringing it to world attention. For these monks and nuns it was an attempt to trade one life for many. There are other contemporary stories of people sacrificing themselves for the sake of others.

Some people kill themselves as a result of deep despair or mental illness. However, our interest here is in those who, with no previous history of insanity, take their lives.

SUICIDE

DEFINING SUICIDE

What we call suicide is defined as "the intentional taking of one's own life; to kill (oneself)."[34] Killing is considered by most, if not all, religions to be wrong. (See "Euthanasia and Religion" for an explication of the reasons.)

SUICIDE AND EGO

Often a high degree of ego is involved in suicide. Venturing to kill oneself is frequently a statement of anger, the result of "a desire to make someone feel sorry for either not doing anything to stop the [suicide] or for causing it in the first place."[35] The act of self-destruction is the suicide's supreme gesture of defiance, a symbolic thumbing of his nose at society—the society that at the same time he is dramatically accusing of having failed him rather than he it. It has been found that many suicidal persons are really ambivalent about ending their life; they seek to make a statement through their attempts at killing themselves, rather than to succeed necessarily with the killing.[36]

There is also a type of death that is called subintentional suicide. A person who constantly takes chances with his life by putting himself in risky situations—such as abusing drugs, playing Russian roulette, or habitually driving fast and recklessly—is an example. "The subintentioned death is one in which the person plays some partial, covert, subliminal, or unconscious role in hastening his own demise."[37] This, too, comes from an egotistic position.

SOCIOLOGIST: But surely you can't say this about an elderly couple who commit suicide because they're old and sick and ready to die, can you?

This is a question that really must be taken on a case-by-case basis. No doubt there are elderly people who can commit suicide with very little ego involved, especially if they are spiritually developed. One such person was Zen master Yamamoto. At the time of his death he was the abbot of a large and respected monastery in Japan. Having grown old—he was ninety-six at the time, if I remember correctly—he was almost completely deaf and blind. No longer able to actively teach his students, he made an announcement that it was time for him to take his leave, and that he would die at the start of the new year. He then stopped eating. The monks in his temple reminded him that the New Year period was the busiest time at the temple, and that for him to die then would be most inconvenient. "I see," he said, and he resumed eating until the early summer, when he again stopped eating and then one day toppled over and quietly slipped away.

SOCIOLOGIST: But how is the story of this man different from that of a couple I read about in Life *magazine? I brought a copy of the article along with me; let me read part of it:*

At the time of their deaths, Lolly and Gronky [it appears that they were called these names by their grandchildren, and the names stuck] were both housebound, under the care of round-the-clock nurses. Lolly had emphysema, was unable to walk, talk or stand up straight without severe breathing difficulties, and was attached 24 hours a day to a machine that delivered oxygen to her through two nasal prongs. Gronky was in the final stages of congestive heart disease; he was subject to hallucinations and could not walk, read, hear clearly, get dressed, bathe himself or control his bladder. If Lolly and Gronky had waited four months they could have celebrated their 50th wedding anniversary, but instead they chose, as they put it, to "terminate their terminal illnesses."[38]

The wife, I believe, was seventy-one and the husband seventy-nine years old, and they were having to take a large number of medicines to keep their illnesses in check. The impression I get from reading the article is that they had had it with their limitations and wanted out. The gentleman's doctor is quoted as saying, "Mr. Martin's body was kept going, but at a price. He had to lead a sharply restricted, highly regulated life. It was pretty darned discouraging. If he'd been a dumbbell, it would have been different, but he was a brilliant man, and he knew exactly what he was losing."[39]

How did they kill themselves?

SOCIOLOGIST: It says here that they drank whiskey laced with crushed tranquilizer tablets.

That was pretty intentional, wasn't it? The Zen master simply abstained from taking nourishment. One might say that he didn't act to continue his life. Yet he didn't act aggressively to kill himself either. His was more a letting go. There was no self-pity, no family to leave behind in shock, just an acknowledgment that his usefulness had ended and that it was time to move on.

A doctor friend of mine who works in cancer wards told me, "You know, when I make my rounds in the hospital, chronically ill, elderly patients will often say to me, 'Doctor, please give me something to end this misery!' and I tell them, 'I don't have to give you anything; all you need do is stop eating.' But you know, I've never known one who did." When I asked him why they didn't, he said, "What these patients really wanted was someone to give them an easy way out—to take the responsibility for their own living and dying off themselves and put it on the physician."

SUICIDE AND PAIN

Ordinary people want to die because they are suffering great mental or physical pain and don't want to endure it anymore. That is understandable—nobody wants to needlessly bear great pain. Such pain is terribly debilitating. On the other hand, according to experts on physical pain, no one need be in great pain these days from, say, a terminal illness, because of the advances in diagnosis and techniques for controlling it.

Too, pain and suffering have the potential for bringing about significant spiritual change in a person. Not only this, but the manner in which pain is endured can have a great moral effect upon those privileged to be attending such a person. There are many stories of people who are physically handicapped to an extreme by illness or accident, yet have a positive and practical outlook on life and do not consider killing themselves an option. Magdalena Cintron, age sixty-nine, has a reputation as a cheerful, kind, and giving person despite being in constant pain as a result of paralysis. She has lived in a room in a hospital in Rochester, New York, for four years:

> She cannot leave, even to attend religious services in the hospital chapel, because she's connected by a hose to a respirator, a machine that breathes for her, pumping in measured amounts of air every minute of every day.
>
> She is also almost completely paralyzed, only able to shrug her shoulders a bit and slightly shift her legs. She must be fed, bathed, turned, lifted and dressed by nurses and therapists, carefully, so her breathing tube isn't disconnected. Her hands and feet are bundled in gauze, to prevent sores or bruises as she is moved.
>
> And yet when questioned, Magdalena Cintron says she has never thought of asking that her machine be shut off.
>
> "No! Because then I couldn't breathe," she explains, looking slightly surprised at the question. "I am used to it, in a way," she adds, her voice hoarse and barely audible, an effect of being on the respirator.[40]

Is Suicide Really an Escape?

The ordinary suicide may think he or she is escaping a life of misery, pain, or financial or other difficulties, but life and death are part of an ongoing process, and anyone who understands this will realize that one does not escape one's misery in one life and avoid having to deal with it in another. (See "Karma" and "Rebirth" sections.) A friend once told me, "Many times I considered killing myself—particularly in my younger days—but each time the idea came up I thought to myself, 'If I think it's bad now, what will it be like if I kill myself? Then, not only will I still have to face what is unresolved for me now, but I will have the added karmic burden of the suicide to deal with as well—not to mention the guilt arising from my awareness of the pain to others that my self-inflicted death caused!' "

COMPUTER PROGRAMMER: Isn't there a difference between killing yourself to avoid a drawn-out, extremely deteriorating, final physical illness—say, something like the case of this Mr. Martin mentioned in the Life *magazine article—and committing suicide because you feel life is unbearable for other reasons, such as a failed love affair, a financial failure, the loss of a job, or a poor self-image?*

Again, one has to look at what's behind the killing. If an individual wants to take his life for purely unselfish reasons—that is, he doesn't want to impose an intolerable financial and emotional burden on his family and friends because of his irreversible illness—certainly the karmic consequences of putting an end to his life would be diminished.

As regards the other reasons you mention for destroying one's life, it's hard to believe they do not involve a strong element of ego: "*I* can't live the way *I* want to, so *I'm* going to kill myself." Too, one who has a weak instinct for self-preservation, a poor self-image, and a failure of will and nerve—some might call it cowardice—would be tempted to opt for suicide as a way to avoid facing up to a painful life situation, usually of his own making. The following case history illustrates the point:

Charles, an engineer, was the father of a large family and a respected man in his community. He fell in love with his young secretary, the daughter of his best friend, and took her as his mistress. He bitterly reproached himself for having seduced her, deceived his wife and betrayed his friend . . . [Yet] he boasted of loving two women at once and leading an apparently successful double life. He said most men he knew would be incapable of such a feat. But he was terribly upset when he learned that his young mistress had become pregnant. He was genuinely sorry for her, but it was rather his own dishonor that frightened him. It was impossible for the two to hide the event from their respective families. Charles did not feel courageous enough to face the complicated circumstances of his life. He felt that suicide was the only way out of his dilemma. He raced his powerful sports car into a huge rock, was thrown into a river, and drowned.[41]

THE STOCKPILING OF DEADLY DRUGS

One of the tragic signs of our time is that many of the elderly are frantically stockpiling deadly drugs in shoeboxes in their closets to kill themselves with if and when they acquire a terminal illness, a permanently disabling stroke, or serious physical and mental deterioration. They are so intent on dying by their own hand, and on focusing all their energies toward preparation for that eventuality, that they stop living in any meaningful way.

DANCE INSTRUCTOR: I saw a TV program about people who collect lethal drugs, and one of them said that just having the option of killing herself at any time took a big weight off her mind! I'd think that these people would feel better because they have that option.

SOCIOLOGIST: Earlier you talked about death meditations. It seems to me that what these old folks are doing is no different from what people who engage in death meditations try to do: symbolically confront death and so make it easier for themselves when it really happens. Why is that so bad?

There's a vital difference. In stockpiling lethal drugs, these people have the *intention* of killing themselves at some time in the future. Even if the suicide doesn't materialize, the intention has karmic significance and is not without its dire effect on others. When we get to the subject of karma, we'll discuss the role of intention in creating negative karma.

SUICIDE AND RELIGION

Over the centuries various religious faiths have taken every conceivable view of suicide, from recommending it to resolutely and uncompromisingly opposing it. Euthanasia has often not been differentiated from suicide. There have been civilizations where the suicide of a wife or servant following the death of a husband or master was expected—as in the Hindu concept of *sati*, where the wife throws herself upon her deceased husband's funeral pyre. St. Augustine, it is reported, felt that suicide for whatever reason is a crime because "suicide is an act which precludes the possibility of repentance, and . . . it is a form of homicide, and therefore a violation of the sixth commandment ["Thou shalt not kill"], not justified by any of the exceptions, general or special to that commandment."[42] Orthodox Protestantism has been just as forceful: "Indeed, its rejection of the doctrine of purgatory makes it still more uncompromising in condemnation of suicide and less hopeful with regard to the future destiny of suicides."[43] Judaism too has repudiated self-destruction in no uncertain terms.

Buddhism is emphatic in its opposition to suicide, chiefly because it holds that only with a human body-mind can one become enlightened and thereby dispel the ignorance that is the root source of suffering. One of the canonical texts quotes the Buddha to this effect: "[Moreover,] a monk who preaches suicide, who says: 'Do away with this wretched life, full of suffering and sin; death is better,' in fact preaches murder, is a murderer, is no longer a monk."[44] Buddhism also teaches that a person cannot avoid by suicide the sufferings which are the result of his former evil deeds—nor can he by killing himself arrive more rapidly at the results of his good deeds. (See "Karma" section.)

"The strong Buddhist objection to suicide," writes Ananda K. Coomaraswamy, internationally known scholar, "is based on the very proper ground that . . . something more powerful than a dose of poison [is needed] to destroy the illusion of I and Mine. To accomplish that requires the untiring effort of a strong will."[45]

SOCIOLOGIST: That seems to contradict the stories I've heard of Buddhists' killing themselves to prove a lack of attachment to their bodies. I've read that monks in ancient China would kill themselves for that reason.

It is important here to distinguish between the canonical doctrines of a religion—in this case those concerning suicide—and their violation by misguided followers who have a perverted understanding of them. It is true that ignorant or disturbed Buddhist monks have immolated themselves as you have indicated. But followers of other major religions—Christianity and Islam in particular—have also sacrificed their lives for what they felt were valid religious reasons. "First in the list," states the *Encyclopedia of Religion and Ethics*, "stand those fanatic beliefs, including degraded forms of Christianity, whose votaries have been impelled to kill themselves, often in most painful ways, to attain a blissful immortality or to avoid something which they regarded as polluting."[46]

DANCE INSTRUCTOR: What I understand from all this is that suicide—and I'm not speaking of euthanasia here because that act seems less cut and dried—is usually considered wrong because it is killing, and killing is wrong. Is there anything more to it than that?

Isn't that enough!

But why is killing wrong? Because it breaks the hidden bonds uniting all forms of life. And taking one's *own* life is wrong because it is destroying what is not ours to begin with. Human life being the greatest miracle of all, it is the most precious.

Furthermore, to take one's own life is a violent act which brings more pain and suffering into a world already teeming with pain and suffering. "The story of suicide is not told in numbers. It is not felt most keenly as a statistical problem but rather as a personal hell by those whose lives it touches."[47] And of course, there is one's own karmic retribution to consider. (See "Karma" section.)

EUTHANASIA

Originally the Greek word *euthanasia* meant "painless, happy death." A secondary meaning is "the act of putting to death painlessly a person suffering from an incurable and painful disease or condition."[48] Increasingly it is being used as a synonym for "mercy killing." It can involve an action that will end life—such as removing the feeding tube from a comatose patient or the respirator from one who cannot otherwise breathe. It can consist of nonaction—that is, not resuscitating a person who has a heart attack or respiratory arrest. Or it can be the painless killing of infants born without limbs or badly deformed.

SOCIOLOGIST: What about any of those situations? Would you call it killing to "pull the plug" on an eighty-six-year-old comatose woman who had had several strokes and was out of her head with advanced Alzheimer's disease before she lapsed into a coma—a woman who was staying alive only because she was being fed through a tube? Would you say it is killing not to resuscitate a man terminally ill with severe emphysema and failing kidneys when he has a heart attack? What can possibly be the reason for keeping these people alive—especially the woman? I feel that the so-called life these people are living is not really life at all; instead, it's a living death. So how can helping them leave it be called killing?

These are thorny problems. The dilemmas created by medical technology are vividly summed up in this passage: "Medical technology has created new heavens and hells for the sick and dying—and a surreal limbo in which souls may hover for days or years, teasing death. But who knows what price we pay for such miracles? Prolonging life, postponing death, we are in the realm of the gods, but our understanding of life and death is hardly godlike."[49]

Some believe there is a moral distinction between active euthanasia (removing a feeding tube from a comatose woman) and passive euthanasia (not resuscitating a terminal patient if he has, say, a heart attack). Presumably the terminally ill man you are talking about had discussed his situation with his family and his doctors, and it was mutually agreed that should additional illness strike him, such as a heart attack, no further treatment would be given and he would be allowed to die. Of course, a patient in a coma could also have had a prior discussion with his or her family about wishing to be removed from a life-support system; such a discussion would alleviate some of the painful consequences which might otherwise result from such a decision.

EUTHANASIA AND THE LAW

As I understand it, this latter (passive euthanasia) has become generally acceptable legally, that is, a patient's basic right to make moral choices, in this case to refuse life-sustaining treatment: "Cardiopulmonary resuscitation, surgery, antibiotics, and even food and water, can be stopped, although the idea of withholding nourishment is still highly controversial . . . Hospitals routinely allow mentally competent adult patients to refuse life-sustaining treatment such as chemotherapy."[50]

As for removing the feeding tube from the comatose woman, there have been cases where legal decisions have allowed such action: "The majority [of justices deciding in a Massachusetts court case to remove the feeding tube from a comatose man], deeming feeding tubes too 'intrusive,' declared that medical advances require a distinction between death as traditionally conceived and 'death in which the body lives in some fashion but the brain (or a significant part of it) does not.' "[51]

So in a purely legal sense, neither of these cases is murder, though the karmic consequences are something else again. On the other hand, there are cases of desperately sick people who despaired of life, and because their entreaties to "pull the plug" on them were refused by either the hospital authorities or a judge, they continued to live and later were grateful to be alive and well. The following story is a case in point:

> "If I ever become so ill that only machines can keep me alive," Jacqueline Cole, 44, told her husband, Presbyterian Minister Harry Cole, "I want you to pull the plug."
> Last spring Cole suffered a cerebral hemorrhage and fell into a coma. Her husband waited forty-one days for her to recover, then asked Maryland Judge John Carroll Byrnes to order doctors

to let the comatose woman die. Byrnes said no, it was too soon to give up hope.

Six days later Jacqueline Cole awoke, smiled, and returned her husband's joyous kiss. "Miracles can and do occur," said the happy minister. "I guess we've muddied the waters surrounding the question of a person's right to die."[52]

EUTHANASIA AND RELIGION

What are the attitudes of the Western religions on this vital social problem?

The Catholic church does not require its members to accept any life-preserving treatment if it would prolong the dying process . . . However, the church says "comfort" care must continue, including food and water. Thus . . . if a patient were in a permanent coma, a respirator could be shut off but feeding could not be withdrawn.

Judaism . . . also condemns any form of active euthanasia but allows the refusal of life supports if they only would prolong the act of dying.

The Lutheran church sees euthanasia as murder or suicide, but allows Christians to "let nature take its course" when they are dying. In other words, dying Lutherans can refuse resuscitation or artificial life supports . . .

Strictly speaking, most black churches favor continuing all treatment—even the [use of] respirators for comatose patients—because of their feeling that every human life, "even life on the border," is in the hands of God . . .[53]

James Rachels, in his book *The End of Life: Euthanasia and Morality*, sees an inherent contradiction in this last contention: "If it is for God alone to decide when we shall live and when we shall die, then we 'play God' just as much when we cure people as when we kill them."[54]

Buddhism holds that because death is not the end, suffering does not cease thereupon, but continues until the karma that created the suffering has played itself out; thus, it is pointless to kill oneself—or aid another to do so—in order to escape.

THE HOSPICE AND EUTHANASIA

PSYCHOLOGIST: I seem to remember that hospices—as opposed to hospitals—are places where dying people are given only comfort care. Aren't they concerned about euthanasia?

In part because of their success in fostering growth in life's final stage, and in part because of their success in the control of symptoms, hospices take away much of the energy from the debate about euthanasia. One strong-minded patient at St. Christopher's hospice told author Sandol Stoddard, "Hospices should be everywhere. All this talk about euthanasia is absolute nonsense. Well-meaning, of course, and I do sympathize, but the fact is, you don't have to kill people to make them comfortable."[55] British hospice director Dr. Richard Lamerton put it this way:

If anyone really wants euthanasia, he must have pretty poor doctors and nurses. It is not that the question of euthanasia is right or wrong, desirable or repugnant, practical or unworkable. It is just that it is irrelevant. We as doctors have a duty so to care for our patients that they never ask to be killed off . . . Dying is still a part of living. *In this period a man may learn some of his life's most important lessons.*[56] (emphasis added)

LIFE'S IMPORTANT LESSONS

SOCIOLOGIST: What's the point in learning life's most important lessons when you're not going to be living anymore?

You're *not* going to be living anymore? There is a certain implication in the doctor's words that at least he believes death is not the end. And he is not alone. A high percentage of people throughout the world believe in some form of life after death, whether it be the continuation of a soul, reincarnation into another body, rebirth (which is not the same as reincarnation), life in heaven or in hell. We'll get into this in greater detail when we discuss rebirth. Rebirth aside, to learn to die well—that is, acceptingly and serenely—is also extremely valuable.

Moral philosophers and medical ethicists have also been part of the ongoing debate on the ethics of euthanasia. Their views have been set forth in many magazine articles and books, which some of you may want to consult. (A few recommended books are listed in the Bibliography.)

4. TO THE TERMINALLY ILL

When a man lies dying
he does not die from the disease alone.
He dies from his whole life.

—CHARLES PEGUY

During a life-threatening illness it is vital that you maintain warm and intimate relations with friends and family members. At the very least, you need a trusted friend in whom you can confide your fears and hopes. Such warm and abiding relationships help stave off the sense of isolation that is strongly felt at this time and help establish an appropriate atmosphere whether you are at home, in a hospital, or in a nursing home.

THE VALUE OF REPENTANCE

Through repentance you can empty your mind of guilt feelings, which often come up with great force at this time, ease your worries and fears, and find peace of mind. Try repeating the following verse:

All evil actions committed by me
since time immemorial,
stemming from greed, anger, and ignorance,
arising from body, speech, and mind,
I now repent having committed.[57]

Repentance is not simply a way of expressing regret for past transgressions. If done earnestly, it is a way of casting out forever the residue of feelings still weighing on the heart. It is unlikely, however, that one recital will eliminate all guilt feelings. The verse, therefore, should be repeated again and again. As an old Jewish saying has it, "You have only to repent the last day of your life, and since you don't know what day that is, you must repent every day."

KEEPING YOUR MIND CLEAR

If you are suffering intense pain, it is well to ask your doctor or nurse to ease it with drugs that do not render you unconscious or semiconscious. Those who are not used to taking drugs and are sensitive to them should beware of heavy drugs—especially painkillers, most of which contain narcotics. Such drugs can induce a respiratory arrest or affect one's mental condition. A patient should not hesitate to ask his nurse whether a painkiller about to be administered could trigger an adverse reaction. Or else a family member can ask. It is common knowledge that in most American hospitals the experience of death is clouded by drugs. When drugs are necessary to relieve pain, there is no alternative, but *heavy* sedatives, tranquilizers, and painkilling drugs are also used for purposes of patient management. Therefore make every effort to avoid them.

BREATHING TO DISPEL ANXIETY

Should you find yourself becoming anxious or tense, the following breathing exercise can bring relief, particularly if you also regularly engage in the breathing exercises described in "Meditations for the Dying Person."

An effective way to arrest the rise of anxiety is to take three long, deep, full breaths, relaxing with each breath, and concentrating only on the breath. In this breathing, expand the abdomen, allowing it to naturally rise with the in-breath and fall with the out-breath. Your eyes may be open or closed.

THE MIND AT THE MOMENT OF DEATH

Your mind state at the time you draw your last breath is crucial, for upon this hinges the subsequent direction and embodiment of the life force. Only with a disciplined and spiritually prepared mind can you hope to resist the pull of old patterns of craving and clinging as your final energies are slipping away. The impulses of thought, feeling, and perception all gather together in this last breath with great potency and can thwart the attainment of a higher level of consciousness and even enlightenment itself. (See "Karma" and "Rebirth" sections.)

VERSES ON THE FAITH MIND

To prepare yourself for the culminating moment, you would do well to read, or have read to you, a sacred text or favorite prayer. Among spiritual literature, the Verses on the Faith Mind[58] has been handed down as one of the most efficacious texts for the liberation of mind from painful bondage to birth and death. It contains the wisdom taught by all fully enlightened ones. The following is the substance of these verses:

> The Way is perfect like vast space,
> where there's no lack and no excess.
> Awakening is to go beyond
> both emptiness as well as form.
> All changes in this empty world
> seem real because of ignorance.

> The Great Way is without limit,
> beyond the easy and the hard.
> Just let go now of clinging mind,
> and all things are just as they are.
> In essence nothing goes or stays.

> To seek Great Mind with thinking mind
> is certainly a grave mistake.
> If mind does not discriminate,
> all things are as they are, as One.
> When all is seen with "equal mind,"
> to our Self-nature we return.

With single mind one with the Way,
all ego-centered strivings cease;
doubts and confusion disappear,
and so true faith pervades our life.
There is no thing that clings to us,
and nothing that is left behind.
In this true world of emptiness
both self and other are no more.

The Way's beyond all space, all time,
one instant is ten thousand years.
Not only here, not only there,
truth's right before your very eyes.
One thing is all, all things are one—
know this and all's whole and
   complete.

When faith and mind are not separate,
and not separate are mind and faith,
this is beyond all words, all thought.
For here there is no yesterday,
   no tomorrow,
   no today.

To prepare yourself through the Verses on the Faith Mind means to reflect upon them daily and to try to perceive their inner meaning with your intuitive consciousness. At the time of sinking into the death coma, intellect ceases to function; thus if the truths of these verses have penetrated the deepest strata of consciousness, they will be available as a guide.

BIBLICAL PRAYERS

Should you feel more comfortable with a prayer directed toward God, try reading, or having read to you, either the Twenty-third Psalm or the following prayer:

Our bodily senses fail us, yea mislead us, when we
seek to grasp the abiding realities of life and its
deeper meanings;
  Teach us, O God, to trust the promptings of
  our heart which strive to wrest from death
  its prey.

Make keen that inner-sense, which reveals us to
ourselves,
> To glimpse that in ourselves which is beyond
> death's reach.
Grant us the intuition to discern in the complexities
of our being that innermost self, of which the body
is only the instrument and outward symbol;
> And the insight to realize that, as the melody
> survives the lute and the meaning the written
> symbol, so the soul survives the body.[59]

The Twenty-third Psalm

The Lord is my shepherd,
I shall not want;
He maketh me to lie down in green pastures.
He leadeth me beside still waters,
He restoreth my soul.
He leadeth me in paths of righteousness
For his name's sake.
Yea, though I walk through the valley
Of the shadow of death,
I shall fear no evil.
For thou art with me;
Thy rod and thy staff,
They comfort me.
Thou preparest a table before me
In the presence of mine enemies;
Thou anointest my head with oil,
My cup runneth over.
Surely goodness and mercy shall follow me
All the days of my life;
And I shall dwell in the house of the Lord
Forever.[60]

REFLECTIONS ON DEATH

While your mind is unclouded and you are relatively free of
pain, reflect on what the spiritually enlightened masters teach
about preparation for the process of dying. Understand that just
as you were born into this world at your karmic hour, so will

you die when your karma decrees it. You have passed through these same shadows many times, though you may not remember, and have experienced many rebirths. While you must enter the kingdom of death alone with your karma of good and evil, there is no cause for trembling. Enlightened ones in all realms of existence wait to guide you. They will not abandon you. They have no other purpose than to release you from the sufferings of recurring birth and death.

WHO ARE THE GREAT ENLIGHTENED ONES?

Who are these fully awakened ones and why should you believe in them? They are those exalted beings who through complete awakening are able to manifest their innate perfection and love; they are those "in whom all spiritual and psychic faculties have come to a state of perfect harmony, and whose consciousness encompasses the infinity of the universe."[61]

Although we all possess the seeds of great love and compassion, without the light of the enlightened ones' wisdom and the waters of their compassion these seeds would never sprout. Or, to change the metaphor, just as a receiver tuned to a specific wavelength can pick up broadcasts thousands of miles distant, so can we receive the boundless aid of the fully enlightened ones if only we open ourselves to their compassion. This is the basis of the responsive communion between these supremely awakened ones and ordinary human beings. For the deepest level of communication is not communication but communion, as Thomas Merton pointed out. Such communion is beyond words and concepts.

This might sound like channeling or communicating with spirits of the dead. The two, however, are not at all the same. Receiving aid from enlightened ones does not mean having some long-dead entity take over the body, speaking and acting through it in order to give guidance to oneself and others. That sort of thing has nothing to do with the world of true spirituality; it belongs to the occult.

In what manner, then, do we open ourselves to the compassion of the enlightened? By having faith in their existence, by grasping the hand being offered us. Unless we cry out for help we can't be heard. In William James' penetrating sentence, "All religion begins with the cry 'Help!' "

Is this hard to accept? Ask yourself, "What happens to the unique consciousness force of the Buddhas and Christs after the disintegration of their bodies?" Science tells us that no energy is destroyed, and the qualities that these saviors embodied—overwhelming love and compassion—are therefore still available to us.

Science on Responsive Communion

If to accept the validity of these statements you need scientific confirmation, consider whether the following from the world of science doesn't bear out what you have just heard:

> As long ago as 1935 eminent physicists have shown that two subatomic particles, having interacted once, can respond to each other's subsequent motions thousands of years later. After investigating the phenomena for several decades, physicist David Bohm suggests that particles *and people* alike may influence each other, because everything in the universe is connected to everything else—past, present, and future—in what he calls "the implicate order." Particles are not really separated, but connected in a way that is invisible to ordinary concepts of reality. In the human domain, he suggests, . . . *"different people who are somehow attuned to each other might develop common notions at the same time."*[62] (emphasis added)

And Michael Talbot in his article "Does Objective Reality Exist, or Is the Universe a Phantasm?" reports:

> [Physicist Alain] Aspect and his team [at the University of Paris] discovered that under certain circumstances subatomic particles such as electrons are able to instantaneously communicate with each other regardless of the distance separating them. It doesn't matter whether they are 10 feet or 10 billion miles apart. Somehow each particle always seems to know what the other is doing . . . Bohm believes the reason [such] particles are able to remain in contact with one another regardless of the distance separating

them is not because they are sending some sort of mysterious signal back and forth, but because their separateness is an illusion. He argues that at some deeper level of reality such particles are not individual entities, but are actually extensions of the same fundamental something . . . [that] all things in the universe are infinitely interconnected.[63]

ONE OR MANY?

SOCIOLOGIST: You've just quoted David Bohm as saying that all things in the universe are interconnected. Before that, you said we had to have faith in the existence of enlightened beings. How do you reconcile such differing views? If we're all One, then who else is there to have faith in?

Although it is true that, from an absolute point of view, we are not separate entities but are invisibly connected, we *perceive* ourselves as physical beings moving through a physical world. But as many perceptive minds have observed, our consciousness encompasses far greater dimensions of reality than most people are presently able to accept. The reality of life is far more complex and all-encompassing than we dare to imagine. As the Eastern religions have long held, and as such scientists as David Bohm and neurophysiologist Karl Pribram (both of whom see the universe as a hologram in which each of the components contains the whole) confirm, the material world is an illusion fabricated by our limited senses, which give us an incomplete, and therefore a false, picture of the true nature of reality.

As I said earlier in this workshop, quoting the Buddha, each one of us is not simply a part of the universe; we are each the whole. Our faith, then, is this: that we can awaken to our intrinsic wholeness.

MEDITATIONS FOR THE DYING PERSON

"Dying . . . can be awful," says Dr. Derek Doyle, medical director of St. Columbus hospice in England, "but the death itself . . . in 99.9% of patients—is peaceful, so tranquil—I'm tempted to say, so beautiful—that one can hardly believe it . . . The tension in the face disappears, labored breathing becomes easy, the tautness of somebody who's suffered a lot and had to be uncannily brave seems to ease away. A lot of the suffering just seems to vanish, yet life is still going on. And for that last few hours or day . . . you have somebody who honestly looks happy and relaxed.[64]

While this may be the case for most patients near death, nonetheless, at some stage of dying certain patients do become tense or agitated. Perhaps this is what Dr. Doyle is referring to when he says dying can be awful. (See the case of Leah in the "Death" section.)

BREATHING EXERCISES TO CALM THE MIND

The moment our body-mind is not actively engaged—that is, completely involved—we fall prey to a whirl of thoughts or fantasies. A valuable exercise for calming the body-mind and inducing a feeling of deep relaxation, and even bliss, is concentration on the breath by counting the inhalations and exhalations, or simply the exhalations. Since ancient times, breath counting has been considered by spiritual masters the foundation of body-mind discipline. Breath is thus the force unifying body and mind and providing a link between the conscious and the subconscious, the volitional and the nonvolitional functions. In fact, breath can be said to be the most perfect expression of the nature of all life. Asked, "What is the length of a person's life?" Buddha replied, "The interval between an inhalation and an exhalation." Each exhalation, it can be said, is a dying; each inhalation a rebirth.

The exercise is performed as follows: Lie on your back with knees slightly raised, the feet and back flat, and a pillow under your bent knees. Lightly clasp your hands, or place them one over the other, on top of the abdomen. If this is not comfortable, your hands can be placed at your sides. Take a deep breath, hold it momentarily, then slowly exhale. Do this once or twice, then breathe naturally.

When you inhale quietly, count "One," and when you exhale, count "Two," and so on until you come to ten. Then return to one and repeat. If you lose the count or go beyond ten, as soon as you become aware of this, return again to one and continue again to ten, counting slowly. If you are by yourself, you may count audibly; if you are with others, count silently.

Another way to perform breath counting is to count only on the exhalation. As you exhale, feel your agitated mind state and negative thoughts evaporating.

VISUALIZATION EXERCISES

Another useful exercise—and this can be done sitting up as well as lying down—is to imagine an elixir slowly descending through the throat, the lungs, the heart, and other vital parts of the body. As it slides through each organ, feel that organ being relaxed, cleansed, and rejuvenated. Simultaneously visualize yourself pleasantly warm and well.

As a further aid in calming your mind, try visualizing the serene countenance of Christ or a saint or the Virgin Mary (if you are a Christian); Buddha or a bodhisattva such as Kwan-yin (if you are a Buddhist); Krishna (if you are a Hindu). Those who follow a religion that does not sanction visualization, or those who have no formal religious affiliation, might find that a certain object, picture, or piece of music instills calmness. Or perhaps a certain prayer. Should feelings of anger or hatred toward any persons arise, mentally embrace that person and radiate thoughts of loving-kindness toward him or her. This may be easier said than done, but if you work at it conscientiously, what seems at first intolerable will gradually become easy.

These exercises are not just for the dying. Don't wait until you have a fatal illness to undertake them. Performed each day for about half an hour, they will do more than simply relax your body or calm your mind; they will transform your whole personality, making it easier for you to live with yourself and others. (See also Supplement 5: "Basics of Meditation.")

EMBRACING YOUR DEATH

Reflect on these words of a Zen master:

Your Mind-essence is not subject to birth or death. It is neither being nor nothingness, neither emptiness nor form and color. Nor is it something that feels pain or joy. However much you try to know [with your rational mind] that which is now sick, you cannot. Yet if you think of nothing, wish for nothing, want to understand nothing, cling to nothing, and only ask yourself, "What is the true substance of the mind of this one who is now suffering?" ending your days like clouds fading in the sky, you will eventually be freed of your painful bondage to endless change.[65]

Imagine yourself, then, fading away, slowly, very slowly, until you remember less and less. Now allow a peaceful, relaxed feeling to take over—not in a hurry but slowly.

5. TO THE FAMILY (OR FRIENDS) OF THE DYING

DYING IN THE HOSPITAL OR AT HOME?

Whether the dying family member will end their days in a hospital or at home is a question of prime importance for them and their family. There are many considerations that should go into such a decision. For example, the family may wish to keep the dying person at home, but are they truly aware of what this entails in their particular situation? Can they stand up to the strain of continuing to work in their outside jobs while coping with, for example, an elderly, incontinent, perhaps semiconscious parent who must be moved about in the bed to prevent bedsores from forming, must be slowly and patiently fed by hand, and must be frequently cleaned up and changed?

Do not, though, refuse to keep a dying loved one at home because you're afraid you may not be up to it. Perhaps there is semiprofessional help available a few hours a day or a few days a week that would lessen the strain, ease the workload, and allow the patient to be in a familiar environment with close and sympathetic family members and friends around them. On the other hand, the dying person may find it easier in a hospital with an understanding, empathetic staff, or in a hospice program, where they could feel relieved that they were not placing the burden of their care on the family. The state of the family finances, too, will enter in, as health insurance has its limitations, particularly with regard to home care.

This and more is discussed in the book *Home Care for the Dying*, by Deborah Whiting Little,[66] and the reader is urged to avail himself of it, as the subject is too complex to be adequately covered here. In the end, the choice is a very personal one for each dying person and their family, dependent on the circumstances at the time the decision is made—and if the circumstances change, so might the decision.

THE LAST HOURS OF THE DYING

Especially in the dying person's last hours, give him your warm support, for each and every member of the family has a karmic bond with him. Be fluent listeners. Pay attention to whatever he may say, neither arguing with nor contradicting him. If he rails against God or the doctor or anyone else, let him do so, though this reaction is unlikely if he has read and reflected upon what we have been talking about. Do not force him to discuss such practical matters as the making of a will if his mind does not move in that direction. For any member of the family to impose his or her own wishes in these last hours, when the dying person needs complete peace to concentrate his dwindling energy for the passage through death, would be karmically harmful to all involved.

The ancients knew what we moderns seem to have forgotten, that dying requires a composed, tranquil mind state to enable the dying to mobilize his dwindling energies for the transition from one plane of existence to another—an occurrence which the ancients never doubted.

REMAINING WITH THE DYING PERSON

Be aware that those approaching death may reach a point where they lose interest in their surroundings and withdraw from those around them into a trancelike state, often seeing or hearing things which others are not experiencing. The family should not interpret this as evidence of the deterioration of the mind or memory of the dying one and assume that he can now be safely ignored. The fact is, his hearing and understanding may be even more acute. Many ancient traditions say that individuals often develop extrasensory perception during severe or terminal illness. Any *excessive* weeping or hysteria on your part, therefore, will almost certainly disturb these sensitive processes going on within the dying; therefore keep these demonstrations as far from the deathbed as possible. Providing a tranquil environment is more difficult in a hospital, where, even though a patient's family may remain calm and centered during the last hours, there can be other patients nearby who are noisy or uncontrolled, along with the ubiquitous television sets going at high volume. All this will make your job harder but not impossible.

Do not, though, interpret the dying person's withdrawal to mean you should withdraw from him. On the contrary, take every opportunity to show your empathy and love by holding the hand of, embracing, kissing, or otherwise touching the dying person and identifying with his needs. Even sitting quietly with him, radiating love and affection, will help dispel the clouds of loneliness and fear that often arise at this time. Even though you observe little body response to your gestures, you can be certain that your caring presence is reassuring to the dying. Abandonment is one of the greatest fears of the terminally ill.

GUIDING THE MIND OF THE DYING

When it is clear that death is imminent, it is well to ask either a close, trusted friend of the dying person or a member of the family to act as primary caregiver. His or her main function will be to read aloud from the sacred writings until the dying one takes his last breath.

You who are to guide the mind of the dying both before and after the death transition—yours is a vital role. Remember, the liberation of Essential-mind from the confines of the body through the death process offers a unique opportunity for awakening.

Both the dying person and the family should be in accord with your role in the dying process. You must fully respect any indication that the dying person wishes to be alone. However, when you do speak to him or begin to read, always address him by name so as to draw his attention.

Create a serene atmosphere for the last hours of the dying, whether in a hospital, a nursing home, or his own home. Obviously, there are more things you can do if the dying person is at home than if he is in the hospital. But this does not mean that you have to surrender your role if the dying person is confined to the hospital. Even if there is more than one person in the hospital room, it is still possible to carry out many of these suggestions.

Arrange the room of the dying one so that there is a feeling of comfortable familiarity. If the patient has a favorite painting, or a photograph of a family member he is close to and who cannot be present, place it where it can easily be seen. It is of prime importance that the channels of communication between you and the dying one be unobstructed by any talk irrelevant to his needs and state of mind.

BREATHING WITH THE DYING PERSON

For you to be composed and concentrated will help the dying person continue with equanimity on his journey into the after-death state. It can be both calming and otherwise helpful to the dying patient for you to share with him the counting of his breath for periods of about twenty minutes, perhaps several times a day, as he nears the threshold of death.

You might begin by holding the dying person's hand as the two of you join in counting. First, however, quietly suggest that he concentrate on relaxing one part of his body at a time, such as each arm, each foot, the neck, and so on, until his whole body has been relaxed. Then begin quietly counting aloud to him as he breathes in and out. Count "One" on the inhalation, "Two" on the exhalation, "Three" on the inhalation, and so on, synchronizing your counting with his breathing. Breathe yourself in unison with the counting and his breathing. After counting up to ten, begin with one again.

* * *

When you observe that the dying person is no longer in a position to do anything for himself, you may begin reciting one of the sacred texts (see "The Heart of Perfect Wisdom" and "Verses on the Faith Mind") or his favorite prayer. This will prevent his mind from drifting aimlessly. Put your lips close to his ear and utter each word distinctly. Keep in mind that the sense of hearing is the last to go. Moreover, since even medical experts are in disagreement over when death actually occurs, do not discontinue the chanting the moment the person is declared dead, but persist for a longer or shorter while, depending on the surrounding circumstances.

6. TO THE DOCTORS AND NURSES OF THE DYING

NURSE: I work in a hospital and am, of course, exposed to people dying. What has always been a problem to me is that medical personnel are generally not trained to deal with dying patients on anything but a purely technical level. A doctor or a nurse spends years in school learning how to treat illness and trauma, but the focus of that schooling is on curing people. Once it's obvious a person cannot be cured, the doctor or nurse is on his own: there are no longer any medical techniques to be put into action to heal the patient, and so many doctors—and nurses, too—lose interest in the case and abandon the patient to die alone. Sure, the doctors are still prescribing painkillers or sedatives and administering them, but these are their only contacts with the patient.

To be honest, most medical personnel don't know what to do in such circumstances: it's uncomfortable, inconvenient, sometimes frightening when you know there's nothing you can do to keep a patient from dying, yet the patient hasn't yet died. You know, this business of having a patient die on you can be very painful. Not only is it a graphic reminder of your own mortality, but since doctors especially are supposed to cure people, it's a personal failure to some when they lose a patient.

Let me give you an example of a situation I experienced just last week. A woman patient in the hospital went into respiratory failure and we made intensive efforts to resuscitate her. About halfway through this attempt her private physician decided that the resuscitation shouldn't be continued. At that point a most disturbing thing happened. Everyone left the room. And so I did too. This patient, who moments before had been the object of intensive efforts, was no longer of medical interest. It was as if she had ceased to exist as a human being despite the fact that she was actually still alive. Not one thought was given to provide medicine for her comfort, much less to spend any time with her.

Why did her physician want the resuscitation stopped?

NURSE: She had an irreversible illness, and the only thing we could do was prolong her life artificially on a ventilator. Her doctor knew she didn't want this. In fact, he specifically said, "I would like you to stop your efforts and let her go peacefully." So at that point everyone left the room.

Why did they do that?

NURSE: They felt that there was nothing else that could be done, since their instructions were to allow her to die. They took their medicines and machines and left her alone to do just that. I know that many patients find it frightening to die alone. This incident really bothers me.

What period elapsed between that incident and the time she was declared clinically dead?

NURSE: About thirty hours.

During that period, did any doctor or nurse remain with her until she died, trying to comfort her? Could they have done that without breaking the rules of the hospital?

NURSE: Yes, they could have, but no one did. It would have been simple to provide her with a few medications to make her breathing easier as well. After I finished my rounds, I returned to her and held her hand, but I couldn't help feeling that the doctors were extremely callous.

On a related subject, I understand that doctors tend to be silent when dealing with comatose patients because the patients don't seem to hear or respond to them. Yet research shows that many comatose patients do hear what is said to them. To react to them as if they were nearly dead is a great disservice to the patients and can become, as one doctor put it, "a self-fulfilling prophecy, influencing physicians to inappropriately withhold or withdraw therapy"[67] even though in some cases the patients may recover.

NURSE: What can you, Roshi, say to the medical profession about the basic human needs of a dying patient?

One has to be careful about making a judgment from this distance. What I can say is that my own interviews with health care professionals bear out the fact that doctors and nurses receive little or no training in how to relate emotionally to dying patients. One hears, too, of some doctors and nurses who do relate emotionally but find themselves burned out after a longer or shorter period of time.

MEDITATION AND THE HEALTH CARE PROFESSIONAL

Any health care professional who takes up meditation on a regular, daily basis will begin to find themself not only better able to relate to a dying patient, but also with greater energy, strength, and emotional resources. Quite a bit of a doctor's or nurse's anxiety around a terminal patient, I am told, comes from the professional's own fear of dying; through regular meditation a person can come to terms with this fear and develop greater compassion. He or she will then be able to know what to do with a dying patient even when medical intervention is no longer useful.

SHOULD PATIENTS BE TOLD THEY'RE TERMINALLY ILL?

NURSE: What do you feel about telling patients they're terminally ill?

Most health professionals I've discussed this question with feel it is desirable to do so. There are, however, positive ways to do this and negative ways. Often one will find that the patient knows without being told, yet the family assumes the patient doesn't know and is afraid to tell them. An example of a constructive approach in such a case is the following:

The doctor, on a visit to a patient, asked if she knew what was wrong with her. She said, "Yes, I've got cancer and I'm probably going to die." He asked how long she'd known this, and she said, "About five or six weeks." The doctor then said to a family member in front of the patient, "Do you know what she's just told me? That she knows she's got cancer, and that she's known it for five or six weeks."

Elaborating on this, the doctor said, "Breaking the silence in this way removes a lot of stress from patients and relatives and avoids a lot of guilt and anxiety for the bereaved later on."[68]

Whether or not impending death is acknowledged in front of patients can also influence the degree of pain they are experiencing. Dr. Robert Twycross and Sylvia Lack speak of a woman patient whose back pain from metastasized cancer was not responding to drug treatment. A frank discussion with the woman brought out the fact that she was quite angry that her doctor and her relatives would not admit that she was dying or discuss the problems this created. Once her condition was openly acknowledged and honest communication was possible among all concerned, there was a marked improvement in the woman's mental state, and the pain in her back no longer troubled her.[69]

DOCTORS, NURSES, AND THE FUNERAL

NURSE: After a patient you've had dies, should you make an effort to go to the funeral home or the funeral itself? There are differences of opinion about this on the part of nurses and doctors.

Let me tell you what a doctor writes about this subject in *The New England Journal of Medicine*:

> It was not easy to make the stop that evening. The holiday season is a difficult time for me to practice medicine; patients are more lonely and depressed, families are under greater stress, and tonight, the bittersweet juxtaposition of holiday joy and the sorrow of death [was] stressful . . .
>
> I started attending [visitations] a few years ago; why, I can't even remember. In those years my experiences convinced me that my participation was essential, and for many reasons. It gives families an opportunity to talk about their experiences surrounding the death. They have questions about what happened in the last days. Second thoughts need to be discussed when the pressure is off. They want to know about the autopsy. They need reassurance and help with their guilt; no one can do that like the physician . . .
>
> The visitation is also personally important to me. My feelings need resolution just as the family's feelings do . . .
>
> I am reluctant, almost embarrassed, to bring this up with colleagues. When I do, they look a bit distant and become quiet. They haven't thought about it much, or so they say. Few with whom I have talked have ever attended patients' funerals, and those that have attended have usually done so under special circumstances . . .
>
> Does our behavior reflect the objective approach toward patients that we learned in our training? Does it [the funeral] remind us of our own eventual death or of our professional failure? Or are we simply insensitive to family needs? Somehow, we must come to realize that our responsibility does not end with the pronouncement of death.[70]

...ATION OR BURIAL?

Six Options for Taking Care of the Body

Long before the dying person breathes his last, he and his family have to decide how his body is to be disposed of upon death. A number of options for body disposition are available. These are succinctly set forth by Ernest Morgan in his excellent *Manual of Death Education and Simple Burial*:

1. Immediate removal to a medical school, followed by a memorial service. Generally this avoids all expense and performs a valuable service. There can be a brief gathering of the immediate family before removal if circumstances permit, but this must be done quickly.
2. Immediate cremation, followed by a memorial service. There may also be a commitment service at the crematory chapel if desired.
3. Immediate earth burial, followed by a memorial service. There may also be a graveside commitment service if desired.
4. A funeral service in the presence of the body, followed by removal to a medical school.
5. A funeral service in the presence of the body, followed by cremation.
6. A funeral service in the presence of the body, followed by earth burial.

The preceding alternatives, which are listed according to cost, with the least expensive first, assume the services of a funeral director, except possibly in cases of immediate removal to a medical school or for cremation.[71]

PREPAYING YOUR FUNERAL

More and more people these days are opting to prepay their funeral. The death of a loved one is a traumatic and difficult time, filled with emotion. Decisions as to burial or cremation, style and expense of casket, whether or not to embalm, and all the other details in regard to body disposal must be made during the most painful part of the period following death—unless they have been arranged for prior to the death. The next of kin may not really know whether you would prefer burial or cremation, a pricey casket or a plain pine box. Moreover, knowing you've taken care of these details and not left them for your survivors can be a source of peace.

There are some things to keep in mind if you are considering prepaying your funeral. The American Association of Retired Persons (AARP) recommends that you plan your funeral and the disposition of your body in advance, but that you be cautious about paying in advance, for three reasons: you may change your mind about what you want, you may move away from the area, or the company providing the services may go out of business before you die.

There are generally several options available for prepayment of costs, including various prepaid plans, a bank account listing a beneficiary (sometimes called a revocable living trust or a totten trust), or a life insurance policy whose beneficiary has been instructed to use the funds for your funeral and related expenses. Prepaid plans can be categorized as follows: (1) guaranteed price, revocable (you can change your mind and receive full or partial refund); (2) nonguaranteed price, revocable (you can change your mind and get full or partial refund, but the amount you prepay may not cover the full costs when death finally arrives); (3) guaranteed price, irrevocable (price is guaranteed but you get no refund if you change plans); and (4) nonguaranteed price, irrevocable (not advised). Whatever you decide, it is wise to put your wishes in writing and make the document readily accessible to those who will be taking care of your body following your death. Do not put the information in your will or in your safe-deposit box as it may not be read until after your funeral. For further information, you may wish to obtain the AARP booklet *Prepaying Your Funeral: Some Questions to Ask* from the Special Projects Section, Program Department, AARP, 1909 K Street NW, Washington, DC 20049.

ARE FUNERAL DIRECTORS NECESSARY?

It is possible to take care of all the details of body disposal without using a funeral director or a funeral home, and some people may wish to do so, especially after reading what one investigative journalist wrote in 1983 about his encounter with funeral directors:

> Twenty years after Jessica Mitford published her classic exposé, *The American Way of Death*, the death industry is unchanged in almost every particular except cost. Mitford found that the average funeral bill, according to industry figures, was $708. When I visited a local mortuary [in New York City] to price a simple burial for a fictitious ailing aunt, the director rattled off a list of probable charges that added up to more than $5,000, flowers and cemetery plot extra. His estimate included $110 for hauling her body two blocks to his establishment and $80 for carrying it back out to the curb . . . Allowing "Auntie" (as he once referred to her) to repose in his "chapel" for one day—something he told me was mandatory, despite the fact that I said I didn't want a memorial service and that no relatives would be dropping by—would be $400.[72]

Lisa Carlson has written a comprehensive book[73] giving a state-by-state listing of laws and regulations covering disposal of bodies, and telling how she dealt with the unexpected death of her husband. She also relates how others have been able to handle burial or cremation of loved ones with few or none of the services of a funeral director. Or, instead of getting information as well as inspiration from this book, one might join one of the memorial societies set up in cities throughout the United States by people banding together in search of a send-off that would not leave their heirs ragged in the streets. Such societies usually offer inexpensive cremations or burials to members. To find the memorial society nearest you, write to the Continental Association of Funeral and Memorial Societies, Suite 530, 2001 S Street NW, Washington, DC 20009.

WAKES AND VIGILS

There are, of course, different ways of saying farewell to a loved family member or close friend. Not uncommon are wakes in which family members and friends stay up most of the night eating, drinking, and reminiscing about the deceased in the presence of his body. The coffin may or may not be open. There is also the rosary wake, in which family and friends stay up all night reciting the rosary.

Then there is the solitary vigil. A sensitive woman friend told me that when her father, whom she hadn't seen for some time because she lived a continent away from him, died suddenly, she had an overwhelming desire to be with him to express her heretofore unstated love for him. So she hastened to the mortuary parlor where his body lay (having first instructed the funeral director not to embalm or cut the body in any way) and then, with an understanding woman friend, she stayed with her father all night. This is what she reported: "My father had died the day before. Throughout the night my friend and I both felt his strong presence. We recited prayers together, chanted, and meditated. I had always thought of my father as a vexed man, but now he looked so peaceful and happy. For me it was truly a spiritual event. Never have I felt closer to my father than that night."

Another woman friend described what it was like to keep an all-night vigil over the body of a close relative, accompanied by his twelve-year-old son:

Charles had committed suicide. But this night as I looked at him lying contentedly in his coffin, the frustration, the hurt, the bitterness of his life had vanished and he looked positively beatific. Even his son remarked on how serene he looked. "I have never seen Daddy looking so happy," he said. "I know he is more peaceful now than he ever was alive. I'm glad I came with you and I'm not the least bit afraid or sad."

THE BODY'S PRESENCE AT THE FUNERAL: A NEGATIVE VIEW

A Unitarian minister who has conducted open-coffin funerals takes a decidedly dim view of their value:

> As far as I am concerned, a commercial funeral for anyone is out; I will never do another. But a *memorial* service is essential. A memorial service is for the people who are left alive, and the best service is one where there is no coffin at all. The immortal things which people leave on earth are their friends, their children, their relationships. These are things that have nothing to do with a . . . lifeless carcass. As far as I am concerned, the custom of the open coffin is not only an economic atrocity which adds hundreds of dollars to every funeral bill, but it gives terrible pain to the survivors. I can't count the times I have had to coax sobbing widows or parents or children away from an open coffin, and for *what*?[74]

THE BODY'S PRESENCE AT THE FUNERAL: A POSITIVE VIEW

Although the sobbing of widows or parents or children before an open coffin may strike some as proof of the unbearable pain such viewing entails for the family, ventilating their grief in this manner can be highly therapeutic. This is confirmed by a psychologist and a psychiatrist.

Ann Kliman, a psychologist in Westchester County, New York, who has been involved in crisis-situation counseling for many years, strongly believes in the therapeutic value of a funeral with an open coffin. She maintains that viewing is a crucial factor in beginning the process of mourning, especially when death is sudden or unexpected. According to her, viewing provides the opportunity to accept the fact of death and to say the last good-byes to the deceased.[75]

The late Dr. Erich Lindemann, professor of psychiatry at Harvard Medical School, also felt that an open-coffin funeral has great value:

When asked, "What do you consider to be the most useful part of the whole funeral process?" [Dr. Lindemann] responded, "The moment of truth that comes when living persons confront the fact of death by looking at the body." When questioned further why he thought this was true, he said, "People tend to deny painful reality. They tend to marshall their mental and emotional resources to deny the fact that death has occurred. But when they experience that moment of truth that comes when they stand before the dead body, their denials collapse. They are facing reality and that is the first important step toward managing their grief. When it is done with other people, the reality is confirmed and at the same time they are encouraged to face the feelings that are basic to the grief response. Grief is a feeling. If you deny it you have difficulty coping with it, but if you face it you start the process of healthful mourning."[76]

One's first-ever viewing of a body in an open casket can be unforgettable. I still remember my vivid impressions of seeing, as a boy of twelve, a body in an open coffin for the first time. In those days it was common practice for mourners to file past the open coffin one by one for a last view of the deceased. You weren't obliged to look at the body, but most did. I was both fascinated and repelled by the reality of death which this type of service represented. The brief ceremonies at the gravesite, the lowering of the body into the earth, the crying and wailing—all this awed and moved me. Such ceremonies, wittingly or unwittingly, provide a way to face one's own grief and a means to ventilate it. The only other experience that has had a greater impact in leading me to ponder the matter of life and death was observing the burning of bodies, many years later, in the ghats of the Ganges River in Benares (Varanasi), India.

WAITING THREE DAYS

In the Buddhist and Hindu traditions, a wait of three days before the body is buried or cremated, to allow the life force to leave the body, is considered vital. For until the life force departs, which ancient texts say takes three days, the body is still considered to be alive. These ancient texts warn against tampering with the body before the life force has left it, since the person who has just died still maintains a close connection with—actually an attachment to—his body. A Tibetan master of old goes so far as to describe the cutting or burning of the body before three days have elapsed as murder.[77]

Some of you may question whether, considering sanitary laws, the health authorities would permit such a wait without embalming. (Embalming involves cutting the body.) Several funeral directors have told me that if prior arrangements are made, the body can be kept for three days in cold storage or in a metal container until it is cremated or buried. This can be done with little additional expense, and it satisfies the demands of the law. In the case of organ donation, however, the value of the retrieved organs would be nullified by a wait of even one day. (See "Organ Donation and the Bodhisattvic Ideal.")

RELIGIOUS ASPECTS OF CREMATION

What are the theological aspects of cremation? Catholicism, several of the mainline Protestant denominations, traditional Judaism, and Islam all favor earth burial over cremation. The Catholic church, according to the *Catholic Encyclopedia* (1975 edition), opposes cremation "because the practice was historically an act of disbelief in immortality by members of certain societies and others, and because cremation does not show reverence to the human body, the temple of the Holy Spirit."

As for Protestantism, most of the arguments advanced by Protestant churchmen are similar to those of the Roman Catholics: that cremation is a pagan custom and thus antithetical to Christian practice. Other churchmen opposed cremation because they found no biblical warrant for it. Burial is further supported by the precedent established in the burial of Jesus Christ.[78]

Orthodox Judaism bases its insistence on earth burial on the Torah: "dust you are and to dust you shall return" (Genesis 3:19) Liberal Judaism, on the other hand, states that there is no biblical prohibition of cremation even though burial was clearly the cus-

the customary practice of the ancient Hebrews. Burial is regarded as a way of respecting the human body and protecting it from desecration or indignity.[79]

Increasingly in modern times, however, these religions are yielding to the wishes of their followers to dispose of their bodies through cremation. The reasons advanced, besides lower cost, are aesthetics and hygiene. Especially if the body has been deformed, wasted by disease, or disfigured, many apparently feel that it is more fitting to burn the body.

Among the Eastern religions, Buddhism and Hinduism both sanction cremation. The Buddha himself was cremated. On the whole, it has been the custom in Buddhist countries to cremate the dead, although burial has also been practiced. Traditionally, Chinese Buddhists have buried their dead; they may or may not still do so.

With regard to Hinduism, cremation began in India as early as the second millennium B.C. In the religion and philosophy of India it is believed that fire resolves the body into its basic elements of fire, water, earth, and air, while at the same time purifying the spirit for its reincarnation.[80]

A CREMATION STORY

Here is a curious story in connection with cremation: It happened that a young Westerner, who was captured by the Japanese during World War II, was imprisoned in Thailand, where he died and was buried. (The story was told to me by a woman who knew his sister.) Not long after the young man's death, this sister and other members of his family began having dreams in which he appeared and complained of the cold. In one dream in particular he asked his sister to bring him his overcoat, which was found hanging on a hook on the back of a closet door in a particular house, just as he had described to her in the dream. The family began to be disturbed by all of this and decided to have the young man's body exhumed and cremated. Once this was done, to everyone's surprise he no longer appeared in the family's dreams. The story is reminiscent of these lines from Robert Service's poem of the Arctic, "The Cremation of Sam McGee":

It's the cursed cold, and it's got right hold
   till I'm chilled clean through to the bone.
Yet 'tain't being dead—it's my awful dread
   of the icy grave that pains;
So I want you to swear that, foul or fair,
   you'll cremate my last remains.

WHERE DOES THE LIFE FORCE GO AFTER DEATH?

NURSE: You have said that three days should elapse from the time of death before the body is cut or embalmed or cremated, so as to allow the life force to leave the body. Where does this life force go after it leaves the body?

Yes, where? To the question "Where does the soul go when the body dies?" Jakob Boehme, the Christian mystic, answered, "There is no necessity for it to go anywhere."

When a Zen master was asked, "All these mountains and rivers and the great earth—where do they come from?" he replied:

"Where does this question of yours come from?"

NURSE: But you did say, or imply, that the life force went to an intermediate place, didn't you?

Did I say it *went* there? When I spoke of the intermediate realm I used the expression "after-death *state*." I did not say it was a place in either a literal or a metaphorical sense.

Many religious traditions teach that upon death the good go to heaven and the evil to hell. Tell me, where is heaven and where is hell?

NURSE: I don't know.

And I don't know the whereabouts of the life force after death. When Zen master Hakuin was asked, "What happens to a person at death?" he replied, "Why ask me?" "Because you're a Zen master!" "Yes," replied Hakuin, "but not a dead one!"

THE MASTERS' RESPONSE

Let us recall how the masters whom I quoted earlier have responded to more or less the same question as the nurse's. Asked to write a death verse, Zen master Ikkyū wrote:

> I shan't die,
> I shan't go anywhere,
> I'll be here.
> But don't ask me anything,
> I shan't answer.

When the Indian sage Sri Ramana Maharshi was asked where he would go upon his death, he replied:

> They say that I am dying,
> but I'm not going away.
> Where could I go?
> I am here . . .

Lastly, consider the response of Hui-neng, an outstanding Chinese Zen master of the T'ang era. When he announced to his followers that he was going to leave the world on a certain date, many of them began weeping. Astonished, he asked, "For whom are you crying? Are you worrying about me because you think I don't know where I'm going? If I didn't know, I wouldn't be able to leave you this way . . . If you actually knew, you couldn't possibly cry, because True-nature is without birth or death, *without going or coming* . . ." (emphasis added)

Observe that these great masters, all of whom were facing death, refrained from saying that they or their soul or life force or consciousness was going anywhere after death. By contrast, we have certain religious authorities making the dogmatic assertion that upon the death of the body, the soul ascends to heaven or else is damned to hell. In ancient times it was asserted that the soul took up abode in the tomb or coffin of the deceased, or that it lingered in or near the grave. But the masters wisely do not try to name or explain. Why not? As an old song sings:

> Fools will give you reasons;
> wise men never try.

ORGAN DONATION AND THE BODHISATTVIC IDEAL

SOCIOLOGIST: If your body had to be held for three days before cutting it, you obviously couldn't donate your organs. In Buddhism, isn't there what is called the bodhisattvic ideal—sacrificing yourself for the sake of others? Wouldn't a real bodhisattva give up his future well-being for the sake of helping people who might desperately need transplants of one or more of his organs? Didn't the Buddha talk about previous lifetimes when he was a bodhisattva and sacrificed himself to save human beings as well as animals? Would a modern bodhisattva do any less?

That's a provocative question. Yes, I believe that a true bodhisattva would be willing to give up his body, or parts of it, even while alive for the welfare of others if he could be assured that his organs would be used in an appropriate, noncommercial way.

PROFITEERING FROM ORGAN DONATIONS

SOCIOLOGIST: What do you mean by "an appropriate, noncommercial way"?

So that nobody reaps a profit from such a donation. I have before me an article from *The New York Times*, by Emanuel Thorne and Gilah Langner, titled "The Body's Value Has Gone Up. Who Should Profit from Organs?"

The article points out that the value of the body, once jokingly said to be about $1.98 (based on its chemical constituents), now exceeds $200,000 and is rising. This is because tissue is being harvested for transplantation, research, and diagnostic and therapeutic products. The article also states that "in 1985, nearly 8,000 kidneys and 20,000 corneas were transplanted; heart transplants are being performed at the rate of 1,200 per year. The value of tissue created by the revolution in biotechnology raises anew important ethical, legal, and economic issues involving how this value is to be shared."[81]

The writers also cite a case in California where a former leukemia patient is suing for the value of his spleen, which was removed during his treatment and used to develop a patentable product subsequently licensed to a biotechnology company. They also refer to a series of articles in the *Pittsburgh Press* which states that in 1984–85, while ten thousand Americans nationwide waited for transplants, nearly 30 percent of kidney transplants at several hospitals were performed on foreigners allowed to jump the queue of Americans. Moreover, surgeons' fees were as much as four times and those of hospitals almost twice as high for foreigners as for Americans. "The Department of Health and Human Services confirmed last month that a high percentage of American kidneys were being transplanted into foreigners who were being charged fees several times that charged Americans . . ."[82] Lastly, *The New York Times* article points out that "if donors believe that middlemen are being unjustly enriched by their donated organs, their altruism might vanish."

Other newspaper and magazine articles have indicated that biotechnology has unwittingly created a flourishing black market for transplanted organs.

To Donate or Not to Donate?

NURSE: But if there aren't enough organs available to meet the demand of people who need them, then even if middlemen are greedy and charge outrageous prices, wouldn't such a shortage still justify a bodhisattva's sacrifice provided someone's life was extended because of his or her gift?

It's a question of balancing: of aiding and abetting greed against the value of extending the recipient's life, yet, according to certain traditional views, adding pain and suffering to a future life of the donor by tampering with the body before three days have elapsed following clinical death (see "Waiting Three Days"), as must be done in the case of an organ transplant. As a practical matter, not many Americans qualify to be organ donors, despite their sincerest wishes. According to those connected with organ procurement programs, a person must die on a respirator to be such a donor. The ideal person is a young man or woman, in excellent health, who has had what proves to be a fatal accident and has been taken to the hospital near death.[83]

Although organ donation is limited to the few people who fulfill the requirements just mentioned, it is possible to donate *tissue* without dying in youth or on a respirator. The donor's medical condition preceding death must be known, and the donation is dependent on that condition and on the fact of his having given legal empowerment to make the donation; but still, a person might die at home and for example, donate his corneas.

SOCIOLOGIST: Given the situation described in the article you read, would a bodhisattva in this day and age donate his organs or not?

My guess is that some would and others would not. With all the complex considerations, each person must decide for himself or herself.

8. CREATING THE FUNERAL SERVICE

> I've a great fancy to see my own funeral
> afore I die.
>
> —MARIA EDGEWORTH

We will now go into the subject of the funeral in greater detail, but before we do, it should be mentioned that those who have specific ideas about their own funeral should make these known before dying, preferably in writing. One of many unfortunate cases where this was not done is vividly described in the following article:

> At Donald's funeral service the eulogist was . . . at sea. "Due to circumstances beyond my control," he said, "I did not know the deceased, but I knew the roots from which he sprang." Faulty logic there; familiarity with the parents of Hitler, Buddha and Babe Ruth wouldn't have told you much about their children. And when the hooey really got into high gear, when the phrases about being "to the manor born" and "facing death with stoic calm" started flowing, I thought back to a very different Donald . . . Puckish lad that he was, Donald would not have liked the generic Irish-Catholic send-off he got, preferring something more Bill Murrayish. But if he didn't want that kind of send-off, he should have said so in his will. He should have said a lot of things, like: Burn this ruined body by sunset, scatter my ashes outside CBGB's, and under no circumstances allow any eulogist to turn me into a nice guy in death that I never was in life.[84]

WHY FUNERAL SERVICES?

In ancient cultures the funeral was considered a rite of passage of the utmost significance to the *departed*. Unfortunately, this is not generally recognized nowadays. It is astonishing to read books on death and dying by authors who profess to believe in the continuity of life, who have much to say on how to allay grief, yet who can offer no guidance whatever to the departed in the crucial after-death state. The funeral ceremonies can, of course, do much to aid the survivors in their new relationships to one another and to the deceased growing out of his or her death; the needs to mourn and to be comforted are essential. But the primary purpose of funeral rites is, or should be, to help ease the deceased's transition to the after-death state. (See "Rebirth" section for a description of the after-death state.)

Sadly, many in our culture shy away from ceremonies larded with rituals. They react badly to what they sense is the hollowness of so much religious ritual; most ritual, they complain, becomes an end in itself. They feel, with Ambrose Bierce, that rites are "ceremonies . . . with the essential oil of sincerity carefully squeezed out of them."[85] But rites that have substance behind them—feeling and understanding—are enriching in that they provide a vivid, not easily forgotten medium for transmitting ancient truths and wisdom.

"Religion originated in celebration and concern," writes Huston Smith,

> and when people feel like celebrating [ritualistically] or are deeply concerned, they get together and act together . . . The impulse to lose and then find oneself in a fluid architecture of form and motion of which one is a significant part runs deeper in life than man: birds fly in formation; and monkeys in high spirits will fall into rhythmic line, draping themselves with rope and banana peels, simian anticipations of the elaborate, needled vestments that will appear at the human level.[86]

If the members of a family didn't at some level of their being believe that the consciousness-energy of their deceased endures somehow, why would they have a funeral service, and then later, perhaps, memorial rites? Or why would any mourners have rites of passage for their dead?

HOMEMAKER: But funeral services are intended to honor the memory of the deceased and console the mourners, aren't they?

Yes, those are two aspects. But let us not forget that honoring the memory of the dead is also a way of discharging guilt feelings; that's why the dead are praised to the sky as the good and the happy.

At a deeper, subconscious level, funeral rites undoubtedly reflect a belief in, or else a "blessed hope" of, another existence, the nature of which is fashioned by karma. If one accepts this, the rite of passage is seen as a means of aiding the deceased in what we sense must be a difficult transition from this side of life to the other.

The funeral ceremony brings home the stark fact of death and is also a means of preserving and extending the link between the departed, the family, and the community. Otherwise, why the chanting, the singing, the benediction, the supplications, the prayers, and the sermon for the repose of the soul by the minister, priest, rabbi, or other officiant? Don't the service and the presence of all the mourners imply that they too believe that the Essential-nature of the departed does not die but somehow continues in one form or another? Isn't the funeral service really a send-off and not a write-off? I repeat: why would a family go through this elaborate ceremony if they believed the deceased was inevitably a corpse, a lifeless bag of bones?

Lyall Watson confirms the deep significance of funeral rites:

Implicit in every funeral practice is the assumption that death is not the end, that it marks some kind of transition. In his investigation of the Malayan death system, Robert Hertz shows how death is not regarded as an immediate or final event, but as only one phase of a gradual development. The Malays and many others recognize a death process that begins early in life, and this belief is reflected in the minds and actions of their communities. The moment that we call death is for them no more than an intermediary stage, a sign that the body should be dealt with in some provisional way . . .

In our society the generally accepted opinion is that death is instantaneous. The only reason for the delay of two or three days between death and disposal is to allow preparations to be made and to give time for friends and relatives to gather. The fact that we are almost alone in this view, and that few other cultures regard death in such a precise way, cannot be accidental . . .[87]

In certain religions—notably Buddhism—the *primary* purpose of the funeral is not to pay one's respects to the deceased or console the family—although these have their place—but to awaken the intermediate being to the true nature of life and death. (See "Rebirth" section.) Solemn funeral services have another vital purpose: they make us think soberly about our own demise.

THE SERVICE

Although families with a religious affiliation may wish to have a member of the clergy hold funeral services in a church or temple or synagogue, an effective spiritual funeral or memorial service can take place anywhere, with or without benefit of clergy. The funerals described later in this chapter, which were actually conducted and can serve as models, do not depend on formal adherence to a religious sect, and yet they can truly be called religious. At the same time, they can serve as well for those who consider themselves agnostics or even atheists. The chanting or reciting of the Heart of Perfect Wisdom, the Prayer, and the Flowers verse, are chiefly for the benefit of the departed. The tributes to the memory of the deceased are mainly to allay the grief of family and friends. To the eulogies may be added music, poetry, additional prayers and psalms, or even dances, depending on the age and personality of the departed, her outlook on life, and perhaps other circumstances.

MEMORIAL OR FUNERAL SERVICES?

It has been said that a funeral is a rite of passage in which the body of the deceased is present, and that a memorial service is one in which there is no body. In the Buddhist tradition, the funeral proper and the memorial services that follow for the next forty-nine days represent continuing attempts to awaken the mind of the departed to the true nature of existence. In this view, memorial services are condensed versions of the funeral, embodying the essential rites.

WHY FORTY-NINE DAYS?

Since in the Eastern religious traditions it is generally agreed that rebirth usually takes place within a forty-nine-day period, the reciting of the sacred texts is every bit as valid during that period as during the funeral proper. These rites are to be repeated every day for the first week and on the death day for the following six weeks.[88] Performed in harmony with the seven-day birth-and-death cycle in the intermediate state, they have as their purpose the awakening of the mind of the deceased before he or she enters the next realm of existence.

These forty-nine-day postmortem rites are not to be dispensed with even when death comes through sudden accident, allowing no time for the preparation of the mind of the victim, or when death overtakes him in a remote or inaccessible location, so that his body or cremains[89] are not present at the funeral. A photograph of the deceased is of special significance in helping those at the service to focus their energies toward the one who died. This focusing, in turn, aids the deceased by making available to him or her increased psychic energy.

THE FAMILY AND THE FUNERAL

The family would do well to participate both in the death rites and in the postfuneral ceremonies which take place in the forty-nine-day interval. In thus reaffirming their karmic link with the deceased they will ease their loneliness and constructively channel their grief. The Mind of the dead and the Mind of the living are intrinsically One. This One can in no way be diminished. Not even the dead can disappear. Where, after all, would they go?

THE FUNERAL OF MARIE—A SIX-YEAR-OLD[90]

This service was for a child of six who died of smoke inhalation. Although neither of her parents had any formal affiliation with a temple or church, they did identify to some extent with the doctrines of Hinduism, Buddhism, and Christianity. On the morning after the death of Marie I was asked by the parents to help organize and lead a funeral service for their daughter. With the assistance of several mourners I hastily put together a simple altar, and on this we placed a large photograph of Marie, as well as handpicked flowers, candles, and some of her favorite foods. In front of the altar Marie lay enclosed in a homemade casket.

The service began with my telling everyone that the main purpose of the funeral ceremony was to aid Marie, and that we could accomplish this by directing our love toward her through our chanting and heartfelt recitations, thereby invoking the wisdom of ancient sages in the difficult transition from this side of life to the other. I also said that while, from an ordinary viewpoint, the death of a young child is considered tragic, we had no reason to feel grief-stricken; Marie was born when she needed to be and she died when she had to die, her karma for this life having exhausted itself, young though she was.

Next we all chanted the Heart of Perfect Wisdom (see "The Funeral of Lillian—An Eighty-four-year-old Writer" for the significance of this inspired text) while one person beat a drum and another periodically struck a small, bowl-shaped gong.

THE FUNERAL PRAYER

Following the chanting we all offered up a prayer, recited with feeling three times in unison, to help invoke bodhisattvic forces for the benefit of Marie. First I recited a line and then everyone repeated it:

O Compassionate Ones,
abiding in all directions,
endowed with great compassion,
endowed with love, affording protection to
sentient beings,
consent through the power of your great
compassion to come forth;
consent to accept these offerings concretely
laid out and mentally created.
O Compassionate Ones,
you who possess the wisdom of understanding,
the love of compassion,
the power of doing divine deeds and of
protecting in incomprehensible measure:
Marie is passing from this world to the next.
She is taking a great leap.
The light of this world has faded for her.
She has entered solitude with her
karmic forces.
She has gone into a vast Silence.
She is borne away by the Great Ocean [of birth
and death].
O Compassionate Ones,
protect Marie, who is defenseless.
Be to her like a mother and a father.
O Compassionate Ones,
let not the force of your compassion be weak,
but aid her.
Forget not your ancient vows . . .

Following this supplication, the following verses were directed
to Marie:

The Flowers Poem

The world is a flower.
Gods are flowers.
Enlightened ones are flowers.
All phenomena are flowers.
Red flowers, white flowers, green flowers,
yellow flowers, black flowers,
all the different kinds of the colors of
flowers, all of the different kinds

of love's shining forth.
Life unfolds from life and returns to life.
Such an immense universe! Oh many lives!
Flowers of gratitude, flowers of sorrow,
flowers of suffering, flowers of joy,
laughter's flowers, anger's flowers,
heaven's flowers, hell's flowers.
Each connected to the others
and each making the others grow.

When our real mind's eye
opens this world of flowers,
all beings shine,
music echoes through mountains and oceans.
One's world becomes the world of millions.
The individual becomes the human race.
All lives become the individual—
billions of mirrors
all reflecting each other.
Marie, there is death and there is life,
there is no death and no life.
There is changing life, there is unchanging
life.
Flowers change color, moment by moment.

Such a vivid world! Such a bright you! . . .
Marie, you were born out of these flowers,
you gave birth to these flowers.
You have no beginning and no ending,
you are bottomless and limitless,
even as you are infinitesimal dust . . .

Marie, you are the flower.
You are love.
All beings shine out of their uniqueness,
all melt into the oneness of colors.
You are one, you are many,
only one moment, only one unique place,
only the unique you.
Beside you there is nothing:
you dance, appearing in all.

From nowhere you came, to nowhere you go.
You stay nowhere. You are nowhere attached.
You occupy everything, you occupy nothing.

You are the becoming of indescribable change.
You are love. You are the flower.[91]

THE FINAL FAREWELL

Upon the conclusion of this verse, all present went singly to the altar and made an offering of a pinch of powdered incense. This over, the 150 or so mourners began walking toward a church a mile away. En route some individuals blew conch shells, while others softly chanted the sacred word "Om," the sounds intermingling. Other marchers quietly chanted sacred verses from the various spiritual traditions.

At the church the small casket was placed on the altar, surrounded by flowers and candles. The proceedings in the church were entirely spontaneous. Different individuals stood up and began singing a folk tune or reciting sacred words. Friends and relatives reminisced about Marie. The haunting sounds of a harmonica played the elegiac "Going Home."

With the conclusion of these informal rituals, we moved to the churchyard, where Marie's grave was dug by close friends. During the digging, participants formed a large circle, joined hands, and began chanting "Om." All the while, conch shells were sounded, providing a rich and meaningful counterpoint—meaningful because in many spiritual traditions the blowing of a conch shell symbolizes the breath of a new life.

Marie's casket was now slowly lowered into the grave as the mourners crowded around. Marie's mother and others who brought flowers began tossing them on the casket, which was slowly being covered with the upturned earth.

When the grave was filled, Marie's mother carefully tamped the earth over it as though tucking her daughter in for a long sleep. As a final gesture, she set in place a wooden cross made by her husband. Once again the large gathering formed a circle, holding hands, and they slowly circumambulated the grave, all the while chanting "Om."

From a financial standpoint, the cost of this funeral was minimal. Apart from the price of the wood to make the small coffin, and what I presume was a donation to the priest for the use of the church and the privilege of burying Marie in the churchyard, the parents had no other expenses connected with the funeral. More important, this kind of funeral, of caring for one's own dead without a funeral director, helped Marie's parents and friends say goodbye in a healing way.

THE FUNERAL OF LILLIAN— AN EIGHTY-FOUR-YEAR-OLD WRITER

Unlike the first model service, which was unrehearsed and held out of doors, this one was formal and in the sanctuary of The Zen Center of Rochester, of which Lillian was a long-standing member. This type of service can be done for anyone regardless of his or her religious affiliation, or lack of it.

Lillian was a writer in her eighties and a well-known person in the community in which she lived. In her will she had stipulated that at her funeral we play the slow movement (the so-called Funeral March) from Beethoven's Third Symphony, the Eroica. Stately and somber, yet not without a sense of struggle and hope, the music concludes on a note of serene acceptance —qualities that mirror Lillian's own strivings for Self-fulfillment.

As family members and friends entered the sanctuary, they were greeted by the strains of this profound music, which set the tone for what followed.

An altar stood at one end of the sanctuary. On this we had placed a large photograph of Lillian, flowers, and her cremains, which had been wrapped in a damask cloth. Since red was her favorite color (she had once said it stood for life), the flowers and the cloth were of this hue. Also on the altar were lighted candles and evergreens—the flames symbolic of infinite light, the pine needles of everlasting life. The photograph enabled those present to focus and direct their energies toward Lillian.

When we started, the music was faded to a soft, background level, and it continued that way throughout the service. I explained that the main purpose of the funeral rites was to help Lillian awaken to the true nature of birth and death and not simply to extol her virtues or lament her passing.

Following this we all chanted the Heart of Perfect Wisdom, which encapsulates the accumulated wisdom of Buddhism's spiritual masters on the nature of ultimate reality. The Heart of Perfect Wisdom is considered a most potent formulation for piercing the delusive mind. It is the kernel, or core, of the message of the wisdom scriptures given by the Buddha. Also referred to as the Heart Sutra, it is to be grasped not through the intellect but with the heart—that is, through one's own deepest intuition. Thus "perfect wisdom" here means transcendental wisdom, as well as the path leading to the attainment of this wisdom, and the text of the teaching conducive to its realization.

The significance of chanting this sacred text is that the deceased, shorn of the limitations of a body and a mind as we ordinarily understand these terms, is now better able to absorb and be guided by its deeper meaning.

The Heart of Perfect Wisdom[92]

Form here[93] is only emptiness,
emptiness only form.
Form is no other than emptiness,
emptiness no other than form.

Feeling, thought and choice
consciousness itself,
are the same as this.

Dharmas[94] here are empty,
all are the primal void.
None are born or die,
nor are they stained or pure,
nor do they wax or wane.

So in emptiness no form,
no feeling, thought, or choice,
nor is there consciousness.

No eye, ear, nose,
tongue, body, mind;
no color, sound, smell,
taste, touch, or what the mind
takes hold of,
nor even act of sensing.

No ignorance or end of it,
nor all that comes of ignorance;
no withering, no death,
no end of them.

Nor is there pain or cause of pain
or cease in pain or noble path
to lead from pain,
not even wisdom to attain,
attainment too is emptiness.[95]

READING AND RITUAL

One of Lillian's close friends now read a poem written on nature and the cosmic rhythm. Upon the conclusion of the poem, Lillian's housekeeper and another friend described joyful moments with Lillian and reminisced about their many years of friendship. The Funeral Prayer and the Flowers poem were then read, this latter being specifically directed toward her.

As the final ritual, each person present went up to the altar, looked intently at the photograph of Lillian, took a pinch of powdered incense from the box on the altar, and offered it on a burning piece of charcoal in the incense pot, making a bow of farewell with hands palm to palm.

This concluded the formal service. Everyone now retired to another room of the Center for light refreshments, where they continued their reminiscences of Lillian.

THE VALUE OF CHANTING

Chanting has a vital place in a funeral service. When it is done with sincerity and zest, the sounds and rhythms of chanting provide a way to circumvent the discriminating intellect and to drive home directly to the subconscious mind of the deceased the essential truths of existence.

CHANTING WITH INSTRUMENTS

It is best to have a drum of one kind or another to set and maintain the tempo of the chanting. It unifies the energy of the service—raising it up or bringing it down, or drawing it together when it becomes scattered. The drummer need not be a professional, nor the drum any special kind, though the drummer should be able to maintain a steady, pulsating beat for the duration of the chanting.

The drummer begins slowly and works very quickly up to the tempo that, once established, must be maintained until the end of the chant. Should the drummer and the chanters not synchronize, the chanting becomes disjointed and the vital energy flow toward the deceased becomes disrupted.

Equally important is the spirit in which the chanting is done, whether with sincerity and vigor or otherwise. Just as lackadaisical drumming can diminish the force of the service, so halfhearted chanting can lessen the impact of the funeral or memorial rites. When the chanting is directed to the deceased, with everyone focusing on the photograph of the deceased, the chanting is especially effective.

Can Chanting Reach the Dead?

HOMEMAKER: You mentioned in your description of Lillian's funeral that she would be better able to absorb the meaning of the Heart of Perfect Wisdom in a disembodied state. How can a dead woman—and a cremated one at that—absorb anything? Who absorbs what?

The point is, she is not dead as we ordinarily understand that term. Her consciousness, or "psychic energy," continues to reverberate.

COMPUTER PROGRAMMER: But a cremated person has no brain and no ears, so I still don't understand how she can absorb anything.

Zen master Hakuun Yasutani points out in his book *Eight Bases of Belief in Buddhism*[96] that a person in the after-death state does have consciousness but not what we ordinarily think of as consciousness in the "alive" state. And he or she also has sensory awareness of a kind not available to us so-called "alive" human beings. This means that the entity can "hear" the Heart of Perfect Wisdom and the other elements of the funeral service, but in a way that cannot be equated with ordinary hearing.

WHAT DO THE SCIENTISTS SAY?

Recall what I said earlier about physicists (such as David Bohm) having demonstrated that two subatomic particles, having once interacted, can respond to each other thousands of years later, and that particles *and people* alike may influence each other, since everything in the universe is connected.

If you apply to chanting what these scientists are saying about the responsive communion between matter and people, you can begin to understand why it is that when you empty your mind of random thoughts and focus all your attention and energy on the chanting and on the person who has died, that consciousness cannot but be influenced.

Some physicians feel that sick people who are prayed for often recover more quickly than those who are not the object of prayers. In an article on religion and medicine in *The Christian Science Monitor* a practicing surgeon comments:

> The use of prayer in medicine is not a groundswell, but there is a willingness to recognize nonscientific interventions. Physicians are no longer bothered about using things whose mechanisms aren't understood . . . In my years in medical practice there are many concrete examples where I would have to give prayer the credit for the outcome, rather than my own intervention as a physician.[97]

And since the dead are not really dead, who can say that chanting and prayer at funeral and memorial services cannot help them as well?

KARMIC LINKS BETWEEN THE FAMILY AND THE DEPARTED

There's another aspect to all this. Who are the people who come to a funeral? The family and close friends of the departed, right?

Through a lifetime of contact and interaction between them, strong karmic bonds have been forged. These bonds are not severed at death.

In the deepest sense there is no one, nothing anywhere with whom we do not have a karmic connection. When the contact was recent (for example, this lifetime) and the bond strong (a relative or close friend), the chanting and the words are greatly intensified. I say "words," but it is really what lies *behind* the words that has the power to rouse and transform. Words that have strong spirit propelling them are like a well-aimed arrow which, once released, will not stop short of its mark.

CAN A DEAD CHILD UNDERSTAND CHANTING?

COMPUTER PROGRAMMER: All right, let's assume it's possible to reach the entity with your chanting. What about that little six-year-old girl, Marie? Even if she did hear you, how could she understand the subtle message of the Heart of Perfect Wisdom?

You say she is a six-year-old girl. But once she has died, is she still six? The knowledge in her subconscious mind—the collective unconscious, if you like—is still functional. So are the karmic impulses that propelled her into the life she just left and that will propel her into her next life. Energy cannot be destroyed; nor can the accumulated knowledge and understanding of countless lifetimes. Forgotten, yes, but not lost.

So what of this young entity? When she dies she is no longer young in the sense of her karmic heritage or physical years—she is ageless. Age is relative, and she is now no longer bound by that restriction. The age of the dead person, then, makes no difference; neither does her sex, her nationality, or even her religion. The only thing that matters is the way in which you chant, that is, whether your chanting has conviction behind it and is focused toward what we are calling the entity or not. We can go even further: it doesn't even matter whether the being who died was human. Animals, too, can be affected by a strong funeral service. All life, having its basis in this universal Mind, is irrevocably connected. In the purest and most fundamental sense there is no difference between a buddha, a six-year-old girl, an elephant, a flea, a redwood tree, and a blade of grass.

FUNERALS FOR NEWBORN BABIES

NURSE: What about when newborn babies die? Or when a woman has a premature birth and they can't save the baby? Or when the baby dies in the womb? A lot of families don't know what to do when this happens. Should there be a funeral or not?

Yes, there definitely should be a funeral in any of those cases. Remember, a child comes to its parents because of the karmic affinity between them. Whether death takes place before birth, in infancy, in childhood, or in old age, the funeral service serves the same purpose. Because of the parents' affinity with the infant, their ability to influence her future life in the after-death state is great. Thus the funeral service represents, as in the case with older people, a once-in-a-lifetime chance to awaken her to the indivisibility of life and death, to the truth that form is only emptiness, emptiness only form—the essential message of the Heart of Perfect Wisdom.

Besides aiding the deceased, as we have said, and providing an outlet for the parents' grief, the funeral service is also a means of allaying possible guilt feelings of family members. And for those who participate in the service wholeheartedly, it can answer questions about the role of karma and the mystery of life and death—questions that inevitably arise following the death of an infant. The darkness surrounding death is thus to some extent dispelled. A meaningful funeral or memorial service awakens our deepest intuitions about life and death. Not only this, but the funeral service gives parents, family, and friends the assurance that they have done everything they can to help the child in the after-death state. This in itself can do much to allay the grief of parents.

SHOULD CHILDREN BE EXPOSED TO DEATH?

HOMEMAKER: You mentioned earlier that the family should participate in the funeral service or death rites. What about children? I know that many people—at least in the United States and Canada—feel that kids shouldn't be exposed to the death of a family member, that they won't understand, or that the experience will hurt them in some way. Some people even go so far as to pretend the dead relative has gone away on a long trip or has gone to sleep for a long time. Would you comment on this, please?

You've heard many times in this workshop that life and death are two doors of the same reality, one marked Entrance, the other Exit. The sooner children learn this, the less they will fear death. And these days even very young children may come up against death through television. To attempt to deny death—particularly the death of a loved one who has played a significant role in the child's life—is grossly unfair to the child and can even do psychological harm. The same is true if one tries to "sweeten" the truth with such statements as "Daddy's gone away on a long trip" or "Grandma has gone to sleep for a long time." People who explain the death of a relative to a child in this way often do so in order to avoid having to deal with the child's inevitable questions and the pain such questions may bring up in themselves.

HOMEMAKER: Then how would you tell a child that a parent or grandparent has died?

This depends on the age and the sensitivity of the child involved. If the parent or grandparent is terminally ill, the child will be aware that something serious is going on. An adult close to the child should indicate, gently but with openness, her willingness to discuss the situation. ("You know, Daddy is very, very sick these days, and he may not get well; in fact, he may die. When that happens, we won't be able to see him anymore . . .") Then when Daddy does die, the child has someone with whom he or she can communicate about the experience. Whether the death is sudden or expected, a child should be allowed—though not forced—to take part in whatever rituals are performed, including viewing of the body and funeral or memorial services, and to join in the sadness and grieving with the rest of the family.

One last thing to be mentioned is that historically, great masters—including the Buddha himself—have come to deep awakening to the true nature of life and death as a result of contact with death. Consider, for example, Zen master Dōgen; his father died when Dōgen was two years old, and his mother died when he was seven. The deep questioning about the meaning of birth and death that led to his enlightenment began when he witnessed his mother's funeral. Many, of course, would regard as tragic the death of both parents before a child's eighth birthday; the child himself might so regard it, brooding on it in a self-pitying manner. But clearly this need not be so. It is not what happens to us but how we *respond* to these circumstances—that is, our attitude toward them—that determines whether they become a thorn or a spur in life.

FUNERALS FOR ANIMALS

HOMEMAKER: What about animals? Would you have a funeral for a pet? If so, would it be the same as for a human being?

Yes, virtually the same.

Let me relate to you a true animal story that happened near Canton, China, in the 1930s. It was reported widely not only in the Chinese newspapers but in the international press as well. The incident went something like this: A hunter, checking his traps, found that he had captured an unusual fox—its body pure white, down to the end of its uncommonly bushy tail. This fox was so tame that it appeared to have no objection to being caught. Impressed by the uniqueness of the animal, the hunter took it home and easily made a pet of it. The animal, though unconfined, did not attempt to escape.

Within the next year, however, the hunter's parents—both quite elderly—died, and so did his uncle. Being of a superstitious nature, the hunter decided he should not keep the white fox around any longer, and he gave it to a Mr. Lim from a neighboring village.

Mr. Lim had not had the fox long when, one night as he was about to fall asleep, he had a vision in which an old man directed him to take the fox to a particular monastery and to set it free there. Disturbed by this because he wanted to keep the fox, Mr. Lim eventually decided to take the animal to the place after all. So early one morning, with the fox in a basket, he hiked up the mountain to the monastery. When he arrived there he told his story to the abbot, Shu Yun. The basket was opened, the fox hopped out, and to the great amazement of the onlookers, it made an unmistakable bow to the figures on the altar. The abbot, suspecting the fox had in another life been a monk of the temple, spoke to the creature and asked if it would like to take the precepts. The fox seemed to understand, and it bowed before Shu Yun, who proceeded with the ceremony. Maintaining a dignified posture throughout the service, the animal bowed once more at the end.

The fox, which appeared quite content to be at the temple, remained there from then on. It is said that the animal became vegetarian and refused to eat if the cook mixed chopped meat with its food. It was also reported that the fox would sit in meditation whenever Master Shu Yun did so, but that if it felt the abbot had sat too long in the cold meditation hall, it would gently nuzzle the old man's cheek until he rose and went to bed.[98]

The newspaper accounts end here, but we can be sure that when the fox died it was given a funeral service, which no doubt included the Heart of Perfect Wisdom.

There are other accounts of animals showing an affinity with a spiritual master—for example, Lakshmi, the calf that followed the late Indian master Sri Ramana Maharshi everywhere and remained at his ashram for several years, eventually dying there. He held a full funeral ceremony for her, and she was buried in the ashram compound beside the graves of the deer, crow, and dog which the master also had buried there.[99]

To some the abbot's attitude toward the white fox may seem bizarre. But we must remember that he was no ordinary abbot, nor was the fox an ordinary fox. Up to the time of the Communist takeover in China, Zen master Shu Yun was one of China's most highly respected spiritual leaders. Sri Ramana Maharshi, too, is renowned by many as modern India's most enlightened sage.

9. GRIEVING

Let us now discuss how we can cope with grief in a healthy, constructive way.

HOMEMAKER: To me the worst kind of grief, the most painful to bear, comes with the death of a child. This is especially true if it's your child and she dies suddenly and unexpectedly. I lost my daughter three years ago and I still haven't gotten over it. I'm not sure I ever will. She was my only child. My sister and one of my closest friends keep telling me, "You've got to try to forget her. You need to go on with your life, and thinking about her just doesn't help." But another friend of mine, who lost a child before my daughter was killed, tells me she doesn't think it's possible—or necessary— to forget. What is your feeling about this?

Can you tell me something about your daughter and how she died?

HOMEMAKER: She was only thirteen. Jenny was coming back from her friend's house on her bicycle, and she was hit by a car driven by a drunk driver. I can still hear my neighbor down the street screaming, "Jenny's been hurt!" I don't remember much after that except sitting in the waiting room at the hospital after the doctor came out and told me she was dead. I couldn't believe it. I just couldn't believe it.
We had the funeral, and I guess I was in a daze for a while. After that, every time I caught a glimpse of her bedroom, or the empty

space in the garage where her bicycle used to stand, I would burst into tears. Thinking of her is so painful! Even now I miss her coming home from school and sitting at the kitchen table, having a glass of apple juice and telling me all about what happened that day.

Yes, it's a terribly painful thing. If you are not a parent yourself it is hard to imagine the hurt that the death of a child brings. Your world suddenly seems empty and your despair never-ending. Hard as it is to reconcile oneself to the death of a sibling or parents, harder still is it to heal the pain of a child's death. For the karma that binds a parent and child is deep indeed. My feeling is you should not try to forget your child but keep your memories of her alive.

COMMEMORATION OF A DECEASED CHILD

HOMEMAKER: How?

An old Chinese verse sings:

> If I keep a green bough in my heart,
> The singing bird will come.

The bird, of course, is Jenny and the green bough your loving thoughts of her. Every time you act in a loving, selfless manner Jenny will appear. Smiling, she will exclaim, "Oh, Mom, I'm so proud of you. I love you so much!" Your love for her will keep you together while you are apart. And through memories you can keep her with you forever.

A MEMORIAL FOR JENNY

DANCE INSTRUCTOR: I heard once of a woman who, after her husband died, kept his pipe next to his favorite chair in a part of the living room she referred to after his death as "Charlie's corner."

Yes. One concrete way to preserve Jenny's memory is to create a special place in your home that you treat with reverence and

respect. Place there a photograph of Jenny and some of her favorite possessions. Keep a vase of fresh flowers there, especially
on her birthday. At that time say a prayer for Jenny or recite a
psalm. Do it on her death day too.

When the family gets together on such special occasions as
Thanksgiving and Christmas, have them join you in these prayers
and blessings if they feel comfortable doing so. Looking at her
photograph, recall moments of her life that brought you both
joy. Besides bringing her alive for you and providing cherished
memories, these family ceremonies will help maintain an unbroken sense of family continuity. But try not to continue to wet
your pillow with tears grieving for Jenny. For all you know, she
may be enjoying great bliss wherever she is.

LIFE AND DEATH: THE ORDER OF NATURE

HOMEMAKER: But what can I do, then?

Reflect that just as Jenny was born when it was time for her to
be born, so she died when it was time for her to die. Her death
may seem to you cruel and entirely unmerited, but remember
that she has her own karma, the workings of which are often
inscrutable. When we come to the subject of karma, many things
about Jenny's death will, I hope, become clear to you. In any
case, you can't bring back the dead no matter how much you
grieve. You have heard me say in this workshop, and have heard
me quote the spiritual masters as saying, that life and death are
indivisible—that they are merely two aspects of one process, both
present at any given moment. Your ability to channel your grief
in a constructive way will depend upon how strongly you believe
this.

Look at Jenny's death this way: she has bypassed the pain and
suffering that are the lot of all of us on this earth. It is your karma
and mine to go on with our lives, to struggle and grow, maintaining normal relations with family and friends. Let her go with
love even as you keep your memory of her alive. *You* must now
live twice as hard, for both Jenny and yourself. To *cling* to her,
to see her death as the end of the world for you, is to create a

barrier between you and everyone else, thereby hurting her as much as yourself.

LOSS, TEARS, AND SELF-PITY

HOMEMAKER: When you've had your daughter with you for thirteen years, it's painful to think of her as not being around anymore. I can't forget she has died. The hurt doesn't go away.

It is natural for you to feel sorrow at Jenny's death; any mother would feel the same emotions at the death of her child. But you must resist falling into self-pity—asking, for example, "Why did it have to be *my* child?" The greatest element in grief is the strong feeling of personal loss; often this is accompanied by a tendency to feel sorry for oneself. If tears well up when you think of Jenny, let the tears flow and you will feel better. But don't allow yourself to be so overwhelmed by your sorrow that you can't eat or sleep well or carry on other necessary activities. Examine your feelings carefully to be sure you are not crying for yourself. (See the story of Satsujo in "The Masters' Reactions to Death.")

DON'T SUPPRESS YOUR PAIN

SOCIOLOGIST: As you know, in our culture public tears—especially from men or boys—are discouraged. From childhood we are taught to "keep a stiff upper lip." There are many men—and not a few women, I'd be willing to bet—who would find it extremely hard to express the pain and anguish that comes when someone close to them dies.

You are probably right. Still, it is vital to feel all the painful and confused feelings that come up in the process of grieving. To suppress the grief, the pain, is to condemn oneself to a living death. Living fully means *feeling* fully; it means becoming completely one with what you are experiencing and not holding it at arm's length. Psychiatrists and grief counselors also say that allowing ourselves to feel our anguish is a necessary step toward recovery, and that to block it psychologically or escape from it with drugs or alcohol is unhealthy. It is through pain and suffering that we can grow, provided we accept and do not resent it. Yet there eventually comes a time when, after you have given yourself completely to the pain, the wrenching episode naturally fades in intensity and you can move on with life—this letting go with love that I spoke of.

THE VALUE OF QUESTIONING IN GRIEF

Beyond all this, if you reflect on Jenny's death, you are bound to ask yourself such searching questions as "Why are we born? Why must we die? What is life worth if someone as full of life as my Jenny now lies cold and lifeless? What is life worth if eyes like Jenny's, which once sparkled with joy, are now closed forever? Some day I will die too. Why?" If you persist in this questioning and probing, one day it will hit you with great force that the *idea* of life and death is an illusion invented by humans to deal with the mystery of existence, and that underlying such a concept is an all-powerful force that rules our lives. Some call it God, others Spirit, and still others True-nature. Marvelously, with this discovery you will laugh and cry with a joy and peace beyond anything imaginable, for you will realize that all life, living or "dead," is interwoven like silk threads in a fine brocade. And this miracle will come about because of Jenny's death.

THE NEED FOR COMPASSIONATE FRIENDS

SOCIOLOGIST: I don't find any problem with what you're saying, but I think you also ought to mention that many people are very uncomfortable around someone who has lost a child or parent or sibling to death, especially if they are constantly crying and carrying on. I suppose it's because they're reminded of their own mortality.

Feelings of grief last much longer than our society ordinarily allows. Yet it is vital for someone who is grieving to be able to talk to a sympathetic person. If one's family circle or friends do not provide such empathy, there are many kinds of support groups, such as the Compassionate Friends (for people who have lost a child, of whatever age), and there are grief counselors. If a support group doesn't exist in your area, it is always possible to start one, for everyone sooner or later is touched by death. There are also several books available that can help the grieving understand what they are going through and, to some extent, guide them through the stages of grief. (See Bibliography.)

THE STORY OF THE MUSTARD SEED

Some of you may be familiar with the story of the woman who came in anguish to the Buddha, carrying her dead child and pleading with him to bring the child back to life. Buddha said, "If you can collect a mustard seed from any household where no one has died, I will do what you ask." Going from house to house in her village in search of such a seed, she of course found no household that had not suffered the loss of a loved one and the grief that comes with it. In this way she was made deeply aware of the universality of death.

CONSOLING THE BEREAVED

MANAGEMENT CONSULTANT: That brings up something else. Recently the wife of a friend of mine died. I went to the funeral, but I felt quite uncomfortable because I didn't know what to say to Ron, even though we've known each other for a long time. What can you say at such a time that doesn't sound trivial or insincere?

The organization Compassionate Friends, mentioned earlier, has a list of do's and don'ts for those who are at a loss for how to express sympathy to a grieving parent, spouse, or other person without offending his or her sensibilities. I think you would find this list helpful. (See Supplement 4.)

THE CONTINUITY OF LIFE

COMPUTER PROGRAMMER: Earlier you said something like "Don't try to forget your child, but keep her alive." I find it hard to reconcile that with the plain fact that she is dead and gone.

We are so materially oriented, so attached to the senses, that we find it hard to entertain the notion, much less comprehend the reality, of discarnate life—of pure consciousness. Yet we lay flowers at the graves of family members and friends who have departed. Doesn't this indicate we believe in our deepest unconscious that they are not dead but somehow continue to survive, out of reach of our ordinary senses? Because our culture as a whole does not yet accept the notion of the continuity of life, and because we don't want to be thought of as superstitious or far-out, we tell ourselves that we do these things out of respect for, or to honor the memory of, the one who has passed on. But if we equate death with extinction, who are we honoring? Such rituals, in my view, reaffirm our own continuity with the departed. They are concrete acts, and we perform them because at some level we feel that the departed still exists in one form or another.

Three: KARMA

Shallow men believe in luck,
believe in circumstance.
Strong men believe in cause and effect.
—RALPH WALDO EMERSON

Chance is a word void of sense;
nothing can exist without a cause.
—VOLTAIRE

1. UNDERSTANDING KARMA

LIFE'S SEEMING INJUSTICE

Ever since the first prehistoric hunters battled a mastodon and one of them lost an arm or leg in the fray, human beings have asked themselves, "Why me and not him?" In all societies and civilizations men and women have struggled to find answers to life's seeming injustice and randomness. Why is one person born deaf or blind, and another free of all physical handicaps? Why is one born with a brilliant mind and another with virtually no mind? Why are some born in the midst of plenty, while others live in poverty and misery? Where is the justice in all this?

For many the answer has been simply "It is the will of God. His ways are mysterious, and we with our limited understanding are incapable of grasping His divine purpose. Therefore 'Ours not to reason why, ours but to suffer and sigh'; we must have faith that in the end God's plan will be revealed." But for countless others these answers satisfy neither reason nor a sense of justice. On the contrary, they often create feelings of powerlessness and resentment which fester and sometimes lead to deep psychological disturbances.

Yet there is an explanation, accepted by millions of people, that opens a window on the why and how of events. This is the doctrine of karma. Though seemingly random and mysterious, karma is a law that functions consistently in dispensing justice. The endless entanglements and contradictions of human existence are clarified by this simple principle, which holds that for every effect there must be an antecedent cause, whose effect in turn becomes another cause, *ad infinitum*. In other words, the doctrine of karma teaches that what we reap accords with what we have sowed.

At the same time, the workings of karma are profound and intricate and their implications not easily grasped. With good reason the ancient symbol for karma is an endless knot.

This sign graphically depicts the infinite network of interrelationships among all forms of existence. It also symbolizes the beginningless and endless causes that condition existence.

THE WHEEL OF LIFE AND DEATH

The process of becoming is also called the chain of causation, the chain of dependent origination, or, more commonly, the wheel of life and death. As the wheel turns (or each link of the chain is activated), the residue of energy from the turn (or link) before gives rise to the succeeding turn, thus keeping the wheel in motion.[1] The wheel of life and death is a representation of the mind of the unenlightened. Buddha taught, "Everything *is:* this is one extreme view. Everything *is not:* this is the second extreme view. Avoiding both these extremes, the Tathagata [that is, Buddha; see Glossary] teaches the Norm of the Mean." Elaborating on this, Coomaraswamy writes, "This [doctrine of the] Mean asserts that everything is a Becoming, a flux without beginning [first cause] or end; there exists no static moment when this Becoming attains to Being—no sooner can we conceive it by the attributes of name and form, than it has changed to something else. In place of an individual there exists a succession of instants of consciousness."[2]

All creatures are tied to the wheel—the ceaseless round of

birth and death—to the law of causation, according to which existence is determined by antecedent actions. This wheel is set in motion by actions stemming from our basic ignorance of the true nature of existence and by karmic propensities from an incalculable past. The wheel is kept revolving by our craving for and clinging to the pleasures of the senses. At the hub are greed, anger, and deluded thinking. The residue of action from each cycle carries forward to the next cycle, perpetually turning the wheel through life and death until we free ourselves from this endless circuit.

WHY BELIEVE IN KARMA?

Belief in the law of causation generates the conviction that just as our past actions shaped the present, so will the life we lead today determine the nature of our future. We *are* the architects of our lives. We *can* change. As the journalist John Walters writes:

Acceptance of the theory of karma and rebirth will settle many problems regarding life which previously seemed insoluble. It brings a reasonable explanation to circumstances and events, to the tragedies and comedies of life that otherwise would make the world seem one vast madhouse or the plaything of a crazed deity. Belief in karma and rebirth results in a lasting sense of calm and understanding. Life ceases to anger and surprise us, death loses its terrors. No longer do we despairingly utter those useless words, "Why does God let such things happen?" When misfortunes strike us, we realize that payment is being made for wrong actions in a previous life. The debts are being wiped out.[3]

KARMA AND CAUSATION

"Karma" encompasses greater meaning than simply "causation." Looked at superficially, this latter term appears to be simple. Let us say my elbow strikes a glass jar on a table and the jar falls to the floor and breaks. The jar fell because my elbow hit it, and the broken glass is the effect. If I am riding my bike and a tire hits a piece of glass and blows out, the cause of the blowout is the glass and the effect is the blown tire. All this is obvious. Somewhat less obviously, a parent, instead of reacting firmly but sympathetically to his unruly child, shouts at him harshly. The child, out of hurt and anguish, attacks his younger sister, continuing the cycle of bad feeling. The parent now has a doubly painful situation—one directly of his own making—to try to resolve. Causation, then, pervades all aspects of our life. In a wider sense, cause and effect is an infinite flux, permeating time and space and linking all beings and all phenomena.

Karma is a more inclusive concept than simple cause and effect because it includes moral—or intangible—causes and effects as well as physical—or tangible—causes and effects. Derived from the Sanskrit root *kri*, meaning to do or to make, "karma" refers to action—often to acts of volition—and deeds. For the *consequences* flowing from such acts, there is the more precise term *karma-vipaka*, although in common practice these days the word "karma" loosely covers both meanings. "Karma" is an evocative word that provides entrance to the subtle and intricate relationships of cause and effect, and to an understanding of the way the pattern of deeds and events fit together and interact.

KARMA AND INTENTION

Every deed performed with an intention behind it—whether it be physical or mental, good or bad—weaves a timeless pattern, leaves an ineffable mark that sooner or later will produce an effect or consequence in our own life and in the lives of others. "This mark will never be erased save by sheer exhaustion of the karma or by the interruption of an overwhelming counter-karma."[4]

However, "intention" must be understood broadly to encompass a wide range of mental activity. Thus acts performed "instinctively" or habitually—such as striking out angrily without premeditation—and acts conditioned by unconscious mentation or emotion, even if we do not understand the motive impulses behind these acts, have karmic consequences. (We know from psychology that even apparently unintentional acts may have subconscious roots.)

Not all experienced effects are products of willed action, or karma. Let us say a heavy branch of a tree falls and seriously injures me as I'm walking along on a windy day. I did nothing to cause the branch to drop, although I experienced the effect of its fall. Nonetheless, I did freely put myself in the place where the branch came down, and to that extent I bear responsibility for what happened to me (perhaps the result of "bad" karma, perhaps not). The cause of the branch falling was the wind and a weakness in the branch; the cause of my injury was being under the branch when it fell. The unexpectedness of the event and my reactions to the severity of the trauma may have a long-lasting effect on me, but this is an effect of a certain cause—my reactions to the incident.

All conditioned phenomena are the result of complex inter-actions of causes and effects. Such phenomena arise when causes and conditions governing them mature. When conditions become altered, phenomena change accordingly.

Volitional acts "are a form of energy which radiates outward from the doer and affects both himself and others. The murderer may never be apprehended and punished by civil authorities, but the dead survive in the present, and sometime, somewhere, the energy of the past act will have an effect on both the murderer and others. The energy is never lost."[5] The late Dr. Sarvepalli Radhakrishnan, one of India's foremost scholars, called karma "the law of the conservation of moral energy." Professor Garma C. C. Chang describes it this way:

Karma is essentially a doctrine of the intricate reciprocation between forces and actions that push forward the turning wheel of *samsara*. When expressed on a cosmological scale this force-action complex is a stupendous power that propels the universe and life; when expressed in the ethical sense, it is an unfailing, impersonal law that effectuates the moral order, "dispensing" natural rewards and retributions. Metaphysically, karma is a creative energy brought forth by the collective actions of certain groups;

it sustains the order and function of a particular universe in which those groups reside . . .[6]

KARMA IS NOT FATE

The Buddha said, "If it be true that a man *must* reap according to his deeds, in that case there is no religious life, nor is any opportunity afforded for the complete extinction of suffering. But if the reward a man reaps *accords* with his deeds, in that case there is a religious life and opportunity is afforded for the complete extinction of suffering . . ."[7]

This passage refutes the erroneous view that all physical circumstances and mental attitudes spring solely from past causes. Furthermore:

> If the present life is totally or wholly controlled by our past actions, then karma amounts to fatalism or predestination. If this were true, free will would be an absurdity. Life would be purely mechanical, not much different from a machine. Whether we are created by Almighty God, who controls our destinies and foreordains our future, or are produced by irresistible past karma that completely determines our fate and controls our life force independent of any free actions on our part, is essentially the same. Such a fatalistic doctrine is not the Buddhist law of karma.[8]

The doctrine of karma, then, repudiates any notion of fate or fixed destiny, since circumstances and our response to them are constantly changing. Karma can be made to sound like fatalism only if one believes that the relation between cause and effect is rigid. Cause and effect, however, are dynamic, the effect always changing according to the circumstances, which are themselves both effects of past causes and causes of current and future effects. Past karma has to be expiated, but through our present actions we have the possibility of changing the future direction of our lives. (Even to speak of past and future may be an oversimplification, but it is a necessary concession to our ordinary way of thinking and perceiving.) Fatalism, with the implication that we struggle in vain against a preordained destiny set by higher authority, is a misconception of the law of causation. If my life is already predetermined, why should I make an effort to live decently? The truth is, nothing is unchangeable, the point being that our capability for the exercise of free will is always present. Clearly, then, everyone has the potential at each moment to alter the course of his future karma. If we did not have that freedom, what would be the point of spiritual training?

PRIMARY AND SECONDARY CAUSES

Karma involves a combination of primary and secondary causes. In the case of a plant, for example, the seed is a primary cause, and fertilizer, rain, wind, sunlight, and attention of the farmer are secondary causes. Take two farmers who plant seeds of grain at the same time. One cultivates his field, fertilizing it with rich manure; the other does nothing but watch the weeds. Obviously there will be a great difference in their respective crops. (Secondary causes may thus be of essential importance.) The principle of primary and secondary causes is always functioning—whether the effect is of minor significance, such as a sneeze, or major, such as death. Similarly, when we pass from this life to the intermediate state at death, though impelled by our desire to be reborn as a human being (the primary cause), we cannot do so without parents, who are a necessary secondary cause of rebirth.

2. CHANGING YOUR KARMA

CAN "BAD" KARMA BE PREVENTED?

Although effects result from causes, we still have the power to influence the ultimate outcome, because running through the chain of causation is our free will. A bad effect, for example, may be turned to a good end depending upon our attitude. Suppose one is sentenced to prison. This is the effect of a previous action. How the individual chooses to deal with the situation, however, is to a large extent up to him. He may have a change of heart and become law-abiding or, as an old offender, tell himself to be more careful and not get caught the next time. He may make prison his spiritual training center by practicing meditation and reading good books. Obviously his attitude toward his confinement will greatly alter its effect upon him.

The life of Robert Stroud, the "Birdman of Alcatraz," exemplifies this principle. After spending fifty-four years in prison, he died at the age of seventy-three. Despite his third-grade education, he was able to teach himself such diverse subjects as astronomy, painting, languages, mathematics, and law. He also planned prison reforms and studied birds, becoming a world authority on bird diseases. Gradually he underwent a change in personality, becoming a loving and compassionate person.

Some of you may also be familiar with the story of the Tibetan master Milarepa. In his youth Milarepa was involved in black magic which directly led to the deaths of many people. Eventually he decided to change his life and began to train under a teacher.

During his training he underwent awesome austerities, subsisting only on nettles and living without clothing in caves high in the mountains. His teacher more than once instructed him to construct a house out of heavy stones and, once it was built, ordered him to pull it down and rebuild it in another location. In the course of these hardships Milarepa came to expiate the karma of having caused the deaths of so many people, and he eventually became a great sage and teacher himself.

SIMULTANEOUS AND PROGRESSIVE CAUSE AND EFFECT

Two other aspects of karma are what might be loosely called simultaneous cause and effect and progressive cause and effect. Suppose I cut my arm badly and cry out in pain. The wound, the bleeding, and the pain occur more or less simultaneously. Later the wound may become infected and the arm may swell, necessitating the attention of a doctor. This is progressive cause and effect.

Then there is the law of small cause and large effect. In this case time is a crucial element: the longer the lapse of time between the cause and the effect, the greater the effect. For example, if you save money, the longer you keep it in the bank, the greater the amount of interest you will receive. Conversely, if you have a debt and do not repay it for a long time, it will become bigger by reason of the interest added to it. Zen master Yasutani has said, "Think of your good deeds as savings and your bad deeds as debts."

VARIABLE AND "CONSTANT" KARMA

Within the period of a single lifetime every being has, in addition to its variable karma, a particular "constant" karma into which it is born, which includes species, race, sex, and certain other congenital conditions—a missing limb, for example. Our "constant" karma is the result of previous actions crystallized at the time of birth and unchangeable until death. For example, to be born white or black or Asian, or as a man or a woman, is unalterable karma. Though set for life, these conditions are then recast at the next rebirth, again in accordance with the individual's ever ripening past actions.

Variable karma is karma which can be modified by one's own effort. Consider the matter of health. A person may be born sickly, but by watching his health, he can make himself strong. Or he may sustain a serious injury which disables him, but by dint of hard work on himself, he overcomes that negative karma. The following story is dramatic proof of this:

A young lifeguard by the name of Doug Heir dove into a swimming pool to save someone crying for help. The force of the dive brought him to the floor of the pool, where he struck his head, breaking his neck and becoming paralyzed. This was a young man proud of his strength and abilities in sports, and now he lay unable to move, permanently disabled. His family worked with him, and he worked hard himself, on his recovery. In time the broken neck healed, and with intensive physical therapy he was able to gradually recover some use of his upper body. Thus inspired, he began weight training and then shotput and javelin throwing, though from a wheelchair. He went on to win a gold medal with a world-record-setting throw in the Paralympics in England, to attend college and then law school, and to live an independent life in his own apartment and drive his own car. In these ways he changed his karma from that of a bedridden, wholly dependent quadriplegic to an active sportsman and professional able to live on his own without help.[9]

Constant and variable karma can be seen in the matter of longevity: constant because longevity is limited by one's genetic inheritance; variable because it is also affected by one's environment and habits. A kind and honest person, one whose conduct is pure, will benefit from the state of mind which his behavior produces. He will be comfortable with himself and secure in his actions. The more humane he is, the more inclined he will be to perform compassionate deeds, and such actions will become instinctive in him. On the other hand, an irascible, cruel, and dishonest man will make both his life and those of others miserable by creating anger and tension. His corrupt acts will become habitual, and he will perform them with increasing frequency.

Moreover, the greater the concentration of thought and will in accomplishing the action, the more lasting the action's effects in the results that follow. Conduct, then, influences states of mind just as states of mind determine behavior.

All actions—whether they do harm or good, whether they are intentional, unconscious, or apparently accidental—affect the doer sooner or later. Every thought, utterance, and deed is a seed that ripens until, under suitable conditions, it comes to fruition as an event or circumstance. The effect can ripen instantly, later in one's present lifetime, or in a future lifetime. Moreover, between each cause and its effect can come succeeding causes which can influence and modify the effect of the original cause. We never know when a particular karmic seed will come to fruition. It is a continuous process, for the way in which one responds to circumstances determines the quality of one's present life as well as that of future lives.

Our moral, intellectual, and temperamental differences are chiefly due to our own actions both present and past; thus karma can be seen as the force giving rise to differences between individuals—differences in abilities, dispositions, and bents as well as in size, color, and shape, and even in one's views of life. Regardless of the time, the place, or the persons involved, the ups and downs of human life are affected and influenced by this law.

TRANSCENDING KARMA

Karma defines and restricts. Simply to have a certain body-mind is already a karmic restriction. We have only to point to the physical capacities of certain animals to see how limited we are in these respects. No human has the speed or stamina of a horse or a cheetah. The arboreal feats of a simian can't be equaled by a human being. A dog's sense of smell is said to be a hundred times more acute than a human's. Every creature is what it is by reason of its karma.

What we all seek, consciously or unconsciously, is release from the limitations and restrictions of the chain of causation pressing upon us. How can this freedom be gained? A deceptively simple koan tells how.

> A disciple asked a master, "When cold and heat come, how can we avoid them?"
> Master: "Why don't you go where there is no cold or heat?"
> Disciple: "Where's the place where there is no cold or heat?"
> Master: "In winter, let the cold kill you. In summer, let the heat kill you."

The master uses heat and cold here, of course, as metaphors for birth, sickness, old age, death—karmic milestones in the life of all of us. These milestones are everywhere. To emphasize that point, the master asks, "Why don't you go where there is no cold or heat?" He is pointing a way out, but the student, not understanding, grasps at straws. "Where is that place?" he asks, and the master tells him: "In winter, let the cold kill you. In summer, let the heat kill you."

In other words, when it is cold, don't wish you were on a beach in the middle of the summer, sunning yourself—give yourself up to the cold. When it is hot, don't spend your time daydreaming of cooling breezes—accept the heat so completely that you transcend it. Pain, disease, old age, death can be overcome, the master is implying, if we don't run away from them but face them with strong spirit. Too often we tend to teeter on the edge of life, hesitant to jump in. It is like contemplating a cold shower in winter. If you *think*, "This is going to be cold!" and mentally brace yourself against it, "Brrr!" you'll start to shiver before the cold water even hits you. But don't *think* of coldness, or anything else—just jump under the shower, drenching yourself. Who then remains outside to say, "I'm cold"? No circumstance, whether bitter cold or stifling heat, whether a difficult family situation or a trying personal relationship, the master is saying, need be unnerving or lasting if we meet it head-on.

So long as one is merely on the surface of things, they are always imperfect, unsatisfactory, incomplete. Penetrate into the substance and everything is perfect, complete, whole.

How, then, do we get to the point where everything is seen as full, whole, perfect? A Zen master tells how:

> Every moment, every existence is causation itself. Outside [them] . . . there is neither I nor the world. This being the case, the man of real freedom would be the one who lives in peace in whatever circumstances cause and effect bring about. Whether the situation be favorable or adverse, he lives it as the absolute situation with his whole being—that is, he is causation itself. He never dualistically discriminates different aspects of the situation; his heart is never disturbed by any outside elements. When he lives like this, he is the master of cause and effect and everything is blessed as it is. The eternal peace is established here.[10]

The way out, then, is the way in.

COLLECTIVE KARMA

Joy or suffering can also follow from collective karma, in which each member of a group reaps according to what the group as a whole has sown. Even as each of us has an independent existence, at the same time we relate deeply to one another. "Given this, there is that." Everything is connected and interrelated; all things are mutually dependent for their existence. "Buddhism holds that nothing was created singly or individually. All things in the universe . . . depend upon one another, the influence of each mutually permeating and thereby making a universal symphony of harmonious totality. If one item were lacking, the universe would not be complete; without the rest, one item cannot be."[11]

We can see this principle operating on a social level. To be a parent requires children. Children need parents for their existence and nurturing. Citizens depend on the police for protection; the police depend on us for economic support. Similarly with the fire department. The city depends on the state for certain services. The state depends on cooperation with other states and on the federal government to protect its inhabitants in a variety of ways. The federal government, for its part, cannot function without the work and support of its citizens, who depend on the nation as a whole for their cultural identity and well-being. Nations, too, depend on one another in numerous ways. In the deepest sense, then, we are all in the same boat—more than that, we are extensions of one another. Karmically speaking, a common lifeline of mutual responsibility binds us all.

It is not always easy to distinguish between collective and individual karma. Suppose I neglect my health and become sick. This is individual karma and no one can substitute for me in this illness; I have to take the bitter medicine alone. However, collective karma would begin to operate if I became seriously ill, perhaps needing an operation, so that my family and friends became involved financially and emotionally. To be a passenger in a plane or car that crashes—this is also collective karma. But the fact that one passenger dies, another is only injured, and still another escapes unharmed—this is individual karma.[12]

Collective karma affects us in individual ways as well as collectively; that is, collective karma also becomes individual karma, and in this sense we often cannot speak of karma as being definitively *either* individual *or* collective. They affect and interact with each other. Think of Hitler—it was his individual karma to be a megalomaniacal mass murderer, but it was also his country's collective karma to decide to make him führer. Another example is the *Titanic* disaster. It was the captain's individual karma to choose to ignore numerous warnings about icebergs and continue on course; but it was also the collective karma of everyone on board to be on that boat with him as captain.

We cannot make predictions about collective karma any more than we can about individual karma. We can, however, look at trends. A person, country, or group holding on to destructive, degrading, self-centered practices, policies, or habits is bound to fall into painful situations. We form a unity. Our collective society, the groups with which we associate, are as much a part of us as we are of them. We can choose to spread peace or hatred.

Collective karma is always in operation, but it functions on a much grander scale than individual karma. This has two implications. One is that we are often not aware of collective karma; it is like a huge painting whose full impact is not evident until one observes it from a distance. The other is that when collective karmic events occur, they can be cataclysmic or of devastating proportions because they involve numerous people.

A distinction can also be made between collective karmic *events* and collective karma. The first is a specific occurrence, such as the sinking of the *Titanic*, the war in Vietnam, or a car accident. The second is the fundamental principle of the workings of cause and effect as it affects a body of people united by situation, location, race, creed, or ethnic group.

Collective karma also involves nations. This is especially evident during wartime when the inhabitants of a country are compelled to suffer for the misguided policies of their leaders. According to the Buddhist scholar Garma C. C. Chang, the doctrine of collective karma provides a plausible explanation for the man-made disasters of history:

> Karma is the creator, maintainer, and destroyer of both history and the universe . . . the mold and nature of any history does not depend upon God's will or plan, but on the nature of the collective karma of the sentient beings in that particular history.
>
> The evidence of collective karma is not lacking in our own world. For instance, the history and fate of sufferers of mankind's inhumanity cannot be regarded as having been planned or caused even *indirectly* by God . . . Even if we give generous allowance to the wistful belief that everything will be taken care of eventually, that a happy ending is definitely in order when the kingdom of God comes, the phenomena of Auschwitz, of Stalin and Mao tse tung, and of the innumerable man-made and natural disasters in history would certainly make any sensible man hesitate to accept this alleged act of creation as both benevolent and wise . . . With the doctrine of karma, however, the problem of evil or moral justice seems to be comparatively easier to explain . . .[13]

THE KARMA OF PARENT AND CHILD

At the most profound level, collective karma involves the parent-child relationship, which is much deeper than that between siblings. The acceptance of their mutual karma by parents and children has far-reaching implications. No child who had been reared to believe in the validity of the law of causation, and who had accepted it, could one day fling into the face of his parents the taunt "Don't blame me! I didn't ask to be born!" for he would know that we all ask to be born and are born through parents whom we *seek* because of a karmic affinity going back before conception. He or she would be aware that the primary cause of our being propelled again and again into "re-becoming" is a clinging to the notion of a separate, individual existence and the desire to be reborn. The conjunction of a mother and a father is only a secondary, or contributing, cause of one's rebirth.[14] Nor could parents with similar awareness and acceptance of the law of causation ever exclaim in exasperation, "We just don't understand how any child of *ours* could do such a thing!" since they would realize that their sons and daughters have karmas—habit forces or tendencies of long standing—which are independent of inherited mental and physical characteristics.

Although adolescence is a time when boys and girls struggle to emancipate themselves from the influence of their parents, and parents at the same time try to maintain their tenuous control over their children, a child who understood the depth of the parent-child karmic relationship would not permanently alienate herself from her parents except possibly in cases where she had been physically or emotionally abused. That awareness would do much to blunt the sharp edges of the inevitable parent-child conflict that surfaces at this particular time. Parents would recognize that they cannot blame their children for the pains of parenthood, while children would realize that the domineering attitudes of their parents are the product of causes and conditions which they (the children) once set in motion. Both would know that mutual respect and love in the parent-child relationship, as in every other, grows from pain as well as from joy.

Although we often speak of "good" and "bad" (painful) karma, the term "karma" is generally used in reference to the latter—as when selfish actions, for instance, are called "karma-producing." In recent years, as the word "karma" has become widely used in the West, several new usages have arisen. Among these is the term "heavy karma," meaning an unusually large debt that must be expiated as a result of pain-producing thoughts and actions in this life and previous lives. The word "karma" may also imply an evil bent of mind growing out of long-standing ego-dominated behavior. We may also speak of "having a karma" with someone, implying a mutual attraction or repulsion that exists as a result of a strong relationship from a previous life. One will also hear the expression, "Karma willing, I'll see you next month," meaning that if my karma decrees that I live at least to next month and make it to our reunion, we'll meet again then.

Inevitably, in certain circles these days, "karma" has become a buzzword, the glib explanation for any out-of-the-ordinary happening. Even in Japan—a nominally Buddhist country—the word is casually tossed about, as witness this story: A high school student showed his report card to his father. Examining the report carefully, the father was dismayed to find a string of low marks. "Why are your grades so bad?" he sternly demanded. The boy offhandedly replied, "Guess it's just my karma, Dad." Whereupon Dad gave the boy a hard slap. "Why did you hit me?" his son protested. "Because that's *my* karma," answered the father.

"Karma" is sometimes used in reference to a relationship that has played itself out, such as a job or love affair that one is no longer interested in. Not infrequently, though, announcing that one's karma with someone has ended is often a lame attempt to extricate oneself from an unpleasant situation. Correctly, karma cannot be used as justification *for doing or not doing anything*. It can only be pointed to as an explanation of something that has already occurred.

LIGHTENING THE KARMIC BURDEN

The workings of karma are complex and often inscrutable. A child is instantly killed by a car, and in their anguish and despair the parents protest, "Why did this have to happen to *our* child? She was such a generous, loving person, with no malice in her. Why did *she* have to die so young and so violently when others whose lives are selfish and cruel die in their own bed at an advanced age? Where is the justice of it?" And if previously they had faith in the goodness of God, they now feel disillusionment and bitterness toward Him. "Why would a loving and just God permit this?" they demand.

Even a person who accepted karma might initially ask such questions when tragedy struck. But on deeper reflection, one would realize that the question was not "Why?" but "How?"— "How can I expiate the karma which brought this about and not create more of it in the future?" The best way to do this is to accept the situation and use it as an opportunity to repay a karmic debt. This does not mean passively accepting whatever misfortune comes your way when you *can* change the situation. By "rolling with the punch," however, one lightens one's pain and lessens one's karmic burden. Furthermore, there is no residue of resentment or bitterness. In families where a child dies, parents who reflect gratefully on the joy and love she brought into their lives eventually find such thoughts a tremendous aid in allaying the terrible hurt. Here, too, our attitude affects our karma.

One who truly understood that the painful events of his life represent the flowering of seeds once planted by him would inevitably say, "I don't know why this has happened, but since it has, I must have helped cause it." This is not the same as saying, "Such and such an experience is happening to me because I need to develop such and such a characteristic"—for example, more compassion.

In the context of an awareness of karma, suffering would be seen as the inevitable consequence of a series of causes and effects that we ourselves initiated. Eventually one develops the faith to accept that whatever happens to us is primarily the result of our own actions. We might make what we perceive to be mistakes, but in an ultimate sense there are no mistakes; we simply live in accord with our past and current karma. To deeply perceive this is to be taught by life rather than overcome by it. By thus accepting and acquiescing in the effects of our actions, we begin to lessen the karmic burden and eventually the pain-producing causes.

Once, a mother whose son had been imprisoned for selling drugs said to me, "What have I done to deserve this? Why *me?*" A physician friend who was present at a talk on karma in which I had related the foregoing incident commented, "Whenever something painful happens to me and I ask, 'What have I done to deserve this?' invariably the answer comes as 'Plenty!' " This has got to be the response of all of us if we are honest with ourselves, for none of us is free from the guilt implied in the question. Yet the sense of guilt may be turned to a positive end by reflecting, "What causes, what incidents brought about the painful result? In what way did my own behavior contribute to it?" Such questioning can be revealing and thus therapeutic. Life does not exist in a vacuum. The more we understand the interconnectedness of all life, the better we understand the motivations behind our actions and the consequences of our behavior. In the end, others as well as we are the beneficiaries.

A Cautionary Tale of Karmic Retribution

The following World War II incident is an extraordinary example of powerful karmic requital:

It was a restless transport [at Auschwitz] . . . Our Polish Jews knew what was up. And so the whole place swarmed with SS, and Schillinger, seeing what was going on, drew his revolver. But everything would have gone smoothly except that Schillinger had taken a fancy to a certain body—and, indeed, she had a classic figure. That's what he had come to see the chief about, I suppose. So he walked up to the woman and took her by the hand. But the naked woman bent down suddenly, scooped up a handful of gravel and threw it in his face, and when Schillinger cried out in pain and dropped his revolver, the woman snatched it up and fired several shots into his abdomen. The whole place went wild. The naked crowd turned on us, screaming. The woman fired once again, this time at the chief.

Schillinger was lying face down, clawing the dirt in pain with his fingers. We lifted him off the ground and carried him—not too gently—to a car. On the way he kept groaning through clenched teeth: "O Gott, mein Gott, was hab' ich getan, dass ich so leiden muss?" which means—O God, my God, what have I done to deserve such suffering?[15]

Although the foregoing is an extreme example of the psychic numbness implied in the innocent-sounding "What have I done to deserve this?" the pattern is quite common. Unhappily, the guilt implied in these words is not something which many can or wish to accept even in the name of justice. Most people obliterate from consciousness their own blameworthy behavior, priding themselves on those actions that put them in a good light. In this way they avoid responsibility for their pain-producing behavior. They are quick to blame others—a wife, a husband, parents, children, friends, society, enemies (real or imagined), an ideology, God, almost anyone or anything but themselves— for their suffering, yet that suffering is the result of their infliction of pain on others. In Solzhenitsyn's words, "Everyone sees how he has been hurt, but does not see how he is guilty."

WHEN OTHERS ARE WRONG I AM WRONG

With the spiritually developed it is otherwise. It would be hard, I think, to find a higher ethical principle than that enunciated by the sixth patriarch of Zen, who said, "When others are wrong I am in the wrong. When I have transgressed I alone am to blame." Such a deep sense of personal responsibility could come only from one who truly understood the law of causation at a profound level. Such a person would know that the network of interrelationships between all forms of life is so vast and complex that we cannot, in a cosmic sense, disavow responsibility for whatever happens anywhere—least of all for the repercussions, on our own and others' lives, of our thoughts, speech, and actions.

Someone once came to me for help in resolving the angry feelings he had for a former girlfriend. I asked him what he had been doing to this end and he replied that he had been directing loving thoughts toward her. I suggested he start reciting a repentance verse and begin directing feelings of contrition toward her. He was taken aback. "Why should I apologize to *her*?" he insisted. "*She* was the one who hurt *me*." "But," I told him, "the fact that you felt pain means you did something to earn it; no doubt you caused her pain as well. You equally share responsibility for this situation."

How do we explain the unwillingness of so many to reflect on their past wrongs which have caused hurt to others, and their failure to see how the tangled web of these actions continues to cloud their lives and those of others? To what can we attribute our reluctance to make a searching and fearless moral inventory of ourselves? Author J. Glenn Gray believes this attitude is traceable to the rise of modern psychology and the predominance of naturalistic philosophers, "who have tended to view guilt feelings as a hindrance to the full development of personality and the achievement of a life-affirming outlook."[16] Worse, people have tended to use such notions to justify antisocial behavior. And so we blame the parents for being too strict or too lenient, but the offender is blameless. Or else we find society at fault and not the criminal. The individual is thus released from responsibility for past deeds and from the hard duty to improve his character. Overlooked is the fact that at every step of the way a person has the choice to follow the honest and moral road or to deviate from it.

3. THE
INTERCONNECTEDNESS
OF ALL LIFE

WE ARE OUR BROTHERS

PSYCHOLOGIST: Having the deep sense of responsibility you mentioned a few minutes ago is not necessarily healthy. It can become an intolerable burden, an oppressive, neurotic sense of guilt that can even lead to deep-seated psychological disorders. I'm not saying your sixth patriarch was a disturbed man, but I don't feel it's advisable for the average Joe to adopt such an attitude.

I'm not suggesting that we go around taking personal responsibility for everything wrong in the world. This would undoubtedly lead to feelings of depression and frustration at our inability to right the many injustices we see. It might also have other unhealthy consequences.

What I am saying is that we need to recognize the interdependence of all life—that we are not alone but move in an intimate dance with all creation. If I move, you move; if you do wrong, I do wrong; if I do good, you too do good. The joys and triumphs of all humanity are also mine as long as I am able to take joy in the good fortune of others without being envious. Similarly, when I am able to cry with the pain of those who suffer, my compassion is working and I do what I can to help those in need. But, as Dolores Leckey observes, "Every time one of us truly rests, the world rests a little, so intimately connected are we with one another." Yet equally true, we come into this world alone and we will leave it alone, sustained by our wholesome karmas and hindered by our unwholesome ones.

> In between [birth and death, writes an anonymous author] we must find whatever meaning we can in our lives. We must reach out to others and celebrate with them those special times in which we honor the past and look with hope towards the future. For it is only in these moments that we transcend our human limitations, break free from the bonds of our solitary existence, and taste the sweetness of life.

To feel that when others are in the wrong I too am wrong, and that when I have transgressed I alone am to blame, doesn't mean that for every wrong committed I must accept blame at a literal level and take the corresponding punishment. Let us suppose you did everything you could to help end the Vietnam War. In that event you might well say, "Why should I feel responsible for the bombings and other horrors that were committed there?" Of course, few people could really say they did *everything* within their power to stop the war. But many did try hard. So where does the responsibility lie? It lies in the need to rid ourselves of greed, anger, and other destructive elements of our personality. It also lies in developing our full potential as compassionate human beings and in actually expressing that compassion throughout our lives. We are our brother's keepers—no, in the deepest sense we *are* our brothers, for we are not apart from them. To take full responsibility for our actions, to accept our karma and work toward a better life for ourselves and others— this is living up to the ideal of the sixth patriarch.

DOES SUICIDE CREATE NEGATIVE KARMA?

HOMEMAKER: Does a person who commits suicide make bad karma for herself?

Yes, very negative karma.

HOMEMAKER: In what way?

Any intentional act that is egoistically motivated has negative karmic consequences. The willful taking of one's life is such an act. Human life is preeminently precious because it is only from that state that we can come to enlightenment and attain true liberation.

HOMEMAKER: I can see where it would be morally wrong to take someone else's life, and that therefore you would have to suffer for it. But why should a person have to suffer karmic retribution for taking her own life? By doing so, you are not reducing the life force any, are you? So what difference does it make if you take your own life?

The injunction not to kill is part of a total effort to prevent destruction of human consciousness and community. No society can be indifferent to the taking of human life.[17] Suicide implies a rupture of human equilibrium in the society of which one is a part; it does violence to our fundamental instinct for life. The Talmud says, "Whosoever saves a single life, it is as if he had saved the whole world." It is true that from the absolute standpoint of Essential-nature, suicide, like any other phenomenon, is void of any fundamental reality. However, the fact is that we exist simultaneously on two levels: the phenomenal (or relative) and the unconditioned (or absolute). Actually, these are not two, though in our speaking about them in the language of our dualistically oriented mind, they seem to be separate. But in moments of utter clarity we may recognize that the phenomenal is the Void and that the formless is the phenomenal. Thus, while in an absolute sense suicide affects no one, since there is no one and nothing to be affected on that level, at the same time, we also exist in the relative dimension of time and space, of human relationships. On this level, the loss is enormously painful to many people—family, friends, and acquaintances. Because my ego-based action—killing myself— was the source of this pain, I am guilty of producing an immense amount of negative karma, the effects of which will adversely influence not only me but many others as well. It is in the world of form that karma is created, manifested, and expiated. To make statements relating only to life on the plane of the absolute, or undifferentiated, is a fatal mistake; it is as blind as seeing only the relative side of life. The formless aspect can never be considered without the differentiated; the two are inseparable.

Speaking of the individual's relation to the community, William James affirms that these two are mutually conditioning: "The community stagnates without the impulse of the individual. The impulse dies away without the sympathy of the community." When the poet John Donne says, "Every man's death diminishes me," he is affirming the spiritual and scientific truth that all life is interrelated, and that what happens in one place can have its repercussions millions of miles away. (See "Science on Responsive Communion.") The individuals who make up a particular society are like the threads of a fine brocade. Remove even one thread and you have marred the entire pattern of the fabric to some extent. It is violent death through murder, suicide, and war that is particularly disruptive.

HOMEMAKER: I am not in favor of suicide, but it seems to me that a person should be able to do what she pleases with her body. After all, it's hers.

Is it really hers? If it were, she ought to be able to control aging and death itself. Obviously neither she nor anyone else can do that. Similarly, if her mind were really her own, she should be able to totally control her thoughts, and she can't do that either. Our body has its own laws, which it obeys regardless of our wishes. So whose body, whose mind is it? Our body-mind is the crystallization of the way we have thought, felt, and acted; it's the gift of our karma, which enables us to be reborn as a human being, with all the joy, pain, and potential attendant upon having a physical existence. Nonetheless, clinging to body and mind as *my* body, *my* mind is the first fatal step on the road to self-imprisonment. As W. H. Auden states in his "Canzone":

> Our claim to own our bodies and our world
> Is our catastrophe.

DANCE INSTRUCTOR: If I take my life, doesn't that mean that the energy that is me will be able to reincarnate in another body and another personality—a self that will be of more use to others than this body of mine filled with pain and misery? Am I not, in other words, doing the life force a favor, if that's the right way to put it, when I step out of this ailing body?

Do you know that as some other person you will be of more use to others? Let's take a look at two men, both blind and suffering from kidney failure as a result of childhood diabetes. This is a true story. They have also lost parts of their extremities to gangrene, and they suffer a loss of feeling in hands and feet, also as a result of the diabetes. One man—let's call him him Jim—lies "encased in a shell of self-pity," angry that he can't play with his children, begrudging the kidney dialysis that keeps him alive. Despite a supportive family environment, when Jim began the dialysis he threatened to kill himself.

The other man, whom we'll call Bob, had also had dialysis, although he eventually received a kidney transplant. Bob arrived home from the hospital after his transplant surgery to discover that his wife had found someone else and wanted a divorce. And now her lover is suing for custody of the man's son, saying the child is really his. In spite of all this, Bob is cheerful and positive. "There are times when I'm alone that I feel a bit down," he says. "But it's not going to make it any better for me to be miserable around people I love."[18]

Both of these men suffered from pain, yet the man who for all intents and purposes had the bigger dose ended up being an inspiration to those around him and a bright star to many others. Had Bob committed suicide when, on top of all his physical suffering, his wife left him, would he have been reborn as a personality who could be of more use to others than he is now? The point is, we don't have to kill ourselves to serve our fellow beings. Our karma can be modified if we strongly will it; we can turn it for the better—or make it worse by adding killing to the list of whatever painful karma we've created in the past.

Intentionally to take one's life for what are plainly selfish reasons is to violently repulse one's own karma and that of others with whom one is connected. Such an act is a descent rather than an ascent in the evolutionary chain. Just think: this body you want to destroy is the product of billions of years of biological evolution and even more of planetary evolution! As human beings, we represent the culmination of the struggle to evolve from the most primitive life forms into this present body, with its highly intricate brain and marvelously complex physical structure. Through the grace of good karma most of us have achieved "a faultless body and a blameless mind." Ours therefore is a sacred obligation to protect them for ourselves and others.

> O man's most wonderful work—
> Just to walk upon the earth!

THE LIFE FORCE WILL SURVIVE . . .

SOCIOLOGIST: What you call this marvelous brain and body have polluted and impoverished the planet and created nuclear weapons so destructive they can wipe out all life on this earth. And if that happens, there won't be an earth to walk on!

Yes, that too. But if you are concerned about the annihilation of all life in the event of a nuclear conflagration, you can stop worrying. The life force will survive. One of the greatest of the Zen masters, Chao-chou (778–897), confirms this: "Before the existence of the world, the Self-nature is. After the destruction of the world, the Self-nature remains intact."[19]

When the karma of our planet has exhausted itself, when the collective karma of all of us living has come to an end, we and the planet will, in our turn, disappear.

SOCIOLOGIST: Small comfort!

KARMA AND ABORTION

HOMEMAKER: Perhaps I'm jumping to conclusions, but you seem to be implying that the taking of life under any circumstances is karmically bad. If this is so, I would assume you are opposed to abortion.

In the most profound sense, neither the doctor's instruments nor anything else can destroy the real life of the fetus, for its ever-abiding True-nature is indestructible. Looking at abortion from a relative view, however, one can see that all the participants in an abortion—that is, the parents and the doctor (or other person) who performs it—share in the effects of that action.

No matter what we do, for whatever reason, we are planting seeds with every single action and will have to deal with their fruit when the times comes. What kind of karma we are creating for ourselves and for others depends on the degree of selfishness, or lack of it, which motivates our action. If a pregnant woman sincerely feels that she is emotionally incapable of lovingly caring for her child, she may create less painful karma by aborting the embryo than by crippling her growing child later on. If she has an abortion because she resents any interference with the gratification of her selfish desires, she inevitably creates painful karma. If giving birth to a baby seriously endangers the life of the mother, then saving the mother's life—she being the more developed one—may take precedence over saving that of the embryo. Clear awareness and affirmation of the law of cause and effect, and complete willingness to assume responsibility for what needs to be done, will help clear the mind of guilt, anxiety, and remorse, which are also seeds for new obstructions.

KARMA AND EUTHANASIA

PSYCHOLOGIST: What about euthanasia? What is the karma of someone—say a doctor or nurse or friend—who in response to the pleas of a sufferer helps him to die in order to spare him further suffering? There's a lot of that going on these days, you know.

Suicide and euthanasia are grave matters—no pun intended. None of us wants to see someone dear to us suffer, of course. But the karma of the one who takes her own life and that of those who aid and abet life-taking are not the same.

Deliberately to take your own life carries with it a heavy karmic penalty, for all the reasons you have heard. To respond to another's entreaties to end his life because of great pain and suffering incurs karmically less serious results. (This latter does *not* include counseling another to take his own life—an action that may have more severe karmic consequences.) It may strike some of you as selfish to be thinking of your own karma when someone dear to you in great pain pleads with you to end his or her life. But that is really secondary to a consideration of that person's karma. Might it not be kinder, karmically speaking, not to accede to that person's request for the person's *own* sake? There are no easy answers to these questions, for each situation is a unique set of circumstances, and each person must make his or her decision based on those circumstances—with the full knowledge that, whatever is decided, cause brings effect.

NURSE: If I am asked by an attending doctor to disconnect a respirator and I do so and the patient soon dies, am I karmically responsible for the patient's death? Or suppose I make out a living will in which I direct a friend to make decisions on my behalf in case I become medically unable to do so myself; and suppose I tell this friend that I don't want to have any ventilators, emergency resuscitation, or surgically implanted feeding tubes to keep me alive if I am in an irreversible coma. Now, if my life is cut short because such heroic measures are not employed, have I created negative karma for myself? Also, let's say I end up on a respirator because I fall into a coma that at first was thought to be temporary. After it becomes clear that my coma is not *going to be temporary, my friend requests that the respirator be disconnected, the hospital permits it, and I subsequently die. What is my friend's karma for getting the respirator disconnected?*

These are ticklish questions. My sense is that if it is part of your job to do such things as disconnecting a ventilator, and you do it with a feeling of contrition coupled with loving and compassionate thoughts directed toward the dying person, whatever negative karma you might incur would be minimal. It is vital, though, that you not distance yourself from the person, but that you try to be as connected with him or her as possible, through empathy and compassion. As for the second example you give, it seems to me that you would be exercising your right *to be allowed* to die, and therefore little negative karma would accrue to your friend. Hospital personnel, I suppose, would disconnect the respirator, presumably after getting legal advice or a court order. But here, too, the attitude of the people involved is of utmost importance in determining the karmic consequences of their actions. The more compassion expressed, and the less self-centeredness, the less negative karma will accrue.

THE KARMA OF "INNOCENT" CHILDREN

DANCE INSTRUCTOR: What about a baby who, the day before it is due to be born, dies in the womb as a result of the accidental malformation of the umbilical cord? This happened to a friend of mine. How can the infant or the mother be at fault?

NURSE: And what about innocent children who die in an air raid or are the victims of a terrorist attack? What did they do to cause their death?

Let's take the last question first. By "innocent" I suppose you assume the children did nothing to contribute to their own death. But don't forget that children come into this life with their own karmic burden even as they are linked with that of their parents. Because of this connection they are compelled to suffer for the sins of their parents, just as parents must pay for the vices of their children. Children are also involved in collective karma.

Regarding the infant born dead: The causal connection between the events of a previous life and those of this one is, of course, obscure. The only thing we can say is that it was her karma not to be born at this time to these parents. It's cases such as this that lead people to ask, "Why is it that good people suffer serious illness and economic misfortune? Why do the merciful often die young and the violent live long? Why do evildoers appear to be happy and the righteous unhappy?" A dialogue between King Milinda, a Bactrian king who extended the Greek dominion into India around 200 B.C., and Nāgasena the Elder, a famous Buddhist monk, may shed some light:

"Venerable Nāgasena," asked the king, "Why are human beings not alike, some short-lived and some long, some sick, others healthy, some ugly and some handsome, some weak and some powerful? Why are certain men poor and others rich? Why some base and others noble, some stupid and some clever? Why do some die early and others live to a ripe old age?"

The Elder replied, "Your Majesty, why are plants not alike, some astringent, some salty, some pungent, some sour, and some sweet?"

"I suppose, Venerable Sir, because they come from different sorts of seeds."

"That is how it is with human beings, your Majesty! They are not alike because their karmas are not alike. As Buddha said, 'Each being has its own karma. Each is born through karma, becomes a member of a family through karma. Each is subject to karma —it is karma that separates the high from the low.' "[20]

AN EYE FOR AN EYE?

Karma is not a matter of an eye for an eye and a tooth for a tooth in the narrow sense; if it were, the world would be full of blind and toothless people. There isn't necessarily a one-to-one correspondence between the evil or good a person does in one lifetime and the results that will be experienced in another. The fact that, in a previous life, one may have cut off a person's hand doesn't necessarily mean that in this lifetime he will lose his own hand. The ever changing events continuously interweave with one another. The currents of karma, both good and bad, inter-mingle, flowing from past lives to the present life and from this life to future lives. Our karma is thus determined by the sum total of our actions, good and bad, and by the larger karmic flux of which we are a part. These actions in turn create a pattern, a predisposition, as a result of which we respond to events in a certain way. That is, our karma creates a pathway, or perhaps a rut, which we tend habitually to follow.

KARMA REALIZED NOW AND IN THE FUTURE

Just as our actions can produce positive, negative, or neutral karma, so the results of karma can occur during three periods in time. Some karma bears its fruit in the present life, or as soon as the act is performed. The effects of the act, though, may not occur until the next lifetime. And in some instances many lifetimes may elapse before an effect is felt. In some cases the karmic force may be so weak that it produces no reaction at all. So retribution experienced in this life is the matured result of karmic seeds sown either in a past life or in the present one; and the accumulated effects of actions in this life, good or bad, are experienced in this life or in subsequent ones.

DANCE INSTRUCTOR: What kind of actions produce positive karma and what kind negative?

Instead of the terms "positive" and "negative," it might be more precise to speak of wholesome and unwholesome volitions. An unwholesome volition is one rooted in greed, hate (anger), or delusion (erroneous thinking)—in a word, in self-centeredness. A wholesome volition is rooted in the opposite of those passions, namely, generosity, love, contentment, clarity of mind.

In the light of what you've just heard about karma realized now and in the future, it may be easier to understand how it happens that one who has led a decent life will suddenly go off the deep end and commit a terrible wrong—to the dismay and consternation of his family and friends, who have always looked upon him as a pillar of virtue. What happened? He has been hit with past karma brought into play by certain causes and conditions.

When we look at human existence from the perspective of only one lifetime, it sometimes seems that the wicked prosper and the good suffer, that the decent person has unhappiness as his lot while the evildoer lives happily. But this is only the outcome of past good and evil karma. If it were possible to track lifetimes, we would see that eventually the evildoers get their just desserts.

PSYCHOTHERAPIST: That's just the point. How *can anyone track lifetimes?*

You can't unless you yourself have paranormal powers, and even then it is hard to determine how accurate your perceptions are.

PSYCHOLOGIST: You spoke about the different time periods in which karmic retribution can take place. How do we know that it happens in that way? I mean, why *should the retributive effects of karma express themselves in future lives and not only in this lifetime? What hard evidence or proof do we have that karma works that way? And* how *does karma caused by my conduct in a past life find its way into my present life as effect?*

We will discuss the last part of your question when we come to the subject of rebirth. For the moment, let me quote the Buddha on karma. When he was asked a question about karma similar to yours, he answered, "I can't tell you *how* karma works; what I can tell you is that it *does* work." He also said:

> If you want to know your past [cause]
> look at yourself now [effect].
> If you want to know your future [effect]
> look at your present [cause].

The Buddha, we know, was supremely enlightened, and this, coupled with his extraordinary paranormal powers, enabled him to see into his own past lives and those of others. He could therefore speak with authority about the different time periods of karmic retribution. But we need not rely only on what the Buddha said. Many men and women today, as in the past, have had ESP experiences and have spoken or written about them.

PARANORMAL ABILITIES

COMPUTER PROGRAMMER: Do many Americans have genuine psychic powers?

Psychic powers are not that unusual. According to a poll conducted by the University of Chicago's National Opinion Research Council, sixty-seven percent of Americans said that they had experienced extrasensory perceptions or some other paranormal events.[21] In fact, I've had several students who have been deeply psychic. Anyone who meditates seriously will, over a period of time, develop ESP to one level or another, simply because meditation, properly and intensively engaged in over a long period of time, develops awareness.

COMPUTER PROGRAMMER: How do you know these students have ESP?

In Zen, students as part of their training are obliged to confront their teacher from time to time in a one-to-one meeting, "eyeball to eyeball." Let me tell you about a certain young student who, while sitting before me, suddenly fell into a trancelike state and with great emotion began to speak in an obscure tongue, moving her arms up and down in an agitated manner. After a while, just as suddenly, she broke out of the trance, rubbed her eyes as if awakening from a deep sleep, and asked, "Where am I?" Observing her intently, I asked, "Do you remember where you were and what you were talking about?" Slowly she said, "Yes, I remember . . . It was in the year 1546 and I was . . ." and then she recounted a stark event in which she had been involved. The manner in which she related this obviously painful experience of a past life—her facial expressions and her general demeanor—convinced me that, at the least, she was not playing a part. She was not the only student to regress to a past life. Other students with paranormal abilities, though not as powerful as this young woman's, have also demonstrated them unbidden.

Obviously those able to see into their own previous lives and those of others will have no doubts as to the validity of karma and rebirth. Such conviction frees them of the mania "You live only once, so what the hell, anything goes!" and affects their behavior in a profound way. (See "Rebirth" section.) Who but a fool or madman would willfully hurt or destroy life if he were absolutely certain that karmic retribution in the form of a hellish existence would follow in this or a subsequent lifetime?

CAN AN ANIMAL CREATE KARMA?

DANCE INSTRUCTOR: My question is, can an animal make karma? Don't you have to have a sense of right and wrong to create karma? Does a fox—even a most unusual one such as the white fox you mentioned earlier—have a moral sense of right and wrong?

Anyone who has lived with animals knows that they may be selfish, jealous, gluttonous, loving, unselfish, aggressive, timid, fierce, and so on. Charles Darwin claimed that the higher animals possess all the emotions of human beings, but in an incipient form.

DANCE INSTRUCTOR: But just because an animal is selfish or loving or timid or fierce doesn't mean it understands the difference between right and wrong. There are even people who are truly unable to grasp the difference.

That's true, yet such people create karma simply by functioning in the world. Morals, as we know, are relative. What one generation forbids, the next permits. Remember, the basic meaning of "karma" is "doing," "action." The actions, emotions, and characteristics of animals express their karma, at the same time influencing and extending it.

NURSE: If a wild animal kills another one for food or some other reason, is that animal making bad karma for itself?

I don't think we can say with certainty what's in an animal's mind when, whether for food or not, it kills another. We know that animals in the rutting season will battle with each other, and that often one or both may be killed. We also know that most animals are territorial and will fight and sometimes kill to maintain their territories. And then there are well-fed cats who will *play* with a mouse and then kill it. But whether there is "malice aforethought" in their mind, as the law quaintly puts it—some mental factor that provides the impulse to kill—I don't believe anybody can say. I certainly can't. What we can say with some assurance is that the actions of animals, like those of humans, are karma-producing. Indeed, only completely enlightened beings, or those in absolute *samadhi*, can be said not to create negative karma (or more precisely, negative karma that would ripen at a future time)—and that is only because the instant such karma is being created it is being expiated. The law of cause and effect is not suspended for any being.

Sri Ramana Maharshi said that it is possible for animals also to be working off their karma, implying that they come into this lifetime with their own burden of karma and either add to it or lessen it. "We do not know what souls may be tenanting these bodies," he is quoted as saying, "and for finishing what part of their unfinished karma they may seek our company."[22]

THE TRANSCENDENT "IT"

At all events, we have been talking from a relative standpoint —time-bound and space-bound causes and conditions. From an *absolute*, undifferentiated point of view, there is no killer and no one to be killed, nothing right, nothing wrong. From the perspective of our True-nature, we cannot postulate human beings or foxes or cows or trees or plants or other forms of sentient life. We can't even speak of karma—good or bad. From that transcendent standpoint there is just *"It"*—not even that, in fact!

PSYCHOLOGIST: If not that, then what?

Just this (clapping his hands loudly)!
Speaking of this "It," a Zen master of old said, "*It* helps you cross the river when the bridge is broken down. *It* accompanies

you as you return to the village on a moonless night. If you call it [True-nature], you will go to hell as fast as an arrow."[23]

THE KARMA OF OPPRESSED CULTURES

SOCIOLOGIST: I'd like to comment on something you mentioned earlier. It's about the fate of sufferers of man's inhumanity to man. Who were you quoting on that?

Professor Garma C. C. Chang.

SOCIOLOGIST: You quoted him as saying he could not accept the idea that such suffering as the Holocaust and similar disasters in history had been planned or caused, even indirectly, by a loving God. And finally he said that with the doctrine of karma the problem of evil or moral justice in the world is easier to explain. What I would like to ask you, and him too, is this: if the oppression of certain cultures is not primarily due to the inbred prejudice, bigotry, and cruelty of their oppressors, from what sort of acts does their bad karma derive? In other words, what evil did they as individuals do that was intrinsically worse than the evil done by other people and that merited the oppression they have suffered throughout history and continue to suffer?

I don't know. Tell me, do you have your own theory of suffering?

SOCIOLOGIST: Yes, at least as far as racism is concerned. We all know that this phenomenon is quite common among different ethnic groups. In our country, the Chinese who came to California in the 1840s when news of the gold rush reached South China, were socially ostracized and exploited. Why? Because they were different—they looked different from us and acted differently. Today Vietnamese, Cambodians, Hispanics, blacks of course, and other minority groups are objects of discrimination in America, and elsewhere too. Look at what's happening in Sri Lanka. There is virtually a civil war going on between the light-colored, native Singhalese and the much darker Tamils, who were originally from the South of India. In this case you have religious and other cultural values of one ethnic group, the majority, clashing with those of a culturally different minority, and that is creating racial animosities. And always there are ethnic jealousies and economic rivalries among different groups. Somehow societies find it impossible to foster ethnic pride without mixing it with hatred for another group that looks different, speaks differently, and perhaps has different religious loyalties. Prejudice and cruelty are so endemic to the human race at this stage of its evolution that we can't get away from them anywhere. Even in a country like India you find strong color prejudice, with lighter-colored peoples trying to exploit the darker-skinned ones. And of course people need scapegoats—always scapegoats.

KARMA: A CONSOLING HYPOTHESIS

Agreed, and it is precisely these ignorant, prejudicial attitudes and behavior patterns that create unwholesome karma and the painful consequences that follow.

But even if we take into account what you have just pointed out, I believe that the doctrine of karma—which holds that basically we are the architects of our fate—is a more plausible, a more consoling explanation of human suffering and injustice in the world than, for example, the notion that a powerful and benevolent God created such pain for His own obscure reasons.

As regards the karma of oppressed minorities, here, too, it would be inaccurate to argue that the prejudice and bigotry directed against them spring only from their own negative karma. Other contributing forces, over which they have no control, may also be operating here. Yet whether we say to another "It's your karma" or not, karma will continue to produce its results, just as the law of gravity operates whether one observes or disregards it. Our belief or disbelief cannot arrest the law of karma in its ceaseless operation.

Karmically speaking, we can't say specifically what past act or combination of acts has brought about the tragedies of these minorities. Perhaps in past existences some of these persons were aggressors who caused large-scale sufferings to others. However, a caveat here: even if one accepts such a hypothesis, it in no way mitigates the oppressors' culpability or the horror of their acts; nor does it mitigate the suffering of the victims. There are, of course, aggressors who justify their aggression by saying, in effect, that they are only helping their victims repay their bad karma. Who would accept such a self-serving rationalization? The point is, it does not follow that those of a particular race, creed, or sex in this life had the same characteristics in their last lifetime. A Nazi who died during the war could thus be reborn as a Jew and later undergo terrible suffering. A white slave owner could be reborn as a black slave, and so on.

Nor can we overlook the karma of obvious aggressors. To be an oppressor or an active bigot is also the consequence of past unwholesome karma. This karma continues to create more negative karma, all of which will have to be painfully expiated sooner or later.

KARMA AND THE INTENTION TO LEARN

NURSE: I've heard it said that the cause of our suffering in this world might be due not to something wrong we did in the past, but to a need on our part to learn something—for example, awareness or humility. Some people even go so far as to say we choose to undergo painful experiences in order to learn from them. Is that so?

These notions are a distortion of the Buddhist teaching of karma. Consider this situation: I start across a busy intersection while the light is still green, and because I am inattentive, I get hit by a car and am badly hurt. My injury did not result from my need to learn the value of mindfulness. Whether I become more attentive in the future as a result of the accident is up to me, but the accident did not happen in order to teach me to be attentive.

Or take another case. Let us say your husband is mistreating you. Through what you did in the past—perhaps within recent memory, perhaps not—you have "earned" the abuse being heaped on you now. But there is a vital difference between accepting responsibility for the abuse being inflicted on you and lying belly up to invite further punishments—taking it without trying to change your circumstances. If you continue to allow your husband to beat you, not only are you perpetuating your pain and grief; you are also helping him perpetuate the bad karma he is creating for himself. Remember, we have the power to change our karma. You could choose to leave the relationship, perhaps moving to a distant area to live, or you could undergo psychological counseling to understand and change your own behavior patterns that may have contributed to the situation, or you can simply sit back and tell yourself, "It's my karma."

NURSE: I have another question relating to karma. May I ask it now?

Yes.

NURSE: I understand many people these days believe that we cause our own illness—karma, you know—and so we also have the power to completely cure ourselves either by willing the disease away or by employing alternative therapies alone. As a nurse, it's hard for me to understand this point of view. What do you think?

Although it is true that our minds and bodies are shaped by our karma—which includes our choice of parents and therefore possible genetic predisposition to certain diseases—we can't overlook the fact of environmental and other influences. A case in point is the recent discovery that many people die from cancer caused by radon gas occurring naturally in their own homes.

We are a very complex interaction of mind, body, emotion, and will. These four are inseparably connected, although for convenience, we divide them into individual components. And so sickness of the body-mind is no simple thing. Take the common cold: it's known that it is caused by a virus, but that physical exhaustion, depression, and stress can also determine whether a person exposed to the virus actually gets the cold. Or take cancer, perhaps the most complex and mysterious of illnesses:

it has no simple origin and no simple cure. While a person's cheerful, optimistic attitude and will to overcome the disease have been known to make a difference in certain cases, they don't at all in others. "Doctors are men," says Voltaire, "who prescribe medicine of which they know little to cure diseases of which they know less in human beings of which they know nothing."

It flies in the face of what we do know about the etiology of sickness to assume that we alone cause our illness and therefore that we can cure ourselves of it. True, an intemperate lifestyle— bad diet, lack of exercise, alcohol and drug abuse, mental confusion, depression, inability to cope with stress, and other factors—can precipitate an illness; it is dangerous to assume, however, that you need only apply some willpower or positive imaging—or even surgery, radiation, and chemotherapy—to effect a cure. For the person who is ill, it can be a traumatic experience to believe he can cure himself—or he's not living right—and then to fail. And it is irresponsible and insensitive to say to him, "You've made yourself sick; just make yourself well! If you can't, something's rotten about you."

This smacks of the religious belief popular in certain times in history, that those who suffer illness and misery do so because they have fallen from God's grace and so are begetting His wrath. If it were true that disease and pain are the outcome of a life of impurity, how do we explain that such an imposing spiritual figure as Sri Ramana Maharshi died of cancer? (See "Sri Ramana Maharshi.")

A CONTRARY VIEW OF KARMA

SOCIOLOGIST: Getting back to what we were talking about earlier, I don't accept the idea that the suffering and evil of the world were planned by God—certainly not by a loving God—for reasons inaccessible to the human mind. Frankly I find the whole notion unbelievable. But the karma explanation of evil is no better. Why? Because it, too, offends human sensibilities. How do you say to a mother whose child was born severely handicapped, "It's the result of your mutual karma—you and your child must have done something terrible in a previous life to have this happen to you now, even though you may not remember what it was you did! It's too bad the two of you must suffer now for what you did before, but if you gratefully accept this misfortune you'll wipe out the bad karma"? Think of how guilty the mother would feel—if she believed you, of course. It's downright malevolent.

Or how do you say to black people in South Africa who are being assaulted by the police and perhaps having their houses burned by white thugs, "Be grateful for your ill treatment. It's all due to the hurt you caused others in past lives. But if you accept this abuse and maltreatment, you'll get rid of your bad karma and have less to feel guilty about in the future"? That's just adding insult to injury.

Or how could you say to a Jew who survived Auschwitz that he, the guiltless victim, and not his tormentors, was responsible for his sufferings? As if the memory of his suffering in a Nazi concentration camp weren't enough without your adding to it by telling him this! Who would blame him if he hauled off and socked you?

Making a victim solely responsible for his misfortune is a way of shutting your eyes to so much that is unfair in life, such as unfavorable social and economic conditions over which he has no control.

In the town where I live a gunman held up a restaurant recently, and in the course of the robbery he shot a fellow dead who tried to escape. That sort of mindless killing is nothing new these days, unfortunately. But the attitude of the person who told me about this incident was most disturbing. In referring to the dead fellow, he said without a trace of emotion, "It's too bad, but that's his karma," adding, "and, of course, the karma of the gunman, too." Not the slightest sympathy for the victim or his family, mind you, or outrage over the acts of the gunman!

With all this talk of karma, that attitude doesn't surprise me. If you accept that all misery is self-created and that in this life you need to accept the consequences of past acts, why empathize with the sufferings of another person? What kind of warm relationship can you have with your fellow human beings when you are convinced that their sufferings are their own fault? For that matter, what kind of sympathetic relationship can you have with yourself if you feel that you are the master of your fate, and yet you can't

even control something like your health? What does that do to your
self-esteem? A person could become completely neurotic.

But this is only half of it. If you concur in the idea of karma,
you've got to believe that by trying to alleviate someone's distress,
you are interfering with his karma and therefore actually hurting
rather than helping him. It follows that you won't do anything to
lessen his pain. You won't help the poor, the sick, the orphans, the
handicapped, because that would be obstructing their karma—you
would be preventing them from expiating it. They alone—and I
emphasize the word "alone"—have to drink their bitter medicine.
You're talking about a pretty sick world if you exclude compassion
and the accompanying urge to help people.

A CONTRARY VIEW REFUTED

It is emphatically not true that in relieving the distress of an
individual, you are preventing him from expiating his karma.
There are, no doubt, people who misunderstand karma that way,
but the notion that karma excludes a compassionate concern for
others is completely false. Compassion and wisdom are two of
the cornerstones of Buddhism, of which karma is a fundamental
teaching. The idea that by alleviating the suffering of another
you are interfering with her karma contradicts this well-known
pronouncement of the Buddha: "One thing I teach, and one thing
only—suffering—its causes *and the way to overcome them.*" (Emphasis added.) And the Buddha was most emphatically not referring only to the suffering of the individual listeners, but to
that of all beings.

Moreover, why would a Zen master on his deathbed reply,
when asked where he wanted to go after his death, "To hell,
because that's where I'll be able to help the most sufferers"? And,
finally, why did the great lay Buddhist Fu Hsi sell his house and
land to buy food for the people in his district, who were starving
because of a famine? Why didn't he say, "It's their karma; I can't
interfere with it," and just let them starve?

Contrary to the view you express, one who truly understood
and accepted the law of karma would be able spontaneously to
offer sympathy, understanding, and help to another in pain, sim-

ply because he would know that he himself at one time or another had had to bear the painful consequences of his own past wrongdoing. The fact is that compassion and karma are not mutually exclusive. To see someone suffering, have an impulse to help, and suppress that impulse would be creating your *own* bad karma.

What Is Compassion?

But what is compassion? Is it merely sympathizing with those in pain, or actively helping to relieve their suffering, like the Good Samaritan who doesn't walk past the injured or the ailing but stops to help? Is it aiding the poor and the homeless? Enlightened compassion involves much more than engaging in such temporary measures. Even if you feed a hungry man, he's going to get hungry again, so unless you teach him how to grow his own food, or teach him a skill so he can earn enough money to buy his own food, your compassion is not of the deepest kind. The same principle applies to the homeless. While they are entitled to help in finding and holding their places in the society of which they're a part and to whose development they have contributed (in perhaps invisible ways), our compassion is not yet truly enlightened unless we can get them to see that their own karma has been a vital element in bringing them to their present condition—that even if society has pushed them to the ground they still have the power to get up and change their karma.

What about the prejudice against minorities? Remember, not every member is discriminated against. Each person has the burden of his or her own karma. We see this fact in a family where children are brought up more or less in the same way by the same parents and are exposed to the same genetic and environmental influences, yet some lead decent lives and one or two become social problems. The following quotation from a letter is such an example: "I have had three normal children. And then I had a baby, a girl who from the moment she was born was evil. My family was loving and close, and now is ruined. She is vicious and spiteful and wants only to hurt other people."[24]

What can one say in response to the story of the fellow who

matter-of-factly characterized the murder of an innocent man as his karma? It *is* disturbing, I agree, to hear someone respond to a killing in such an insensitive way. But this fellow's indifference no doubt was due to his equating karma with fatalism—the belief that everything is preordained and that therefore, in this case, there was nothing that could have been done to prevent the killing. But that's a misunderstanding of karma, as you've heard. It may also be true that had the dead man not tried to escape he probably wouldn't have been shot. In that sense he had some responsibility for his death; it was by no means preordained. Still, no feeling person would view a brutal killing with such cold indifference.

You ask, "If you accept that all misery is self-created, and that in this life you need to atone for past misdeeds, how are you going to empathize with the sufferings of another person?" The law of cause and effect does not imply that all misery is self-created. What happens to one of us affects all of us, though the effect isn't always obvious.

Nor is it accurate to say we are here merely to atone for past wrongdoings. We are here to work out past karma, both positive and negative—a statement which has a much broader implication than that of paying off past karmic debts. You can think of our present life as a huge school or arena where we seek to develop ourselves physically, mentally, morally, and spiritually —in other words, to raise the level of our own consciousness and the consciousness of others. That is why we are strongly attracted to certain parents and to certain other people, including a spouse, whose actions often pain us and whom we in turn pain. The development of our full potential necessitates undergoing pain and struggle. We may resent that pain, and we may hate the person or persons we blame for it, yet our karma propels us toward such persons precisely because at this stage of our life the pain is essential for our growth and spiritual advancement. If we gratefully accept the pain and see it as an opportunity to grow, to purge ourselves of past unwholesome karma, we have already taken a giant step upward.

It's all too easy to throw around the arcane word "karma" with an air of omniscience. The fact is, all ego-motivated acts create karmic consequences, but that doesn't mean those acts have no other implications. Let us say a man and his child are brutally murdered in a terrorist hijacking of a plane. Was this their karma? Yes, because they chose to be on the plane and so become the victims of the collective karma of all those on board. To say this, however, is not to excuse the horrors and evils of terrorism or make light of the tragedy of such killings. If we see somebody suffering, we need to help her if at all possible. That person's karma *might* be pain and poverty; nevertheless, we must act. This is *our* karma. We cannot ignore individual suffering, for only by responding to it do we express our compassion and demonstrate our humanity. Would a compassionate, undeluded individual, when confronted with human misery, turn away from it with the thought "It is self-created; it's no business of mine"? The answer is a flat no. Why not? Because enlightened compassion is not the outcome of conscious choice; it is the upwelling of a deep instinct in all of us, which if not obstructed by deluded thinking operates freely. Besides, to be helped may be a person's karma as much as his suffering is.

To say, "It's my 'bad' karma" after an unhappy event in one's own life is a positive thing, especially if it leads one to reflect on the significance of the shifting circumstances of his life. But to say "Too bad, but that's your karma" gratuitously to someone in misery is not only insensitive but, in many cases, only partially true. Besides, common decency—respect for another's feelings —is a social imperative in any civilized society. An individual may have brought on his sufferings by past misguided actions, or his sufferings may be due to collective karma. Nonetheless, a truly sympathetic human being would act immediately and directly to do everything he could to alleviate another's pain and suffering. Helping another would be helping himself. No man's karma is exclusively his own, and no one's suffering is exclusively her own. A web of relationships sustains and nourishes each of us.

One's Karma Constantly Changes

The truth is we can never know precisely what our karma is because its origin may be obscure. It is constantly shifting, adjusting, moving, being expiated, and being newly formed. This old Chinese story about a farmer whose horse ran away illustrates the dynamic quality of karma. When his neighbors came over to console him, sighing, "Too bad, too bad," the farmer said, "Maybe." The next day the horse returned, bringing with him seven wild horses. "Oh, how lucky you are!" exclaimed the neighbors. "Maybe," replied the farmer. On the following day, when the farmer's son tried to ride one of the new horses, he was thrown and broke his leg. "Oh, how awful!" cried the neighbors. "Maybe," answered the farmer. The next day soldiers came to conscript the young men of the village, but the farmer's son wasn't taken because his leg was broken. "How wonderful for you!" said the neighbors. "Maybe," said the farmer.

Obviously, then, trying to extrapolate future karma from a certain event would be as foolhardy as looking at pictures of babies you've never seen before, singling one out, and attempting to describe what her future will bring.

The answer to the question "How do you say to a mother who has given birth to a seriously retarded child, 'It's your karma'?" is obviously "You *don't* say it," for the reasons already given. A mother who understood the play of karma would not need to be told this, for she would know that every child comes into the world with its own karma, for better or worse, and that it is one of the main determinants of her child's personality and character—along, of course, with genetic and enviromental influences (which are themselves the vehicles of karma). Aware of that, she would not burden herself with a lifelong guilt over her child's sad condition; she could console herself with the conviction that her child's affliction is a form of karmic retribution— partially due to the mother's actions in a previous lifetime, but mainly attributable to the child's past behavior. Present karma must not be overlooked; the mother's lifestyle also enters into the total picture. A pregnant mother's drug abuse or drinking or smoking is bound to have harmful effects on her fetus, as much research has disclosed. Still, there are mothers (and fathers too) who lead healthy lives yet have mentally or physically impaired children. Conversely, a dissolute mother may bear a normal child.

Here again, the wholesome karma of the infant may produce normality, nullifying the effects of the mother's intemperate lifestyle.

COMPUTER PROGRAMMER: Here's a somewhat different story I wish you'd comment on: A young woman I knew always believed in the goodness of God and of course tried to live a good and moral life. Her husband was a decent young man whom she loved dearly. They were not long married before he was inducted into the Army and sent over to Vietnam. He had been there less than three months when he was killed in action. At the same time a neighbor of the family—a man who had led a despicable life, causing a lot of pain to everyone around him—also was sent to Vietnam. At the end of the war the second man returned without so much as a scratch. This woman told me she couldn't understand how a just and loving God could punish goodness and reward evil in this way. As a result of these incidents she lost her faith in God completely, and she admitted to me that she had even turned to hating Him. How do you say to her that her husband died his early death because of something he did in the past? To me this translates as "He deserved it!" Is that so different from saying, "It's God's will"?

You ask, "How do you say to her that he deserved his death because it was retribution for past wrongdoing?" As with the mother of a retarded child, you do not say such a thing. No one but a callous or misguided person would make such a bald statement. Why? Because it would not comfort the woman even if she already believed in the law of causation, and if she did not, you could never help her by making such an insensitive remark.

The complexities of karma are such that we must be wary of giving simplistic interpretations to any event. For example, collective karma, the workings of which are often much harder to discern, also exerts a pervasive effect upon us. Take the case of the soldier who died during the war. Collective as well as individual karma may have been involved. These two types of karma cannot always be separated. It is individual karma to be part of a collective karmic situation or group—for example, being born to a certain race or ethnic group. Remember, not everything painful that happens to us is the outcome of our personal karma alone. A wartime death may in fact be the result of collective karma in which our nation's aggressive actions cause us to suffer dislocations simply because we live in that country. Or a combatant might suffer death or injury as a result of his own actions. Whether the young soldier who was killed in the Vietnam War would fall into this last category would depend on a number of collateral considerations. Did he enlist or was he drafted? Did he volunteer for a mission in which he was killed? Did he kill before he himself was killed? If so, did he do so with hatred in his heart or "no-mindedly"? These circumstances would bear on whether personal or collective karma was involved, or both, and to what extent. As you have heard, personal and collective karma often overlap. In any event, it would be exceedingly bad taste to say offhandedly to a widow that her husband's death was due to his karma and hers. Given the right time and place, one could tactfully raise the subject of the role of karma in the lives of all of us, and encourage her to bear her misery bravely and without rancor as a way of expiating her own karma.

SCIENCE AND KARMA

COMPUTER PROGRAMMER: But can you prove karma?

I suppose you mean scientifically prove. It would make more sense for science to give credence to causation from the perspective of karma. Science, I understand, admits of proof only in relation to the physical world, although its understanding of what constitutes that world is now radically expanding. Validating a law of cause and effect that applies to all planes of existence, not just the physical (as it is now understood), is beyond the scope of science as we now know it. It must be remembered that the method of scientific verification by experimental means is limited, as are man's senses.

In this connection, Professor Huston Smith asks:

Why should the West, dominated to the extent it currently is by scientific modes of thought, go to school to a perspective forged before the rise of modern science? Some think the answer lies in the extent to which the Buddhist cosmology anticipated what contemporary science has empirically discovered. The parallels are impressive. Astronomical time and space, which irrevocably smashed the West's previous world view, slip into the folds of Buddhist cosmology without a ripple.[25]

HOW TO CREATE GOOD KARMA

NURSE: How can we live so that we make good karma and avoid bad?

A good question. Insofar as we free ourselves of greed and anger, cultivate compassion and wisdom (seeing things as they really are) and immerse ourselves in *all* the circumstances of our life, we accumulate wholesome—or at least not unwholesome—karma. The Buddha's precepts provide excellent guidelines: (1) not to kill but to cherish all life; (2) not to take what is not given but to respect the things of others; (3) not to engage in improper sexuality but to practice purity of mind and self-restraint; (4) not to lie but to speak the truth; (5) not to cause others to use liquors or drugs that confuse the mind, nor to do so oneself, but to keep the mind clear; (6) not to speak of the shortcomings of others but to be understanding and sympathetic; (7) not to praise oneself and condemn others but to overcome one's own shortcomings; (8) not to withhold spiritual or material aid but to give it freely where needed; (9) not to become angry but to exercise control. There are others, but these are the most important.

Although observance of this or any other moral code is the first indispensable step on the road to a genuine spiritual life, only an awakening to the true nature of life and death can provide unshakable contentment—in this or any other life.

To sum up: One's life situation is not ordered by either gods or devils but is the consequence of one's own actions, arising from our thoughts, speech, and emotions, whether we are aware of the meaning of good and bad or not. These actions echo within us and influence our personality. When our attitudes change, our circumstances likewise change.

Our horizons would expand and our lives would take on fresh meaning if we began training ourselves to see that even the minutest event in our lives has karmic significance. We would gain a new awareness of our own power and dignity even as we became more humble, for we would realize that we are not isolated fragments thrown into the universe by a capricious fate, but part of one vast ocean in which all currents intermingle. Wonder and joy would replace boredom and discontent.

Four: REBIRTH

I am just as certain as you see me here
that I have existed a thousand times before
and I hope to return a thousand times more.

—GOETHE

After all, it is no more surprising to
be born twice
than it is to be born once.

—VOLTAIRE

All life is phoenix-like,[1] recreating itself
again and again from its own ashes.

—AUTHOR UNKNOWN

1. THE CASE FOR REBIRTH

WHAT LIES BEYOND?

"As far back as I can remember I have unconsciously referred to the experiences of a previous state of existence . . . As the stars looked to me when I was a shepherd in Assyria, they look to me now a New Englander . . . And Hawthorne, too, I remember as one with whom I sauntered in old heroic times along the banks of the Scamander amid the ruins of chariots and heroes."[2]

Perhaps you've heard or read statements such as this before and dismissed them as no more than the fantasies of a starry-eyed New Ager or an Eastern guru. Surely no one with both feet on the ground could believe that he had lived in other bodies in times past, and that he even remembered those lives. Yet these are not the ravings of a lunatic or the pseudophilosophic musings of someone strung out on drugs. These are the words of Henry David Thoreau—a man of lively mind, to be sure, but as American as apple pie.

THE INTERMEDIATE REALM

It is the teaching of sages from Buddhist and other cultures that at the moment of death we begin our transitional existence, which is the intermediate realm between death and rebirth. This realm is very different from the physical plane, but in one respect it is identical. For just as our ego-based perceptions affect the way we relate to and interact with our environment and events in this world, similarly does our karma, stemming from both the last and many former existences, affect the way we relate to the experiences of an intermediate life.

There are said to be three primary stages in the transitional state. The initial stage consists predominantly of physical sensations of freedom and is relatively short in duration. At this point a tenuous connection to the physical body still remains. One may be acutely aware of the actions and words as well as the thoughts of living loved ones. This sensitivity and awareness mean that any words *directed to the deceased* at this time—as in chanting, for example—can bring about an awakening.

The second stage encompasses diverse sensory experiences and lasts longer than the first. In the final stage the entity is drawn, according to its karma, to a particular rebirth. The process from death to rebirth is said to take place in cycles of seven days or multiples thereof—usually forty-nine days. But this figure is not fixed. It can occur in a day or a week or not until many years later. Presumably the time of rebirth is determined by, among other factors, the attraction of the being to parents with whom it has a karmic affinity.

PSYCHOLOGIST: How is it possible to know about such things as this? You're talking about what happens after someone is dead.

Some extremely psychic people have the capacity to recall all the stages of death leading from one life to the next. There is also the testimony of some of the ancient masters in the Tibetan *Book of the Dead*, a text which traces a person's journey from dying to rebirth and teaches the art of dying peacefully in order to obtain a propitious rebirth. This book leads one, in vivid detail, through the various stages of that journey. Valuable as it is, it has the disadvantage of being written in language too quaint or esoteric for modern readers.

NURSE: Since some people are able to remember these things, there must be some sort of sensory consciousness that remains after death.

As I mentioned earlier, the seventh, eighth, and ninth levels of consciousness do survive death. (See "The Nine Levels of Consciousness.") Or you could say karma, or the force of will, continues in its cyclic propulsion through death, after-death, and rebirth. But we also possess a semblance of our other senses in the intermediate existence. At the moment of death the first six levels of consciousness become transmuted from a physical orientation to a nonphysical. Until we take on a "solid" body again, sight, hearing, smell, taste, touch, and intellect are incipient, functioning in a tenuous way. Without a body as a vehicle they cannot be fully utilized, but neither are they completely absent. Zen master Yasutani explains it this way:

> This intermediate being is constantly changing and does not have any rigid form. It is said to be much superior to present-life existence. It is like an electric current: it can pass through all obstacles and even fly hundreds of miles in a moment. It is also said to have intellect, emotion, and will of a tenuous nature as well as the five sensory organs.
>
> It is said that the intermediate being has some mysterious power to see, feel and find its parents, and that it is able to see the sexual intercourse by which it may be conceived.[3]

DANCE INSTRUCTOR: Can you tell us in more detail about this realm?

It is as difficult to give a precise description of the *intermediate state* as it is to give one of this world—only more so. Since, as I've said, the experience of passage is colored by our karma, it will differ from person to person. However, it is possible to give what might be called an Everyman's (or -woman's) description of this state.

Let me capitulate in some detail the masters' accounts of the stages of the journey from death to rebirth. During the first stage the most striking element is the thought of how easy it is to die. Unlike the sometimes prolonged act of dying, which may be difficult and painful, death itself is as simple, easy, and natural as a leaf's fluttering off a tree. Many people see their whole life played out rapidly before them in the instant before physical death. Soon after that, as the intermediate state of existence is entered, there may be a feeling of floating or flying, similar to sensations people often have in dreams. There is an awareness of great calmness and tranquillity, a sensation of relief and utter ease. One might even wonder, "What was all the worry about?" With the last breath all worries and cares of the mundane world are cast aside. The entity may then be drawn to a tunnel of bright white light and may sense that loved ones or a wonderful experience lies in wait at the end. The feeling is like that of walking into a lover's embrace, or like the joyful anticipation of a child waiting to open presents on Christmas morning.

The events and experiences of this first stage are substantially the same whether a person has very negative, pain-producing karma or relatively good karma. However, the way a person with bad karma relates to these experiences will be considerably different from the way a person with good karma does. The former might, for example, feel cynical, suffused with apprehension and suspicion. At first such a person may feel that he "got away with it," that is, with the crimes and evil perpetrated in his life, but he will soon become uneasy. What is happening will be perceived as a loss of control, and his anxiety will grow.

The second stage of passage is deeply influenced by a person's mind state at the time of death. Also of great importance are the life experiences of the being both in its last previous lifetime and in its many former lifetimes, as well as the kind of guidance received in the immediate post-death state. Here again, is where strong, meaningful chanting at the funeral can be effective. (See "The Value of Chanting.") Thus the experience of the second stage varies extensively from person to person. The experiences encountered, however, are all projections of one's own consciousness, and if this is understood and firmly imbedded in the mind, one will not be frightened by the apparitions that may appear.

HOMEMAKER: Since the first stage of dying is so pleasant, why can't a person who wishes strongly enough just remain there?

Because merely having the desire is not enough. More important is great spiritual strength. The scholar Evans-Wentz, translator of the Tibetan *Book of the Dead*, explains it this way:

> If, when dying, one be familiar with this state in virtue of previous spiritual training in the human world, and have power to win Buddhahood at this all-determining moment, the Wheel of Rebirth is stopped, and Liberation instantaneously achieved. But such spiritual efficiency is so very rare that the normal mental condition of the person dying is unequal to the supreme feat of holding on to the state in which the Clear Light shines; and there follows a progressive descent into lower and lower states of the *Bardo [see Glossary]* existence, and then rebirth . . . In the realm of the Clear Light the mentality of a person dying momentarily enjoys a condition of balance, or perfect equilibrium, and of oneness.[4]

For most people, then, it is inevitable that they enter the second stage. When it begins, the intermediate entity may feel confused, as if awakening from a deep, drugged sleep. Everything will seem vaguely familiar and dreamlike, as though the being were caught in a constant state of déjà vu. Many different things may happen now. The senses, which were once accustomed to the simple and mundane things of the physical world, will be assaulted by various frightening, terrible, or exquisitely beautiful sights, sounds, and smells. Loud, startling noises, sudden bangs, cracks, and rumbles will be heard. Howling wind and raging fires may appear. The entity may feel as if it is sinking into an abyss or becoming paralyzed. Words are spoken, but no sound is heard; sounds are heard, but no words are spoken. Thoughts wander randomly, as in a delirium. It is not possible to focus on objects, because they move away or become transparent. Nothing appears solid, nothing has substance. It is possible to move like a flash of lightning, at great speeds through objects. All of the senses, though of a tenuous nature, are present, but they are no longer attuned to the physical realm.

HOMEMAKER: Would even a young child or an infant experience these frightening things?

It depends entirely on its karma. Remember, after death there is no such thing as age or even sex. In this sense, death is the great equalizer. What *does* remain, though, are the conditioning karmic seeds that were planted throughout many lifetimes. Also of extreme importance is one's last thought at the time of death. If a child died peacefully—say, in her sleep or in her mother's arms—the chances are her last thought would be a positive one. If, on the other hand, she died violently, her last thought would very likely be filled with fear, confusion, hatred, or other turbulent emotions. It is a mistake to think of a child as "only" a child. In one sense, of course, he is only as old as his physical body, but in another, a child is as ageless as the universe—as we all are. A person's physical form, looked at from birth to death, is no more than a temporary stopping point, a momentary embodiment. One should not be misled by it. An infant of two months, a man of seventy years—at death there is no difference between them other than their self-created karmic load.

It is vital to understand that the way an individual reacts to the transitional experiences greatly depends on the kind of life he led before dying. Whether he is frightened by these experiences or unmoved by them depends on the degree to which he saw through his clinging attachments to the material world. And his reactions to events now will determine much of what is yet to come.

The masters have assured us that everything one experiences in this state is as unreal and devoid of substance, as empty of all abiding reality, as what is experienced in the dimension of waking consciousness. All lights, visions, and apparitions of every kind should therefore be regarded as mere projections and reflexes of the entity's mind states. Since the terrifying things it encounters cannot cause harm, it need not cower before them. The being should now remind itself of the need to be free from all clinging attachments to objects as well as experiences. If the entity was experienced in meditation during former existences and developed concentrative powers to a high degree, it will still have the ability to focus its mind. It is possible to accomplish this if there is single-minded concentration on the truths one has understood. Although the entity may feel as if it is in the midst of a raging storm, it can become tranquil and centered through the concentrative power of its mind.

When the second stage draws to an end, the third stage begins. As with the first two stages, here too karma plays an all-important role. This is the time when one, so to speak, looks into the mirror of her karma and finds herself committed to a particular course of action. According to the causes and conditions established, the entity will be drawn to one of a number of realms in which rebirth will take place. Those who have led destructive, pain-producing lives will be inexorably drawn to a rebirth that will entail great suffering. Those who have led more wholesome lives will also be drawn toward rebirths that are in accord with their deeds.

It should be emphasized that the impulse to be reborn is devoid of all self-conscious reflection or cognition. It is rather a blind yearning toward the mother-to-be on the part of one who will be reborn as a male, or toward the father-to-be for one who will be reborn as a female. This instinct is governed by our karma, which induces us to be attracted to a particular type of environmental and physical existence—well-to-do or humble, male or female, human or nonhuman, dark- or fair-skinned, Chinese, Mexican, African, or American. The body can thus be described as a crystallization of thought patterns conditioned by our karma—a process that began before birth and that will continue after it in an infinite expansion of life.

We can rightly say that we contain the seeds of past memories and the vestiges of recollections of former lives, not excluding the former lives of others. The scholar John Blofeld describes this well:

What we call "life" is a single link in an infinitely long chain of "lives" and "deaths." Perhaps, if our unconscious could be raised to conscious level, we should be able to perceive the entire chain stretching back far enough to exceed the most generous estimates of the length of time human beings have populated this earth. (And why just this earth? Why should not many of our previous lives have been passed upon other earths contained within this stupendous universe?) Perhaps the recollection would include hundreds or thousands of millions of lives lived here or elsewhere, and at this or other levels of consciousness, perhaps in states of being previously unsuspected.[5]

BELIEF IN AFTERLIFE

It can fairly be said that no notion has persisted for so long and in so many guises as the idea that the death of the physical body is not the end of individual existence. That all living beings, including the unseen inhabitants of other realms, have previously existed in some form or another and will continue to be reborn was almost universally accepted in the ancient world. Even in prehistoric times, people have clung to a belief in the hereafter with fierce tenacity, refusing to believe that a person's influence ended at death. The pervasiveness of these beliefs is seen in the diversity of civilizations which believed them: civilizations in Egypt, India, Ireland, Greece, and South America. Through myths and legends, through sacred texts and rituals, faith in the continuity of existence has been handed down to the present time. According to the noted anthropologist Sir James Frazer, individuals in primitive societies no more doubted their immortality than they did the reality of their conscious existence.[6]

Ancient Egyptians did not question the reality of an afterlife, and they made certain that the dead wanted for naught, furnishing them with a prodigious amount of paraphernalia for their journey and eventual encounter with Osiris. The dead were, in a sense, as alive as the living, for why else would such solemn religious rites as animal sacrifices and offerings of food and wine be made?

The Greeks were heartened by the concept that their souls, newly released from the body, would fly like freed birds to the bliss of Elysium. Early Christians, prior to the Second Council of Constantinople in A.D. 553, believed in re-becoming, a conviction that was in accord with the Gnostic belief that angels may become men or demons, and that from the latter they may rise to become men or angels.

CONTEMPORARY BELIEF IN REINCARNATION

In our own time, too, we persist in refusing to accept death as the incontrovertible end. According to a Gallup poll taken in 1980–81, nearly 70 percent of Americans believe in life after death.[7] While most people's concept of an afterlife is based on a union with God, reunion with loved ones, and/or life in a heavenly realm, a surprising 23 percent believe in reincarnation. What is surprising is not that such a great number believe in the continuity of existence, but rather that so *few* Americans embrace what is, for a large proportion of the world's population—Hindus, Buddhists, and Jains, as well as others—incontrovertible.

Many outstanding individuals of our age—Carl Jung, Ralph Waldo Emerson, Albert Schweitzer, Henry David Thoreau, and Mohandas Gandhi, to name just a few—believed in reincarnation, transmigration, or rebirth (terms which, though used interchangeably, are not really identical—see "Rebirth Distinguished from Reincarnation"). Belief in reincarnation, if not rebirth, is not inimical to contemporary Christian and Jewish beliefs. Dr. Leslie Weatherhead, minister of London's City Temple for almost three decades, felt that reincarnation offered a key to unlock many problems for Christians. He pointed out that Jesus never denied it, that it was a prevailing belief in Jesus' day, and that it was an essential part of the Essene teachings.

Passages in the Old Testament and the Kabala, sacred texts of Judaism, contain references to metempsychosis, or transmigration. It is also universally accepted by the Hasidic movement. Commenting on the origins of Jewish belief in transmigration, Rabbi Moses Gaster says, "There cannot be any doubt that these views are extremely old [in Judaism]. Simon Magus raises the claim of former existences, his soul passing through many bodies before it reaches that known as Simon . . . The [Hebrew] masters of the occult science never doubted its Jewish character . . ."[8]

To the ordinary modern Westerner, however, rebirth, which is commonly misunderstood to be synonymous with reincarnation, is perceived as no more than a superstitious fantasy, something to be relegated to the domain of the channeler, spiritualist, and

New Ager. Few prominent people in the sciences or the humanities will say forthrightly, as did Dean William Inge, "I find it both credible and attractive."[9]

IS REBIRTH THE GOAL OF LIFE?

PSYCHOTHERAPIST: Why bother living if the only goal of life is to die so that you can start over again with a clean slate?

Rebirth is *not* the goal. The ultimate "goal," to use this imprecise term, of a person with an aspiration to awakening is not rebirth—and with it the inevitable pains and sufferings attendant upon a body—but the unconditioned state of pure consciousness. What the true aspirant seeks is release from the pain and frustrations of numberless lives, from the endless wheel of rebirths, both for himself and for all beings.

As author John Blofeld has written:

It is the outflows resulting from our varied responses to the play of phenomena which harness us to the wheel of life—"the torture wheel upon which the victim's bones are broken one by one and his flesh lacerated until, in his ignorance, he prays for the permanent death that is forever denied him. Bound by our own folly and stupidity to this wheel, we are dragged upwards and downwards through realms of life and death; every phenomenon produces a reaction within us, leading to some sort of outflow from our minds, which acts upon phenomena and causes them to react upon us yet again, and so on, endlessly, until wisdom is painfully achieved."[10]

As this vivid description makes clear, yet another rebirth is nothing to look forward to.

Simply stated, what propels us again and again into rebirth is the desire, the craving, the will for another body, coupled with the tightly held notion of oneself as a discrete entity. Rebirth, then, is the inevitable consequence of our not having attained full awakening and total integration in this lifetime. At the same time rebirth is another opportunity for awakening, assuming of course that one incarnates as a human being again. Remember, it is only through a human body that we can come to enlightenment—this is why human life is so precious. "Reexistence," then, is a halfway house on the way to one's true home. As Gandhi said (speaking of attaining the goal of *ahiṃsā* or nonviolence), "I cannot think of permanent enmity between man and man, and believing as I do in the theory of rebirth, I live in the hope that if not in this birth, in some other birth I shall be able to hug all humanity in friendly embrace."[11]

REBIRTH DISTINGUISHED FROM REINCARNATION

DANCE INSTRUCTOR: I am confused about the difference between reincarnation, which I take to be the transmigration of souls, and rebirth. You said they were not the same.

The doctrines of transmigration and reincarnation imply the existence of a soul and are simplifications of the teaching of rebirth, which is, admittedly, more difficult to grasp. The problem lies in the key term "soul." What we call our soul, or our self, is actually no more than a current of consciousness comprised of "thought-moments[12] of infinitesimal duration succeeding one another in a stream of inconceivable rapidity."[13] The speed and progress of this process, although always of lightning-fast duration, change according to the nature of the stimulation. If the catalyst is slight, the process functions without full cognition.

We can compare the process to a movie: the illusion of motion is created by numerous still frames moving in swift progression. It is also like a river: the body of water rushing before us is in reality made up of innumerable droplets of water flowing together.

DANCE INSTRUCTOR: Doesn't what you are talking about differ from what we think of as soul?

The Buddhist scholar Francis Story explains "soul" more precisely:

Much misunderstanding of the Buddhist doctrine of rebirth has been caused in the West by the use of the words "reincarnation," "transmigration" and "soul" . . . "Soul" is an ambiguous term that has never been clearly defined in Western religious thought; but it is generally taken to mean the sum total of an individual personality, an enduring ego-entity that exists more or less independently of the physical body and survives it after death. The "soul" is considered to be the personality-factor which distinguishes one individual from another, and is supposed to consist of the elements of consciousness, mind, character and all that goes to make up the psychic, immaterial side of a human being.

The Buddha categorically denied the existence of a "soul" in the sense defined above. He recognized that all conditioned and compounded phenomena are impermanent, and this alone makes the existence of such a "soul" impossible.[14]

Reincarnation implies an independent, migrating soul substance that embodies itself in a new form. The teaching of rebirth, or the continuity of life, repudiates such a notion.

WHAT PASSES OVER?

PSYCHOTHERAPIST: Then how can you say that a certain individual is reborn? What is there to distinguish the consciousness of, say, my grandmother from all the consciousnesses that are not her?

Ah, your grandmother again! Clearly she still lives in you. In Original-nature no such distinctions as my grandmother or your grandmother, self or other, this or that can be postulated.

PSYCHOTHERAPIST: If that's true, why do you say she continues to exist? Doesn't there have to be a thread of continuity identifiable as my grandmother's consciousness?

While there is no thread of continuity tangible to the senses, there is nonetheless a stream of continuity which can be called neither different nor identical. As the scholar T. R. V. Murti explains, "Rebirth does not mean the bodily transportation of an individual essence from one place to another. It only means that a new series of states arises, conditioned by the previous states."[15]

Many analogies have been used to describe the transmission process. Take a flame. If you light a candle with a match, is the flame in the candle the same as or different from the flame of the match? We have to say not the same and yet not different. Another analogy, one used by Ananda Coomaraswamy, is that of a billiard ball's rolling against another such ball. "If another ball is rolled against the last stationary ball, the moving ball will stop dead and the foremost stationary ball will move on . . . The first moving ball does not pass over, it remains behind, it dies; but it is undeniably the *movement of that ball*, its momentum, its karma, and not any newly created movement, which is reborn in the foremost ball."[16]

If life is a sequence of moments linked in a chain of causation, the moment beyond death is the next link in the chain. As there has been a sense of continuity and yet no continuous self, there is nothing surprising in that sense of continuity's extending beyond the moment of death. Life is a series of events or happenings, and death takes its place in the series of events, giving rise to the next event. Thus there is no self that is reborn; there is an ongoing continuity of "again–becoming." In each moment of life the individual is born and dies, yet he continues. The same is true of the moment of death.[17]

So rebirth, or better, "again–becoming," does not involve the transfer of a substance but is better described as the continuation of the process which occurs at every moment of consciousness, continuing to operate to both affect and effect our rebirth.

We can't, then, say that the being that has just been reborn *is* your grandmother, nor can we say that it is *not*. The karma energy of the last thought of this life is the precipitating cause of our next life. This present life provides the basis for the quality of our death, which in turn conditions the nature of our next life.

NURSE: Just what is *it, then, that is reborn?*

To give it a name is to twist the truth to suit ourselves. An enlightened master said simply, "Not he, yet not another." Buddhaghosa, another sage, said, "It is a mere material and immaterial state, arising when it has obtained its conditions . . . it is not a lasting being, not a soul."

NURSE: If I understand you correctly, you are saying that it is a no-thing *which passes over. Then what happens to all the forces and energies that gave rise to the body?*

The energy embodied within us does not simply vanish with the death of the physical body. Within each of us there resides tremendous untapped energy, a force which can influence not only this life but succeeding ones as well. If we wish to give it a name, we can call it, from a psychological perspective, the seventh, eighth, and ninth levels of consciousness. (See "Death" section for a full explication, with diagrams, of the nine levels of consciousness.) From a spiritual perspective it can be called the force of karma. This energy survives our physical death, is germane to the process of rebirth, and is the main determinant of the nature of our next embodiment. But while karma is tied up with rebirth, karma per se is not what impels us to rebirth. What does bring us to re-becoming is the craving for perpetuation of the self or, more precisely, the illusion of self.

ALL IS CHANGE

Consider the law of the conservation of energy, which, as you know, states that energy is never consumed but only changes form, and that the total energy in a physical system cannot be increased or diminished. The forces within us, including our thoughts, are another form of energy and do not dissipate with our passing. As the physicist Gary Zukav writes in *The Dancing Wu Li Masters*, "Every subatomic interaction consists of the annihilation of the original particles and the creation of new subatomic particles . . . Transient forms sparkle in and out of existence, creating a never-ending, forever-newly-created reality."[18] This is a vivid description of life on every level of existence: all existence is birth and death—instantaneous, unending phenomena. At every moment we are undergoing change, or momentary death, but although things change, nothing is ever lost or destroyed. Since all compounded things are impermanent, everything is in a state of flux. Perhaps this is easier to understand if we take the example of the electronic billboard in the middle of Times Square in New York City. The daily headlines are announced by what appears to be writing in motion, actually made up of hundreds of light bulbs rapidly flashing on and off to give the appearance of words moving in a line. Similarly, all change, when broken down to its most minute elements, takes place with inconceivable speed—so much so that there is never an obvious demarcation point between states of being: all beginnings are endings, all endings are beginnings. Nothing is, everything is becoming.

DANCE INSTRUCTOR: How can you say that there are no demarcation points between states of being? Certainly you must admit that it is obvious whether a person is alive or dead, and that these are completely different states of being.

Actually, it is not so obvious. No one yet has passed the final word on exactly when death occurs. Is a brain-dead person dead? What about those who have been declared dead but who have been revived? And what about those unfortunates whose bodies are sound, but whose minds are so benumbed and shocked by mental disease or congenital conditions that their lives are no more than wisps of smoke? Remember, too, that ancient Buddhists and Hindus placed strict taboos on tampering with a body for at least three days after clinical death. Why? Because the body is not considered to be truly dead during those vital few days when the life force is still unable to fully sever its attachment to its prior physical form.

INTUITION VERSUS SCIENTIFIC PROOF

DANCE INSTRUCTOR: It seems to me that much of what you theologians are saying relies on intuition. There's nothing wrong with that, of course, but you seem to imply that scientists should be willing to accept on pure faith what you have learned through intuition. But intuition can never be proved.

True, intuition, which is the faculty of immediate and direct cognition, is not amenable to proof by the methods of science; yet it is inherent in all of us and needs only to be developed. As Emerson points out, the sacred books of each nation are the sanctuary of the intuitions. Since intuition is the means by which we fathom transcendental religious truths, it should be respected as another mode of cognition. As an aspect of the mystical, it cannot be conceptually grasped. Science, too, partakes of the mystical. Einstein and other outstanding men of science have said that their greatest discoveries came, not through logical thinking, but through an intuitive leap.

Science deals with the time-space dimension, with the world apprehended by the senses and the intellect; religion deals with the *scientist*, with his longing for self-transcendence and Self-fulfillment. The spiritually awakened know that the phenomenal world, the province of science, is only one half—or more properly, one aspect—of reality and that inner peace, more certainty, and true wisdom come when this world of forms has been transcended *but not abandoned*.

Science and religion need not be rivals; they can be mutually reinforcing. Science without a spiritual outlook is barren and socially dangerous. Religion bolstered by science is better able to keep its feet on the ground while its head is in the heavens. Dr. Robert Jastrow, himself a highly respected scientist, affirms in vivid language the central role of religion: "For the scientist who has lived by his faith in the power of reason, the story ends like a bad dream. He has scaled the mountains of ignorance; he is about to conquer the highest peak. As he pulls himself over the final rock, he is greeted by a band of theologians who have been sitting there for centuries."[19]

Also be aware that as regards proof, there is a fundamental difference in philosophic outlook between the cultures of the East and the West. The attitude of Western philosophy is that "what is *not proved* is to be treated as false." The attitude of Eastern philosophy is that "what is *not proved* may be accepted as true until *proved* to be false,"[20] particularly if supported by our intuition, experience, and/or reason.

THE POWER OF WILL

PSYCHOLOGIST: You mentioned in passing that the force that continues after death can be designated the power of will. Could you explain this further?

The power of will is a tremendous force to be reckoned with. Anyone who has had a two-year-old can attest to that. This will has the power to extend through lifetimes.

A parable illustrating this principle goes like this: A man was determined to empty all the water from a vast lake in order to find a priceless pearl lying at the bottom. After two or three days of the man's emptying bucket after bucket of water, a huge dragon appeared and said to him, "I am the lord of this lake. What are you doing?" The man answered that he was searching for the lost pearl and that he intended to empty every drop of water from the lake until he found it.

The dragon laughed at him and said derisively, "You will never find it. It is impossible for you to empty all the water, even were you to do nothing else for your entire life." But the man kept on emptying bucket after bucket. "You are wrong," he said. "I will succeed. For even if I don't empty the lake in this life, I will die with nothing else on my mind than to get the jewel. In my next lifetime I will return to the lake and continue my work. When I die, I will again be reborn and will again persist. Even if it takes me one hundred, one thousand, ten thousand lifetimes, eventually I will succeed and the pearl will be mine." The dragon, struck by the man's fierce determination, realized that nothing could stop him and that he (the dragon) would eventually lose not only the jewel but his lake as well, so he gave the pearl to the man.

Swami Vivekananda (1863–1902) wrote vividly of the will that perseveres through successive births:

Such a gigantic will as that of a Buddha or Jesus could not be obtained in one life, for we know who their fathers were. It is not known that their fathers ever spoke a word for the good of mankind. The gigantic will which manifested Buddha and Jesus—whence came this accumulation of power? It must have been there through ages and ages, continually growing bigger and bigger until it burst on society as Buddha or Jesus, and it is rolling down even to the present day.[21]

Of all the needs we have—to create, to know, to experience life—nothing can compare with the will to develop oneself spiritually in order to free oneself and others from suffering. Yet it takes countless *lifetimes* of dedicated effort and single-minded determination in order to develop one's potential to the fullest so that this can be accomplished. It is impossible to burst full-blown into the world as a completely enlightened person without such preparation. Since the will to live again is conditioned by a need for self-development, a person will very likely be drawn to the state of existence most conducive to that activity. Remember: it is the *desire* or craving for a continuation of life, and the clinging to a notion of a separate individuality, that propel us again and again into new rounds of birth and death. This is why, when the Buddhist sage Nāgasena was asked by King Milinda whether or not he would be reborn after death, Nāgasena replied, "If when I die I die with craving for existence in my heart, yes; but if not, no."[22]

REBIRTH ISN'T ALWAYS A STEP UP

SOCIOLOGIST: Well, if we've been reborn so many times, how come we're not better people? Why do we still kill and maim and generally ruin this planet we live on?

Don't forget that a person's succeeding life isn't always a step up. If that person has set up negative causes and conditions in the past, they will ripen eventually, and that could mean a drop to a much lower rung on the ladder of existence. Given most people's limited vision, it is extremely difficult and painful to continue to do the things one needs to do to develop into a fully grown human being. A person who has truly seen into his True-nature—and this is possible for each one of us—has the advantage of knowing what he or she has to do. This is often accompanied with the strength—developed through steady and regular practice of meditation—to transcend the pain and difficulties that may accompany self-development.

The Will to Live Makes Man Re-live

DANCE INSTRUCTOR: Do we actually have the power to choose the type of existence into which we will be reborn? It almost sounds as if you are saying that you'd better watch out, because you'll probably get what you want.

That's not far from the truth. Remember the song that went something like "You can't always get what you want . . . But you might find you get what you need"? Well, that's closer to it. What we *think* we want is often just a reflection of our superficial desires. Our deepest yearnings push and pull us on a subconscious level and drive us to what we truly need—even if it's not what we *think* we need or want. Oscar Wilde expressed this perfectly when he said that there are two kinds of unhappiness in the world: not getting what you want, and getting what you want.

There is another element also at work here. We could call it the principle of "like attracts like." The subconscious mind exerts a tremendous power to draw to itself others of similar inclination. People feel most comfortable with those who share similar interests and values: artists enjoy hobnobbing with other artists, musicians enjoy the company of musically inclined people, and the spiritually minded will commune with those who share their interests. On the other hand, thieves associate with underworld characters, drinkers with alcoholics, drug addicts with pushers; neurotics seek the company of other neurotics, and the mentally disturbed gravitate toward people who are unbalanced. On both a conscious and subconscious level we create our environment even as we participate in it.

So long as there is *desire* for rebirth, repeated rebirths will take place in various existences. Indeed, attachment itself, the craving, brings about the next birth. V. F. Gunaratna puts it epigrammatically: "The will-to-live makes man re-live."[23]

SOCIOLOGIST: If all it takes to be reborn again and again is to want to be reborn, you'd think that this fact would relieve the anxieties of a lot of people who think death means extinction—the end.

Oddly, in our culture not too many people believe that it is possible. But a belief in rebirth *would* relieve one's anxiety about dying if one felt that in his life he had not created unwholesome karma. The hitch is that one's next existence will be on a lower or higher level, depending on the kind of life one has lived— whether a pain-producing one or a more or less selfless life. An employer, say, who was the epitome of greed, exploiting his employees and others mercilessly, might find himself in a hellish existence in his next life, suffering retribution for his inhumane behavior.

On the other hand, if you are able to die free of the fear of dying and without the conscious or unconscious wish to be reborn—merely asking yourself in the words of an ancient Zen master (Bassui), "What is the true essence of the Mind of this one who is now suffering [dying]"—you will eventually be freed of your painful bondage to endless change.

SOCIOLOGIST: So what happens to such an individual?

I don't know. I suppose the ancients would call him a divine immortal. For most living beings, though, the attachment to life is so strong that escaping from the pull of endless rounds of birth and death is immensely difficult. While still a bodhisattva (see Glossary), Gautama (the Buddha-to-be) is said to have been reborn into animal and human realms some 550 times before attaining full Buddhahood.

HOMEMAKER: Suppose a person doesn't want to be reborn because she is frightened of the results of negative things she did throughout her life.

A deeply spiritual person is not frightened of being reborn, because she understands the root cause of birth and death and calmly accepts the consequences of her actions, be they good or bad. It is only because such a person is without fear that she can die free from thoughts of body or not-body. Then, too, a highly developed person might willingly be reborn, taking on a body out of love—love and compassion for those who are still suffering and who need help to come to true understanding.

Your question brings up another important point. It is impossible to live a life full of fear, anger, and pain-producing actions and then, at the moment of death, escape from karmic retribution by having a "good" thought. Although a person might be afraid of rebirth and try to suppress the desire for another body, it is not possible to do so, because the habit forces of many lifetimes are still operating at the moment of death. The last thought of a dying person has an initial impact on the rebirth, but the cumulative effect of the events of his or her life exerts a tremendous additional influence. With respect to the person you mentioned, her next rebirth would be conditioned by her fear of retribution in that life. Accordingly, she might be reborn agoraphobic or severely repressed, or as a withdrawn, timid individual afraid of her own shadow. But in any case, she certainly would be reborn. Fear is a clinging to that which we fear; perversely, it is this clinging that brings us the very thing we fear or would most like to avoid.

CAN FEAR BE CARRIED FROM LIFE TO LIFE?

PSYCHOLOGIST: Are you implying that a person can come into life with fears already established?

Yes. There are many cases of people who have severe, unexplained fears that have been present from their earliest childhood. Children sometimes have aversions that border on the hysterical. I remember one mother telling me about her child. She said that he had been petrified of large bodies of water from the time he was an infant. He would be fine in the bathtub, but if they went on an outing to the beach, he screamed in such terror that they had to leave. He is a teenager now and he still does not enjoy being around lakes or oceans, although he is no longer as visibly frightened.

How would you explain such a phenomenon? If you look at the problem from the point of view of rebirth, it is entirely possible that the young man died at sea in a previous lifetime and took with him into his current life a terror connected with the experience. Naturally, there can be other interpretations for such fears, but this one is seldom, if ever, considered by traditional psychoanalysts.

Nonetheless, a number of therapists do concur in the belief that many of our fears and neuroses actually stem from causes in prior existences. Such people, who call themselves past-life therapists, hypnotically regress their patients into one or more previous lifetimes to search for the trauma that is creating a problem for them in this life. In his book *The Case for Reincarnation*, Joe Fisher talks about Dr. Alexander Cannon:

> Cannon, an Englishman awarded degrees by nine European universities . . . specialized in discovering hidden complexes and fears engendered by traumatic incidents in past lives. Holding that the work of the great psychoanalyst Sigmund Freud had been "outflanked" by reincarnation, he declared: "The majority of people do not benefit from psychoanalysis because the trauma lies not in this life but in a past life."[24]

NEGATIVE ATTACHMENTS

PSYCHOLOGIST: You talked earlier about how an attachment to something draws us to that very thing. Well, what happens if the attachment is a negative one? For instance, if a father abused his daughter and caused her death, would there remain, after the girl's death, any attachment to the situation or to her father? Is there still a karma there, if that is the right expression?

That is an interesting problem. The Ven. Mahasi Sayadaw, a Burmese master, tells of a case in Sri Lanka concerning a woman who persuaded her lover to murder her husband. The husband was reborn as the woman's own child and would have nothing to do with her. He left home as soon as he could, eventually becoming a monk.

Quite possibly the last thought in the mind of this unfortunate being was one of hatred for his former wife, and this violent emotion created a strong attachment which brought about his rebirth at the very site of the attachment. Some people, of course, would view this account as no more than a morality play, a cautionary parable of the tribulations caused by a violent disposition. If one accepts re-becoming, however, it is not difficult to believe that such strong emotions as hatred and anger could destroy our powers of objectivity to the point where we would be drawn obsessively to the very being we most detest. These words, attributed to the Buddha, are germane here: "Holding on to anger is like grasping a hot coal with the intent of throwing it at someone else: you are the one who gets burned."

REMEMBERING PAST LIVES

SOCIOLOGIST: What you say is all very fascinating. I don't have any problem believing that before this existence all the matter and energy that is currently arranged as me had always been there in one form or another—that I was the clouds, the trees, the birds. And of course, when I die the cycle will continue. But that's very different from assuming that my personality, including my memory of this existence, will continue. For that matter, I don't remember any previous existence.

Do you remember all you did and learned in high school, or even in college? Yet you know that you were there. How many people remember all the incidents of their childhood, much less their birth itself? Few indeed. Yet they never doubt that they were born. Many people cannot even recall their dreams of the night before. Since people's memories vary greatly in their capacity for both vividness and recall, memory is but shallow and inadequate proof of happenings of the past. Commenting on this phenomenon, Lama Govinda writes:

They forget that active memory is only a small part of our normal consciousness, and that our subconscious memory registers and preserves every past impression and experience which our waking mind fails to recall.

There are those who in virtue of concentration and other yogic practices are able to bring the subconscious into the realm of discriminate consciousness and thereby to draw upon the unrestricted treasury of subconscious memory wherein are stored records not only of our own past lives but the records of the past of our race, the past of humanity, and of all pre-human forms of life, if not of the very consciousness that makes life possible in this universe.[25]

Anyone who has had a loved one suddenly die knows that it is often very difficult to remember the events that took place immediately following the death. At such a time, everything may become suspended, vague, blurred; one may be in a state of shock. How much more difficult, then, must it be to remember the events of one's own death and subsequent rebirth. Also keep in mind that after death the consciousness-energy goes into an intermediate state, in which sensory impressions are not registered as clearly as they were during the physical existence. (See "The Intermediate Realm".)

Nevertheless, there are numerous case histories of people who have remembered one or more of their previous lives. One of the most convincing, thorough, and meticulously researched books on this subject is Ian Stevenson's *Twenty Cases Suggestive of Reincarnation*.[26] Dr. Stevenson has been Carlson Professor of Psychiatry at the University of Virginia Medical School and has served as chairman of the department of neurology and psychiatry. He currently heads the division of personality studies. While Stevenson's research does not provide proof in the conventional scientific sense, it offers persuasive testimony in a uniquely unbiased way, testimony that is devoid of the bizarre or supernatural trappings with which so many of these stories are presented elsewhere. Much of Stevenson's research was done in the Near and Far East, but he has also pursued cases in Africa, Europe, and this country. The focus of his studies is primarily children between the ages of three and five who spontaneously began talking about a previous lifetime.

SOCIOLOGIST: How do you know that these stories were not deliberate fabrications? Perhaps their parents just put the words into the children's mouths.

That's very unlikely for several reasons. First, the family, including the child, had nothing to gain from setting up such a ruse. There are no financial rewards given to people who report these memories, nor is there much in the way of publicity. Remember, in many cultures of the East memories of previous lives are not looked on as anything unusual. Since rebirth is accepted as a fact, it is a common assumption that some people will remember who they were in another life.

In a number of cases, moreover, the parents of these children were downright angry with them for persistently babbling on about their other family, the one they used to live with. Some parents punished their child for continuing to insist she had lived another life in another city. Stevenson affirms this when he says, "Even in cultures where reincarnation is accepted, parents sometimes think such memories are harmful. They are often upset by what the child remembers. Parents would not be particularly pleased to have a murdered child, not to mention a murderer, reincarnate in their family."[27]

In most of the cases reported by Stevenson, however, it was the child's determination to see the family of her past, and her unwavering stance about the facts of that existence, that finally forced the parents to ascertain whether or not what she said was true.

Another point is that there were usually a great many witnesses to the truth of the statements these children made. Stevenson and his coworkers cross-examined several children over a long period of time, and their stories proved amazingly accurate when verified. Any discrepancies in their accounts are recorded, and often these involve such minor things as mispronounced names or the statement that a house was green instead of blue.

Finally, much of the information related by these remarkable children was of such a nature that no one in their family could possibly have had access to it. Just think: A child of four announces that his real name is not Edward but John. He gives his address in another town; neither he nor his parents have ever been there. He gives the names of his former parents, their occupations, and the stores where they commonly shopped. Then he relates various incidents that took place during that life— usually family events of a mundane nature, but occasionally peculiar occurrences. His parents eventually track down the address where the child used to live and take him there. Along the way he is able to recognize various landmarks and point out the house where he used to live—despite its having been painted in the intervening years. In some cases the child has picked out relatives from a large crowd of people. In other instances, he has pointed out changes in the house or surrounding area that only someone familiar with the vicinity could have recognized. In still more unusual cases, the child has spoken idiomatic phrases, or even carried on long conversations, in the language of his former existence, a language with which neither he nor his parents were even marginally familiar.[28]

Do you really suppose all these incidents could be a matter of deception and nothing more? Why would anyone in his right mind bother? The parents were uncomfortable with the idea that "their" child might "belong" to someone else, much less *be* someone else. And for the child it is often confusing and sad to think about his former family. I personally find it hard to believe that anyone, much less large numbers of people, would want to do all this just as a hoax.

EDGAR CAYCE

DANCE INSTRUCTOR: Do adults ever remember past lives?

It is less common for adults than for children, but there are some who do have this ability. Edgar Cayce, arguably the most noted and gifted psychic of our time, is an example of someone who was able to see into not only his past lives but those of others as well. His "readings," which illuminated in detail the workings of the law of causation and rebirth, are world famous. Cayce was born in 1877 on a Kentucky farm and raised by strict fundamentalist Christian parents. Although uneducated beyond the ninth grade, at age twenty-one he learned to induce extraordinary medical clairvoyance through self-hypnosis. After twenty-two years of healing others—frequently strangers living thousands of miles away—he discovered that his powers could be enlarged to see into their past lives. At first these "life readings," as they came to be called, caused the humble and self-doubting Cayce considerable anguish, for the doctrine of rebirth seemed to him in conflict with his literal interpretation of the Bible. But once he reconciled them, he devoted the rest of his life to helping many thousands of people trace their afflictions and limitations in the present to specific conduct in the past.

Scores of such cases, with the details confirmed, are presented in *Many Mansions* by the psychologist Gina Cerminara. Also included in the book is the case of a man anemic since birth who had, five lifetimes previously, seized political control of a country, shedding much blood. Another man's chronic digestive weakness was traced by Cayce to two previous lifetimes of gluttony. And in another case, a woman's poverty and misfortunes were seen as caused by her misuse of authority and wealth in a previous life in which she was part of French royalty.

ESP and Spiritual Training

In my years of teaching I have had several students who, I was convinced, had the ability to recall previous lifetimes, as I told you earlier. In Zen, however, there is no encouragement or emphasis given to this type of endeavor, since the purpose of spiritual training is not the development of psychic abilities but rather Self-realization, or enlightenment. It is very easy to get sidetracked from the path of spiritual discipline when one has strong psychic perceptions. It was for this reason that the thirteenth-century Zen master Dōgen said:

There are those who have the supernatural power to know their past lives, whether as humans, animals, or some other form of sentient life. However, this supernatural power is not acquired by becoming enlightened . . . but is rather the result of bad karma in past lives . . . Even if you can understand the events of five hundred lifetimes a little, it is not really much of an ability.[29]

One of my students, who had many such memories, told me she was happy when the memories began to fade in intensity, enabling her to concentrate on what needed to be done in *this* life.

A TALE OF THREE LIVES

Nevertheless, these recollections can sometimes be helpful. One student told me the following story. For years she and a young man with whom she worked closely—he was one of her supervisors—had an extremely antagonistic relationship. Try as she might, it was impossible for her to overcome her negative feelings for him. One day while she was meditating she suddenly saw herself dressed in unusual garb. She knew she was somewhere in middle Europe in the thirteenth century. (She told me the exact location and date.) Next she saw herself leaning over a cradle and looking at her baby boy; with anguish she realized he was deaf, blind, and mute. She then saw herself strangling the baby and feeling the baby's anger, which was directed toward her. When she remembered this, she was filled with horror and self-loathing. An instant later she saw herself in her next lifetime just as she was being condemned to burn at the stake by the very same being she had murdered in her previous life. She looked at the man with abhorrence and was shocked to see that it was the man whom, in this lifetime, she found so hard to tolerate.

Soon after she had this recollection, painful as it was—she told me she cried in despair for hours remembering the horrendous thing she had done—she decided to tell her antagonist about the memory. She told me:

I was very apprehensive about telling John these things. I wondered if he would think I was a weirdo and our relationship would become worse than ever. But I felt it was our only chance to change the terrible karma we had been building together. When I told him the memory, he began to cry. I was crying too. Afterward he said to me, jokingly, "Well, Mom, I guess we've got a lot to work out. But knowing now that what we did to each other in the past is what is affecting our relationship today—this will make it easier to bury the hatchet." From that time on we became close friends.

Another case involved a husband and wife who were going through a painful divorce. The wife in particular was filled with bitterness toward her husband, who had been not only unfaithful to her but also, she felt, mentally abusive. One day the woman came to me and said that she remembered being with her husband in another lifetime, this time not as his wife but as a woman who wished to marry him. When he told her that he would not accept her, she became enraged and tried to poison him. After remembering this, she told me, she felt that she had a karmic debt to pay her husband, and that this was why she was suffering so much in their current relationship. She also said that she felt it imperative that they come to some accord in this lifetime, or else the negative karmic pattern that they had built up would be perpetuated. She and her ex-husband, it might be mentioned, now have a cordial relationship.

Stevenson mentions one case where a woman's memories of having committed suicide in her previous life deterred her from killing herself again. The knowledge that nothing would be over or solved and that she would have to face her problems in her next life was enough to make her reconsider and change her life.

HOMEMAKER: You said that you don't encourage people to develop the psychic ability to recall past lives. Yet from what you have been saying, it seems to me that it could be very useful to remember what we did in the past, especially for helping us see into blockages we might be experiencing in our present life. Knowing more about our past lives might also help us make better decisions concerning the direction of our life this time around.

For many people it is a kindness that they *don't* remember what they did in the past. Let me tell you about an incident that took place about fifteen years ago. A young man came to our center who was not very stable psychologically, but who felt a need for spiritual practice and tried hard to meditate. One day he was persuaded by a friend to see a psychic. That was the last we saw of him until he reappeared several years later—disheveled, destitute, and seriously disturbed. He had been told by the psychic that in his last life he had been a Nazi responsible for the deaths of many people. That information, along with some other events, was so traumatic that it precipitated a severe psychological collapse—one from which he has never recovered. This is an extreme example, but it probably is not unique.

Many people would be horrified to learn of the terrible things they had done in previous existences, and unless they had some means of understanding and atoning for their actions in past lives, they would become ill or very depressed. Emerson warned about dragging around "the corpse of memory." And Gandhi, in speaking of this same subject, said, "It is nature's kindness that we do not remember past births. Where is the good . . . of knowing in detail the numberless births we have gone through? Life would be a burden if we carried such a tremendous load of memories. A wise man deliberately forgets many things . . ."[30] Owen Rutter expressed the same sentiment when he wrote, "The obscuring of memory is surely merciful. The remembrance of all the wrongs we have done and all the wrongs which have been done to us, throughout our chain of lives, would be an intolerable burden. Most of us have enough to contend with in this life without burdening ourselves with the recollection of the dangers, the fears and the hates of other lives."[31]

HOMEMAKER: It still seems as if it could be useful to know what we were like in the past. You wouldn't deny, would you, that people who went to Edgar Cayce were helped by his insights? If you accept the fact of rebirth, it is only natural to want to know what you did in those other lives and try to seek out the details.

There are very few people alive today with the psychic abilities of Cayce. In this day and age of spiritual supermarkets, you never know what you will get when you approach someone for a past-life reading. How can you be sure that the information you receive is accurate, not to mention relevant? Let us say someone tells you that in a previous life you were Queen Victoria. Does that mean you should move to England and try to reclaim the crown jewels? Or suppose you learned that you were an Egyptian living at the time of the pharaohs—should you decorate your home in the style of ancient Egypt?

Many people, even those who are psychic and able to recall their own previous lives, make the mistake of believing that the only other lifetimes they lived were the ones they remember. They become very attached to those lives and say with pride, "In my last lifetime I was such and such a person." Unfortunately, all too often people who claim to have genuine memories of previous existences exhibit a singular predilection for lifetimes in which they were famous personages. Just think of all the people who have claimed to be Napoleon in a previous life! And he, ironically, often said, "Do you know who I am? I am Charlemagne." But in the greater scheme of things, what difference does it make? *Everyone* has had *innumerable* previous lifetimes—"as many as the sands in the river Ganges," as the ancient texts say. All life is life after death. It is folly to speak of the remembered lifetime as the only one! Nor should one identify with a remembered life of fame or power more than with one of humble circumstance.

Another important element is this: it is very difficult, if not impossible, to accurately interpret the data from former existences unless one is of a psychic bent himself. Even then mistakes can be made. Karmic connections and motivations are often vague, as I said earlier when we were discussing karma, and rarely can you easily relate a cause in one lifetime with an effect in another.

2. FURTHER IMPLICATIONS OF REBIRTH

THE MORAL EFFECTS

There are many other examples that could be given, but as you can see, evidence of rebirth is circumstantial at best and does not provide incontrovertible proof. Nonetheless, it should be clear that the memories of previous lives affected a number of the protagonists in a positive way. There are obvious moral implications inherent in the law of rebirth and its other half, karma. To remember the pain-producing actions of one's previous lives, and to see their consequences in subsequent lives, lead one to the inescapable conclusion that in a basic sense we are the masters of our destiny. We ourselves are responsible for our life situation, be it good or bad. The salubrious effect of this belief has not been lost on the millions of Buddhists and other believers who look to themselves as the cause of their tribulations. One who is certain that sooner or later—if not in this life then in some other—what is reaped will be in accord with what has been sown will think twice before committing some evil.

The noted Orientalist Max Müller, speaking of rebirth, wrote:

Whatever we may think of the premises on which this theory rests, its influence on human character has been marvelous. If a man feels that what, without any fault of his own, he suffers in this life can only be the result of some of his former acts, he will bear his sufferings with more resignation, like a debtor who is paying off an old debt. And if he knows besides that in this life he may actually lay by moral capital for the future, he has a motive for goodness . . . Nothing can be lost.[32]

There is more evidence of the moral effect this belief exerted on people in times past. A British census of approximately one hundred years ago gave these figures on crimes committed in India: "Among Europeans, 1 conviction for every 274 people; among native Christians, 1 in every 799 people; among Buddhists, 1 for every 3,787 people."[33]

WHY ARE WE RESPONSIBLE?

SOCIOLOGIST: I am disturbed by what you said earlier concerning the moral aspects of the doctrine of rebirth. If we can't remember what we did in our former lives, what possible moral significance could those actions have in this life? For example, if I rob a bank and then am caught and jailed, at least I know that I was the perpetrator and therefore deserve my sentence. Or take the case of a drunk driver who kills someone in a car accident. Such a person may have no conscious memory whatsoever of the events leading up to and immediately following the crash; still, he is clearly guilty of the crime, since the results are evident.

Now take the case of someone who is accused of a crime of which he has no memory and the effects of which are not even evident. How could such a person possibly feel contrite? Angry, resentful, hateful, yes; but repentant, impossible! Yet you are saying that because of the law of rebirth I should feel responsible for actions which I supposedly committed but will, most likely, never remember. And, to top it off, you can't even say it is the same "I" who committed those crimes that I am in this lifetime!

Not the same, true. But not different either. No, it doesn't seem fair, on the surface of it, to have to expiate or feel repentant for sins we are not aware of having committed. Yet there is a deeper principle at work here: the law of cause and effect, of which I spoke earlier under the heading of karma.

What you are proposing is that we should not be held accountable for the results of our actions unless we can identify the causes of those results. Even in a court of law such a proposition would not hold water. What judge would pardon the accused simply on the basis of the latter's alleged lapse of memory? Consider this situation: A person begins smoking cigarettes when he is fourteen years old. At the age of fifty he is in a car accident and suffers a severe head injury, which wipes out much of his memory of his early years, including the fact that he had ever smoked. A year later he develops lung cancer. Is he responsible for his condition even though he can't remember what caused it? Of course he is. That we can't remember some of our actions doesn't make us any the less responsible for them, nor does it mean that those actions have not affected us. The same principle holds true from lifetime to lifetime.

Two indispensable elements produce the deep awareness essential to establishing moral behavior. They are a concern for the karmic consequences of our actions in subsequent existences, and an uncertainty about the fruits those actions will bear. To be unable to establish the specific incident from a previous lifetime which produced our suffering in this life, and yet to affirm, "My own acts are the ultimate cause," is indicative of a deeply spiritual orientation. The man who has forgotten, the man who protests his innocence, the man who suffers—he cannot be separated from the karmic impulses he set into motion so many lifetimes ago.

REBIRTH AND THE MOTIVATION TO LIVE RIGHT

DANCE INSTRUCTOR: Doesn't belief in rebirth diminish the importance of this *life because it gives us further chances to make good in our next life? If you knew that all you had was this one life, and that was it, you would work harder to make it amount to something.*

Would you? Or would you, as I said earlier, just "live it up"? What would there be to make you accountable for your actions? Every life we lead is equally important because it determines the nature of our subsequent lives. How can you get to the top of a ladder without climbing each rung in sequence? If there were no other lives to come, our actions, both good and bad, would be lost. In reality, though, nothing is lost. Nor do good deeds die even if the doer does not believe. As Christian theologian Geddes MacGregor says, "There are no cosmic free lunches."

HEREDITY, ENVIRONMENT, OR KARMA?

MANAGEMENT CONSULTANT: There is something about rebirth that bothers me. If it is the same person or life force that is being reborn, why don't we have the same appearance from life to life? Our physical and emotional characteristics clearly come from heredity and environment—rebirth has nothing to do with it.

Physical characteristics are not intrinsic to the life force or thought force that passes over from death to rebirth. What is inherited from our previous lives is manifested through genetic constitution, external circumstances, and certain tendencies. Fears, affinities, and various other emotional inclinations may also pass over. The interplay of external conditions with karmic forces molds and influences the new being, who also has the power to alter his circumstances. While it is axiomatic that a baby born to black parents will be black, or one born to Caucasians will be white, there is nevertheless a wide range of characteristics over which the individual's attitude has its pull. Francis Story describes it this way:

> Here the principle of attraction comes into play; the thought force gravitates naturally towards what is most in affinity with it, and so to some extent creates, and certainly modifies, its circumstances. These also act upon the awakening consciousness, so that heredity and environment both have a share in molding the new personality. If the past karma was bad, these external conditions will reflect that "badness," so that it is only by a new effort of will that the mind can rise above their influence and fashion for itself a better destiny.[34]

Of course, some people might look similar, if not the same, from lifetime to lifetime—provided, of course, they are born as humans each time. There are many intriguing cases of people with unusual physical characteristics who claim to have had those identical marks in a previous life. Birthmarks, too, may well be an inherited physical karmic tendency, since no one knows why certain people have them and others do not. Stevenson has been doing some fascinating research on birthmarks for over a decade. Comparing the past-life memories of children who have unusual birthmarks and birth defects with postmortem reports of injuries in their alleged previous life, he has found a correlation between the injuries in the previous life and the birthmarks in the present. He feels that these records will "provide the strongest evidence we have so far in favor of reincarnation."[35]

THE QUESTION OF GENETICS

If our physical and emotional characteristics come solely from heredity and environment, how do you explain the unusual circumstances surrounding identical twins separated at birth? Studies have shown the astonishing similarities of these twins' behavior, including such things as the names of people they married, dates of marriage, names and ages of their children, and predilections in clothing, food, hobbies, and occupations. Even if it were true that all these coincidences were purely a result of their shared genetic background, there is still room for consideration of karma and rebirth's having exercised an influence on their lives. Why is this so? Because everyone *chooses* his or her future parents. Thus, from a Buddhist point of view, we also choose the appropriate genetic influences, as well as the immediate pre- and postnatal environment, that will affect our future behavior.

It can be said that heredity and environment are, on the physical plane, the manifestations of the spiritual laws of rebirth and karma. Since it is virtually impossible to isolate which of the factors—karma, genetics, or environment—is exerting the most influence on a person's life, all one can do is to say the data supports both explanations, and to bear in mind that karma is transmitted in part through heredity and environment. As we know, the genes an individual receives from his ancestors through his parents are only one contribution to the personality.[36] The extent to which they affect the individual is dependent on additional factors, such as the modifying influences of the prenatal and postnatal environment. And, from a Buddhist perspective, karma as well.

How do you explain, for example, such occurrences as early childhood phobias, the spontaneous development of extraordinary abilities in children, incidents of transsexuality, idiot savants, childhood autism, child prodigies born to ordinary parents, and even exceptionally strong preferences dating from infancy? Those who believe in rebirth have no trouble accepting that these phenomena are related to or stem from incidents that took place in past lives. "It is only if rebirth is taken to mean the transmigration of a 'soul,'" writes Francis Story, "that there is any conflict between [rebirth] and the known facts of genetics."[37] One geneticist with whom I recently spoke told me, "No geneticist who is not a Nazi would try to make a strong case for the immutable determination of behavior by the genes. There is hard evidence that our genetic makeup may predispose us to certain *patterns* of behavior. Nevertheless, other factors also play important determining roles.[38]

Clearly, then, biological and sociological explanations still leave many questions unanswered.

HOMEMAKER: What is your theory, then, as to why some identical twins separated at birth follow similar patterns in their lives?

It would appear that their karma in past lives was extraordinarily alike. Perhaps they were together for many lives as siblings who had only each other for comfort and friendship, or they might have been very close friends who remained loyal to the end of their lives. Possibly their love for each other was so great that in different lives one sacrificed herself for the sake of the other. Whatever their pasts were, we can assume they took strikingly parallel courses. In the case of fraternal twins, there are many other possibilities, including that of a mother and young child who died together, or perhaps a husband and wife with an extraordinarily deep attachment to each other. However, except in the case of identical twins, the attraction and karmic bonds between siblings are not nearly as strong as those between parent and child.

HOMEMAKER: What makes the karmic bonds between parent and child so strong?

Since parents are the vehicles for our births, we owe them a tremendous debt of gratitude. We are attracted to and born through parents (one or both) with whom we have a karmic affinity. That affinity also forges the bond between them and us. In healthy family relationships it is the unconditional love children feel from their parents that supports them throughout their lives. Human children have an exceptionally long period of total dependence, and without the love and help of parents or another adult, they cannot survive. It has actually been shown that infants who are deprived of love will fail to thrive and may even die. They become depressed and withdrawn, showing signs of both physical and psychic distress.

Think of all the times you've seen movies or heard stories of a young man on the threshold of death calling out to his mother or father. For better or worse, our parents' influence—their presence or absence, their care or lack of it, their morals or debaucheries, their ideals or hypocrisy—pervades our lives, even as we simultaneously affect our parents.

MISCARRIAGES, STILLBIRTHS, AND ABORTIONS

NURSE: If beings are so strongly attracted to their parents, how do you explain miscarriages and stillbirths? Or, even more puzzling, why would a mother abort her child?

The great anguish these events cause for the parents, especially the mother, is evidence of the strong attraction that exists between the parents and the unborn child. Only the rare mother-to-be is indifferent to the fact of her pregnancy and the child she carries. It is not uncommon for women to be more careful of their bodies during this time: they stop drinking alcohol and caffeine, stop smoking, start exercising, and begin eating more balanced meals—all for the sake of their babies. Unfortunately, there are also cases of mutually negative attachment, such as when the being-to-be is drawn to a drug addict who makes no attempt to cure her addiction for the sake of the baby.

Negative mutual attachment is also evidenced in cases of abortions undergone without coercion. Although the unborn being is attracted to a particular set of parents, the mother, because of karmic circumstances at the time of conception, is unable to acquiesce in the being's choice of her as a mother. Talking with women who were contemplating an abortion, I have seen the confusion, anxiety, and pain which they faced. Their decision to abort was made in anything but a casual or indifferent manner and was arrived at after much deep searching. There was an undeniable bond between the mothers and these unknown beings within them—a bond that was severed with great pain. It is important to recognize that more than one set of causes must be present for someone to be reborn, the will to live being only one cause. Also indispensable are parents who are physically able to reproduce, and the mother's willingness to carry the baby throughout the pregnancy. This is not to say that the mother is responsible for miscarriages and stillbirths. There can be, however, contributing factors of both a physical and a karmic nature that make the pregnancy impossible to continue. Remember that the being-to-be is only one half the picture. While it has its karmic impulse to be born, the mother also has her karma, one which might not include having a child at that time.

Another possibility is that the karma of the unborn child was not strong enough to carry him throughout the pregnancy. Perhaps his karmic bond with the mother was tenuous; or perhaps, due to effects stemming from causes in previous lifetimes, he was only able to sustain a short existence in this life. We really don't know.

In the case of early miscarriages, it may be that the life force never joined with the ovum and sperm to produce a viable embryo. But this, too, is conjecture. Orthodox Buddhist psychology believes that from the moment of conception the being-to-be has a mind that is aware at a "bare state of subconsciousness identical with the . . . adult consciousness during dreamless sleep."[39]

You can see, then, that the sad occurrences of miscarriages, stillbirths, and abortions do not mean that the craving for life and attraction to the parent is absent; rather, these events mean that there are additional karmic factors at work.

NURSE: So there can be many reasons why a particular being chooses a set of parents?

Any number of reasons.

AFFINITIES AND APTITUDES

DANCE INSTRUCTOR: Might the child be attracted to certain parents on the basis of their mutual affinity with, for example, music, dance, science, or a sport?

That is certainly possible. Don't forget that the force of will exerts a tremendous power that transcends what we call death. A person who is immersed in a certain endeavor throughout his life—for example, mathematics—can become so obsessed with the subject that it becomes the focal point of his existence. The same can be said of music, dance, art, sports—the list could go on and on. Such a passion would decidedly affect a person's karma and subsequent rebirth.

As we know, there are many children who seem to inherit the aptitudes of one or both of their parents for such things. If a father is an artist and his daughter is similarly inclined, someone is bound to say, "She gets her talent from her father." And if neither the father nor the mother has a skill that their child displays, you will probably hear, "It must have come from Grandpa," or Great Auntie, or someone else in the family tree. But occasionally a child develops a talent that cannot be so easily explained—no one in the family has ever had this ability to anyone's knowledge. Might it be possible that the child possessed his or her talent even *before* being born into this life?

CHILD PRODIGIES

Consider the uncanny abilities of child prodigies. From ancient times to the present there have been numerous instances of remarkable children who have displayed extraordinary precocity in such fields as music, art, language, science, or mathematics. It is common knowledge that Mozart, who was born into a musical family, was composing by the age of four, but we must also consider Handel, whose interest in music was roundly discouraged by his parents. There are many other cases of children who developed outstanding talents at an early age, such as Giannella de Marco, who in 1953 at the age of eight conducted the London Philharmonic Orchestra; Dimitris Sgouros, who at the age of seven gave his first solo piano recital, and at the age of twelve graduated from the Athens Conservatory of Music with the first prize and the title of professor of piano; Marcel Lavallard, who was an accomplished artist by the age of twelve; and Tom Wiggins, the blind child of a slave, who was a concert pianist by the age of four, despite the fact that his intelligence was so low he could barely speak. Yet never has science adequately explained why such phenomena occur. Is it not more plausible to believe that these remarkable cases stem simply from accomplishments in a former life? Dr. Leslie Weatherhead suggests that rebirth is the answer:

> Is it an accidental group of genes that makes a little girl of eight a musician far in advance of grown men and women, who have slaved for many years in that field? Is it a piece of luck that a boy of fourteen can write perfect Persian? If so, life seems unjust as well as chancy. Or is it that they have been here before? Plato believed wholeheartedly in reincarnation, and his famous "Theory of Reminiscence" asserted that "knowledge easily acquired is that which the enduring self had in an earlier life, so that it flows back easily." In the dialogue *Meno*, Socrates shows that an untutored slave boy knew mathematical facts which in this life had never been taught him. "He had forgotten that he knew them . . . To Socrates it was self-evident that the boy's capacity was the result of an experience he had had in a previous lifetime."
>
> One wonders why men have so readily accepted the idea of a life *after* death and so largely, in the West, discarded the idea of a life *before* birth.[40]

COMPUTER PROGRAMMER: But can you explain the method by which someone could retain such a vast wealth of knowledge and experience even after dying? If you can, I'd like to know how, so that in my next life I can take off from where I am now, rather than having to go through all my schooling again!

Even if I could explain the method of this particular action—which I cannot—it would not tell you the reason *why* it happens. And that, you will agree, is equally, if not more, important.

There are myriad things the workings of which we cannot explain, yet which we do not question. If a switch is flicked, for example, a light goes on. By this act, one implicitly accepts the reality of electricity, even though one may know nothing about wiring a house and very little about the nature of electricity itself—other than that Ben Franklin was lucky not to have been electrocuted when he flew his kite. Millions of people who work with computers every day haven't the vaguest notion of how the computer does its job. Innumerable examples can be cited of people's using things, doing things, being in step with and being led by forces about which they know little or nothing. So not understanding the workings of something or the method by which it accomplishes its task does not preclude the existence of that thing or force.

NEAR-DEATH EXPERIENCES

NURSE: I suppose you've heard of cases of people who have had near-death experiences. This often happens after a cardiac or respiratory arrest, while doctors and nurses are frantically trying to resuscitate a person. After the patient has been revived, it is not uncommon for him to say that he observed the resuscitation efforts as he was floating pleasantly out of his body. These people typically describe feelings of deep calmness and tranquillity. They didn't want to go back into their body with all its pain and problems, and they did come back only with the greatest reluctance.

I wonder if you could comment on this. Would you say that these people were on another plane of existence similar to what you were just discussing? Or were they experiencing some other type of consciousness? If nothing else, these incidents certainly seem to support a belief in life after death.

Yes, I have heard of these experiences, and I have been to conferences where they were discussed with great interest. It was primarily the research and writing of Dr. Elisabeth Kübler-Ross in the mid-1970s that brought these phenomena to light. She stirred up a great deal of controversy when she claimed that the extraordinary similarities in hundreds of stories from people who had had near-death experiences proved that there was life after death. At first she found that many people were reluctant to discuss their experiences for fear of being labeled insane. But when they did talk about what had happened to them, she was struck by the harmony and beauty of what others assumed was an ordeal.

In the last ten or fifteen years, so many people have reported these episodes that there are now even clubs where people can compare what happened to them. In a 1982 Gallup poll it was reported that "35 percent of those who had suffered a brush with death had felt the near-death phenomenon. Using those figures, Gallup estimated eight million Americans have undergone such experiences."[41]

Kübler-Ross claimed that many of the people who underwent these experiences "resented our desperate attempts to bring them back to life. Death is the feeling of peace and hope. Not one of them has ever been afraid to die again."[42] Other studies have shown that people who have undergone a near-death episode become more sensitive, more religious, and less materialistic than they were before. Experiencers often find themselves consumed with a desire to be of service to others. Dr. Bruce Greyson, a psychiatrist at the University of Connecticut Health Center, says that "The most common aftereffect is that they no longer are afraid of dying. They are freed up to live their lives."[43]

A couple of years ago I talked at some length with one of my students who had had a near-death episode. He was in the hospital when he stopped breathing. He said that he felt himself gently float out of his body and that he watched the frantic efforts to resuscitate him. He told me he was able to read a small sign on the other side of the room. He could also see his doctor's distraught face, even though the doctor's back was to him, and he was able to read the doctor's thoughts. Later, when my student was past the crisis, he spoke with his doctor, who verified what he (the doctor) had been thinking at the time. My student said he felt great peace and wondered what all the fuss was about. In the end, the thought of leaving his wife and children made him decide to return to his body, albeit reluctantly.

The experience had a dramatic effect on this man. Soon after he regained his health, he sold his business and went into a different line of work—one that he had always wanted to be in but that had before seemed impossible. He also made several other major changes in his lifestyle—all for the better. And he told me that the experience totally erased all fear of death. "Death," he said, "has completely lost its mystery for me. I am absolutely not afraid to die."

What is going on here? Some physicians dismiss these reports as no more than hallucinations caused by chemical reactions in the brain—reactions induced either by lack of oxygen or by drugs in the system. Others admit that they really haven't the foggiest notion as to what's going on, but that obviously *something* is happening.

From a spiritual point of view, something indeed is going on. What these people are experiencing is the initial phase of the journey to rebirth, the *first* stage of death. The near-death experience is analogous to taking an airplane trip to a foreign country very different from our own and barely getting out of the airplane at the airport. Many experiences await you, as they do for everyone else on board, but until you actually leave the airport and begin your sojourn, your experience and those of the other passengers are roughly equal. Many people who have had a near-death experience, and researchers too, mistake these experiences as *the* afterlife, not realizing that there are stages to death leading to inevitable rebirth in another existence.

A CHILD IS BORN

NURSE: What happens to the intermediate being after conception? Aside from the obvious physical changes, what effect does prenatal development have on the infant?

With its entrance into the womb, the intermediate being simultaneously dies in the transitional realm and begins its rebirth into the human realm. You could say that its period in the womb is yet another type of existence into which it was born and from which, at birth, it will die. There is an astonishing amount of both physical and psychic growth that takes place during this time. Perhaps this is why, in China, human life is calculated from conception, not birth.

With the intermediate being's entrance into the womb, a growing subconscious awareness of its body slowly robs it of the innate purity of its senses as they once again become attuned to the physical world. Hearing in particular develops rapidly, but the fetus is also aware of light and, to a certain extent, the mother's emotions. By the time the infant is ready to be born, its senses have once again developed to a point where they will begin to color the child's perception of reality. The links of the chain of being have all been filled—from birth to death to the intermediate state to rebirth—and the circle of life continues on its path. (See Diagram 4.)

We see in the laws of karma and rebirth the very keynotes to the evolution of humankind. Swami Paramananda superbly summarizes the beauty of these laws:

Reincarnation is not, as is supposed by many hasty thinkers, a pagan doctrine; it has its roots in the very foundation of the spiritual world. It explains the incongruity of life in the light of reason. It offers us consolation in the deepest sense. It makes clear that our disadvantages and our sufferings are not imposed upon us by an arbitrary hand, but are the fulfillment of just laws. Also it teaches us that our lost opportunities are not taken away from us forever. We are given new chances that we may learn, that we may evolve . . . Nothing of real value is ever lost, nor our misdeeds, our cruel and treacherous acts, forgotten until we have atoned for them. It is not that some being is keeping account of our thoughts and deeds, but we ourselves keep a complete record . . . and we reap the sum total of these thoughts and deeds in our every embodiment.[44]

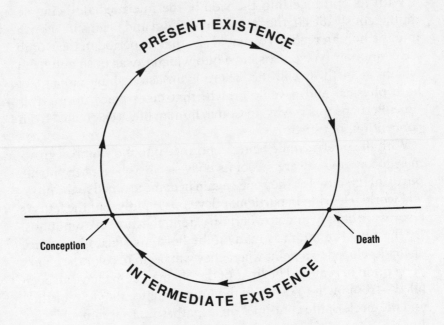

Diagram 4: The Circle of Continuing Existence

The most profound mysteries of life and death are within our grasp. If we understand that life holds the secret of death, just as death embodies the secret of life, we can live with greater peace in our hearts and greater love for all living beings.

Five: SUPPLEMENTS

1. LIVING WILLS

"It was Socrates who, according to Plato, saw painful disease and suffering as good reason not to cling to life. In the *Republic* he condemns the physician Heroditus . . . [for] 'inventing lingering death.' "[1] Today, through a medical science whose techniques advance more and more each day, it is even more possible to maintain biological life in bodies which have otherwise long since died.

CPR [cardiopulmonary resuscitation] has saved countless lives, but it has also increased the number of coma patients who would have died before the stunning developments in emergency medical treatment . . . Forty-six-year-old Rosemary Pugh had a seizure, her first, on the back of a Denver bus. She eventually got CPR, but never recovered. She's been comatose for seven years . . . Evelyn Morganstein [another patient at the same nursing home] . . . was an attractive woman who worked in a VA hospital in Los Angeles, raised dogs, played the violin and was married twice. She became senile, eventually living in her car . . . she later had a stroke and [has] never regained consciousness.[2]

Terminally ill, incompetent and often comatose people have had their lives prolonged for considerable and even extended periods of time, affording them no satisfaction, causing suffering both to them and to their relatives, and necessitating great expense, sometimes borne by the patients themselves, often to the complete exhaustion of their resources.[3]

"The biggest frustration I have is resuscitating people who shouldn't be resuscitated," says a veteran Maryland nurse. "We have ridiculous situations. Very, very old people are resuscitated and put on a respirator, even though there's no hope of them ever coming off of it . . ."[4]

How can one die naturally—that is, without months or perhaps years of subsisting by means of ventilators, emergency resuscitation, and surgically implanted feeding tubes?

THE RIGHT TO REFUSE MEDICAL TREATMENT

A number of states now have laws on the books which recognize the right to die naturally and without heroic measures to prolong life; others are debating such legislation. As for common law, according to *Changing Times* magazine, one has the right to refuse medical treatment if one so wishes. In fact, "some courts have held that forcing treatment on an unwilling person constitutes assault and battery."[5]

On the other hand, we hear of forty-seven-year-old Thomas Wirth dying of AIDS. It seems that Mr. Wirth "signed a living will with notarized instructions saying he wished to be allowed to die with dignity and without 'extraordinary measures,' . . . and designated a friend to make medical decisions in the event that he became incapacitated." Nonetheless, when Mr. Wirth fell into a coma as his illness progressed, and his friend then attempted to stop the aggressive medical treatment being given to Mr. Wirth, his doctors refused to do so and a state court upheld their decision.[6]

LIVING WILLS

What is a living will? Just as a person, while of sound mind, makes an ordinary will that determines how his possessions will be distributed upon his death, so can he make a *living will* that would come into effect while he is still alive, specifically to prohibit the prolonging of his life artificially should he find himself

in a terminal medical condition from which there is no reasonable expectation of recovery.

LIVING WILLS: THE NEGATIVE SIDE

The language of living wills is sometimes too vague to be acted
upon. Take the case of Mr. Wirth. The term employed in his
living will was "extraordinary measures." What may be extraordinary measures today might well be commonplace tomorrow,
or what one person would consider extraordinary measures
might not be so to another. In addition, your particular living
will may not be legal in the state in which you find yourself when
you need it, simply because it is not written in the language and
according to the form required by that state.

A more subtle danger arises when a person makes a living will
while he is still distant from the event or events that the living
will is intended to guard against. At that last minute, will he
really *not* want that resuscitation? There are, after all, plenty of
stories of people who were thought to be drawing their last
breath, or were thought to be in a condition from which they
would never recover, yet they did: Bill Inman, in his twenties
when he suffered massive brain damage in an automobile accident, was in a coma for a year. His mother was told he would
be a vegetable. Four years later he was living in his parents' home.
His language ability was back to normal, he was able to feed and
dress himself, learning to walk by himself again, and planning
to finish a degree in astrophysics he was working on before his
accident.[7] And he is not the only case of miraculous recovery.

A fear of those who have argued against living will legislation
is the possibility that such a will may leave an elderly patient at
the mercy of an unscrupulous nursing home administrator, who
might want to hasten the patient's death by withholding treatment prematurely.

And finally, unless the existence of your living will is known
or pointed out to the doctors and nurses at the hospital in which
you are being treated, and to your friends and relatives, it obviously cannot be acted upon. At least one state (New York)

requires that, once called, ambulance medics must administer life-saving measures.

LIVING WILLS: THE POSITIVE SIDE

On the other hand, living wills are legally recognized in many states when drafted in accord with certain requirements. Similarly, a durable power of attorney—the appointment of a proxy to act after a person becomes incompetent—is recognized in most of the United States. Many physicians, too, knowing that a patient has executed a living will will respect it even if state law is unclear on the subject. This brings up a crucial point: a patient should always talk with his or her doctor about both the patient's and the doctor's feelings well before a living will would be employed.

HOW TO MAKE A LIVING WILL

Standardized forms are available from Concern for Dying[8] and from the Society for the Right to Die, both listed at 250 W. 57th Street, New York, NY 10107. For those readers living outside the United States, a World Federation of Right to Die Societies, which is composed of such societies in many nations throughout the world, was established in 1980 in Oxford, England.

You may wish to have your lawyer draw up your living will. Or you could adopt the sample immediately following.[9] In either case, it is advisable to have your will witnessed by two adults and notarized. And it is just as important to give copies to your doctor, lawyer, closest family members, and anyone else who might be in a position to make a decision about your medical treatment.

SAMPLE

Directions for My Care

I wish to live a full and long life, but not at all costs. If my death is near and cannot be avoided, and if I have lost the ability to interact with others and have no reasonable chance of regaining this ability, or if my suffering is intense and irreversible, I do not want to have my life prolonged. I would then ask not to be subjected to surgery or resuscitation. Nor would I then wish to have life support from mechanical ventilators, intensive care services, or other life-prolonging procedures, including the administration of antibiotics and blood products. I would wish, rather, to have care which gives comfort and support, which facilitates my interaction with others to the extent that this is possible, and which brings peace.

In order to carry out these instructions and to interpret them,

I authorize _____ to accept, plan, and refuse treatment on my behalf in cooperation with attending physicians and health personnel. This person knows how I value the experience of living, and how I would weigh incompetence, suffering, and dying. Should it be impossible to reach this person, I

authorize _____ to make such choices for me. I have discussed my desires concerning terminal care with them, and I trust their judgment on my behalf.

In addition, I have discussed with them the following specific instructions regarding my care:

(please continue on back)

Date _____ Signed _____

Witnessed by _____

and _____

2. THE HOSPICE MOVEMENT

Healing a person does not always mean curing a disease. Sometimes healing means learning to care for others, finding new wholeness as a family—being reconciled. Or it can mean easing the pain of dying or allowing someone to die when the time comes. There is a difference between prolonging life and prolonging the act of dying until the patient lives a travesty of life . . . We hold fast, but with open hands, because sometimes the most important part of loving can be knowing how and when to let go.[10]

The hospice movement, which has so revitalized the care of the terminally ill in England and America, was begun by health care professionals who were dissatisfied with the quality of care available to those whose diseases could not be cured and who were nearing death. Typically, these patients find themselves in the intensive care unit of a hospital, treated more like an object or a disease entity than a dying human being despite the very best of intentions. Instead of being lent support and comfort in their last hours, they are stripped, willy-nilly, of their dignity and composure by the very institutions and machines that are designed to help them. Alternatively, dying patients may be at home, perhaps in great pain, isolated from loved ones by mutual exhaustion, by uncertainties and guilt, by the disease and its pain, or by the sedation prescribed to blunt that pain.

Dying people are frequently abandoned by their doctors, who feel they can do little to help them and who have many other patients for whom a cure is still possible. Even hospital nurses may abandon the dying in the press of other responsibilities that seem more vital and less personally troubling. One recent study found that nurses took, on the average, twice as long to respond to the call bell of dying patients as they did to the summons of patients who were apparently recovering.[11] In any case, hospital nurses can only spend, generally, an hour or so per day with any given patient, and this may not be enough to develop the trust and rapport so needed by the dying patient.

Meanwhile, the family of the dying patient may well be beset with stresses—physical, emotional, spiritual, not to mention financial—that very often lead to disease, both physical and mental, in the bereaved. Not uncommonly, these stresses are exacerbated by medical protocols and an institutional environment designed for those who will recover, and not for those who die.

The search for a better context in which to care for the dying led to a rediscovery of the medieval concept of hospice. The word "hospice" comes from the Latin word for hospitality; and the medieval hospice, or place of hospitality, opened its doors to those who most needed help: the pilgrim, the traveler far from home, the sick, and those with incurable diseases. Some hospices were large, well appointed, and famous—such as the hospice of the Knights Hospitallers at Rhodes—while others must have been the simplest of cottages; but all had in common the ideal of service. Whether run by monks or nuns, members of lay orders, or simply those who felt a vocation of caring, hospices at their best embodied a spiritual attitude that has all but vanished in the evolution of the modern hospital.

"In medieval times," writes Sandol Stoddard,

> dying persons were seen as prophetic souls, voyagers and pilgrims valuable to the community in a number of ways, not least in the opportunity they provided those around them for service and spiritual growth ... The dying were seen as individuals useful to mankind, not in terms of what organs they might contribute to those after them, or as objects of scientific speculation, but as beings moving forward, more rapidly than others, on the metaphysical plane.[12]

This view of the dying is all but absent from our society and its institutions, even those institutions created for the sick. This is because our society largely denies death. Death undercuts, by definition, all secular achievements, both individual and cultural, and to be conscious of death is to be conscious that all our common pleasures and accomplishments are at best temporary. In a society increasingly concerned with desires and possessions far in excess of those we were born with, to acknowledge death is profoundly subversive. Death threatens our cherished myths—of technical omnipotence, of the ever-fresh and conquerable frontier, of the permanence of our productions. As Arnold Toynbee put it, "Death is un-American."[13]

Our denial of death amounts to a denial of life, and in this milieu the modern hospice has arisen as a compassionate affirmation of life, with power to heal the living as well as the dying. Hospices, both ancient and modern, are built on the quiet confidence that death, like life, is a kind of pilgrimage, though a beginningless and endless one.

Modern hospices are centrally administered, physician-directed programs characterized by (1) knowledge and expertise in the control of symptoms (including physical, psychological, social, and spiritual manifestations); (2) a coordinated, interdisciplinary approach to care, typically involving doctors, nurses, pharmacologists, social scientists, clergy, and volunteers; (3) home care in conjunction with inpatient facilities; (4) the patient *and the family* as the unit of care; and (5) the availability of services at any time of the day or night, as well as after the patient's death.[14]

Hospices differ in their degree of autonomy from other institutions. Many of the most well-known and successful hospices are completely autonomous programs, to which application for admission is made by the patient, his or her physician, and the family. Others have degrees of autonomy within a larger institution. It is difficult, though in some cases not impossible, to provide the hospice atmosphere within a hospital setting.

In a hospice setting, the patient is seen not as a person with an incurable and terminal disease, but as a person with symptoms (for example, pain) that *can* be treated and usually controlled to a great extent. This palliative care is aimed not at extending life at any cost, but primarily at increasing the *quality* of that life. Symptoms are treated as synergistic; that is, they are not regarded as being in isolation from each other. As one British hospice director says to his staff: "Don't just treat the pain, treat the situation."[15] All this results in a positive attitude both in the hospice worker and in the patient and family. The foremost goal of hospice care is an alert, pain-free existence for patients in order to help them live as fully as possible until they die.

Some patients will prefer to stay at home, and in many cases the hospice team can make this a viable option, without the exhaustion and uncertainties the family usually faces under that circumstance. Most hospices, in fact, encourage remaining at home where this is appropriate, since inpatient care—though significantly less expensive than corresponding hospital care—is expensive, and inpatient services are usually very limited by space to those who most need them. More importantly, where the family can provide a substantial portion of the care, there is a greater chance for growth, for resolution of long-standing family problems, and, after the patient's death, less chance of guilt and self-criticism.

Not every hospice program has inpatient facilities; most hospices begin, in fact, as home-care programs. It is still too early to see whether most hospices will remain solely in this mode, working in conjunction with hospitals as needed, or whether residential hospices—considered by many in the field to be the format that most fully embodies the hospice concept—will become the rule. In a residential hospice, a sense of community grows up that is of great benefit to patients, staff, and the larger community. And of course, many patients simply cannot be cared for at home, especially as their death approaches, yet taking the patient to a general hospital may involve compromises in the quality of care as well as increased costs relative to a residential hospice.

It is the aim of hospice programs to provide services without regard to the family's ability to pay; this has been a feature of the hospice concept since medieval times. In the 1970s, the average per-patient cost over the last three months of life for five

hundred patients served by The Connecticut Hospice, Inc., of
New Haven, Conn. was only $750.[16] This was home care. It has
been reported that residential-hospice care, despite its much
more personalized nature, costs in the neighborhood of 27 percent less than ordinary hospital care. No doubt this is due to the
hospices' considerably lower investment in high-technology medical devices and their support systems.

An important part of a well-run hospice program is the volunteers that are attracted to it. At St. Christopher's volunteers
attend team meetings and are very much respected for the distinctive contribution they make. Volunteers meet a patient on
the patient's own ground, as Dr. Sylvia Lack, director of the
hospice in New Haven, says; because no one is paying them to
work, they are uniquely able to help a patient keep his or her
sense of self-worth. Volunteers are an important part of the spiritual atmosphere of a hospice, and they frequently become closer
friends of the dying than paid professionals are able to.

For the patient, the dying process represents an exceptional
time for spiritual growth if that process is not thwarted by overwhelming pain or technical interventions, and especially if the
patient is aided by an atmosphere of honesty and compassion.
Hospice workers often encounter patients able to resolve emotional problems and long-standing difficulties in the final period
of life, when impending death provides the impetus for
settlement—an impetus so often lacking under the circumstances of ordinary counseling or psychiatric work. Hospices are
very much oriented toward facilitating this process, for the sake
of both the patient and his or her family and friends. In the words
of one St. Christopher's patient, who was dying of incurable cancer after a life of abandonment and rejection, "Here at the hospice, you see, things are so different from all that I am used to.
I have to go over my whole life again, it seems, sorting it out . . ."
This kind of growth occurs, perhaps not so much as a result of
particular techniques of care (though hospice team members will
not be oblivious to these techniques), but as a result of the unconditional acceptance that is part of the hospice concept.

Those who are interested in hospice care should investigate,
as much as possible, the quality of care provided and the degree

to which hospice principles are followed in a given hospice, using the same care they would exercise in choosing a doctor. In time, hopefully, communities will be as familiar with their hospices as they are with their hospitals, and through patients, families of patients, and volunteers, the ideals and experience of hospice will be an everyday part of many people's lives.

Lastly, it needs to be mentioned that, in the United States at least, many hospices will not accept a patient whose doctor does not certify that in his opinion the patient has no more than six months to live. As many doctors are reluctant to predict such a limit in certain kinds of illness, this can restrict one's chances of entering into hospice care.

The following organizations supply information on hospice care:

Children's Hospice International
1101 King Street, Suite 131, Alexandria, VA 22314;
(703) 684-0330

National Hospice Organization
1901 N. Fort Meyer Drive, Suite 307, Arlington, VA 22209;
(703) 243-5900

3. WHAT TO DO UPON SOMEONE'S DEATH: A CHECKLIST

The following is a list of things that need to be done immediately following a death. It was compiled, in part, from Ernest Morgan's *A Manual of Death Education and Simple Burial*[17] and Deborah Whiting Little's *Home Care for the Dying*.[18] If organs are to be donated—and organs can only be accepted under certain circumstances of death and condition of the body—the family should let the hospital know before death. The hospital will contact the appropriate transplant coordinator, who may get in touch with the family. The organs of a person who dies at home are not suitable for donation.

1. Call the person's physician within an hour after the death. If the medical examiner or coroner must be notified, ask the doctor to do so.

If the death occurs in a hospital, advise the nurse that you believe the person has died. The nurse will call the doctor to have the person declared dead. Generally, unless organs are to be donated, the family will have plenty of time to say their final farewells before the body is removed from the room, especially if the mortician is not notified until the family has finished.

2. If the body is being donated to a medical school, call the

school, inform them that the donor has died, and arrange for transportation.

3. If funeral arrangements have already been made, notify the mortician as to when you want the body to be transported.

4. If pallbearers are to be used, select and notify them.

5. Notify anyone else who is to have a role in the services.

6. Arrange for family members or friends to take turns answering the telephone and the door at the home of the deceased. Keep a careful record of all calls.

7. List immediate family, close friends, and employer or business associates of the deceased, and inform them by telephone of the death.

8. Coordinate the supplying of food for the next few days and take care of other things that need to be done, such as cleaning. When coordinating the food supply, keep in mind the presence of possible out-of-town relatives and friends.

9. If child care is required, arrange for it.

10. Arrange accommodations for visiting relatives and friends.

11. Decide where memorial gifts can be sent if flowers are to be omitted. If flowers are to be accepted, decide what is to happen to them after the funeral.

12. Write an obituary for the newspapers. This commonly includes the age, place of birth, cause of death, occupation, college degrees, military service, organization memberships, any outstanding accomplishments, names of survivors in the immediate family, and names of any memorials set up in lieu of flowers. It is unwise to list publicly the date and time of services, as this gives a clear indication to thieves of when the house of the deceased will be empty.

Deliver the obituary to the appropriate newspaper offices; there may be a charge to print it.

13. If the deceased was living alone, notify the utilities and the landlord of the death; notify the post office and indicate where to forward mail.

14. Notify the lawyer and the executor of the estate. Get original copies of the death certificate, as these will be required by several institutions.

15. Notify by mail any distant friends and relatives.

16. Investigate possible insurance and death benefits (Social Security, credit union, trade union, fraternal, military, and so forth) and any income for survivors from these.

17. Review all debts and installment payments. There can be delays in the transfer of assets and in other financial settlements at the time of death; if such delays will occur, make arrangements with creditors to delay any payments that do not carry insurance clauses that would cancel further payments outright.

18. To those who telephoned or sent flowers or other memorials, as well as those who helped with food, child care, or other matters, send appropriate acknowledgments and thanks. Include any nurses or other health care professionals who helped care for the person prior to death.

19. If the person died at home, arrange for return of any rented equipment.

4. CONSOLING THE BEREAVED: DO'S AND DON'TS[19]

1. DO let your genuine concern and caring show.

2. DO say you are sorry about what happened to their loved one and about their pain.

3. DO allow them to express as much grief as they are feeling and are willing to share.

4. DO be available to listen, run errands, help with children, or whatever else seems needed at the time.

5. DO allow them to talk about their loved one as much and as often as they want.

6. DO talk about the special memories and endearing qualities of the one who has died.

7. DO reassure them that they did everything they could, that the medical care their loved one received was the best, or with whatever else you know to be *true and positive* about the care given to the one who died.

8. DO, in asking how they are, be specific. "The last time I talked to you, I remember . . ." "I've been thinking about you a lot, and wondering how things are going for you since . . ."

9. DO thank them for sharing their pain.

10. DO send them a personal note.

11. DON'T say, "It was God's will," "I know how you feel," "Time will heal."

12. DON'T say, "God is teaching you to trust Him and increase your faith."

13. DON'T say, "Be strong; others need you."

14. DON'T say, "It could have been worse; at least your wife lived," "At least one child made it," "The baby was a girl and you wanted a boy," "The baby would have been retarded."

15. DON'T say, "These things don't just happen; there has got to be a good reason."

16. DON'T simply say, "How are things going?"

17. DON'T let your own sense of helplessness keep you from reaching out to a bereaved person.

18. DON'T avoid the grieving because you feel uncomfortable.

19. DON'T avoid mentioning the deceased person's name out of fear of reminding the bereaved of their pain.

5. MEDITATION

WHAT IS MEDITATION?

Although there are many kinds, meditation at its highest is a form of mental and spiritual training that aims at stilling and focusing the normally scattered mind, establishing a measure of physical and mental repose, and then becoming an instrument for Self-discovery. Meditation can also be a method of cleansing the mind of impurities and disturbances, such as lustful desires, hatred, ill will, indolence, restlessness, worry, and cynical doubt. When the dusts of these hindrances are wiped from the mind mirror through disciplined meditation, we come to see things as they are in their True-nature, undistorted by our mental or emotional colorations. A lesser fruit of meditation is the strengthening and calming of the nervous system, and the tapping of physical, mental, and psychic energies. This last is analogous to a generator-battery; a special kind of energy (called samadi power) is generated and stored in the meditator's lower belly, enabling him or her to respond instantly to urgent situations without strain or wasted effort. Gradually the winds of anger, greed, and folly subside and the meditator is returned to the stillness of the world of no-thing–ness, the luminous Void, our true home. In correctly practiced meditation, the practitioner develops greater vitality, equanimity, mindfulness, and a responsiveness to the circumstances of his life. Meditation, then, is a healing practice in which the heart is calmed and the spirit strengthened.

MEDITATION AT REST AND IN MOTION

Broadly speaking, meditation embraces much more than formal sitting (the more common designation for this type of meditation) in a stable, motionless posture and trying to concentrate the mind. To enter fully into every act with total attention and clear awareness is no less meditation. "Meditation is to be aware of what is going on—in our bodies, in our feelings, in our minds, and in the world."[20]

The two, formal meditation and meditation in motion, are mutually supportive. If you "sit" every day for a certain period, a special kind of energy develops; this energy enables you to perform your daily tasks with singlemindedness and clear awareness. Conversely, if you perform your daily tasks mindfully—working on a computer, attending meetings, laying bricks, cooking dinner, and playing with your children—it is easier to empty and concentrate your mind when you sit in meditation.

Meditation can be done by anybody; it requires no special talents. Being free of any philosophic or religious content, it is for anybody and everybody. If you are already meditating, you can easily adapt your spiritual practice to the meditations that follow. (Meditations on death and specific meditations for the dying person at the point of death and during the intermediate state between decease and rebirth are described in the "Death" and "Dying" sections, respectively.)

Don't wait until you become seriously ill before beginning to meditate; start while you are still in good health. Faithfully pursued, meditation will add depth and clarity to your life.

When you are ready to meditate, choose a secluded area—the privacy of your own room, a basement, an empty attic, a corner of the backyard, or any similarly isolated place. Since the most intrusive sounds are those of the human voice, whether heard directly or on TV or radio, such sounds should be avoided if possible. Natural sounds, on the other hand—such as a bird's singing, a cricket's chirping, a cat's meowing, or a dog's barking—are ordinarily not a disturbance to the meditator. Especially felicitous is the pitter-patter of rain or the steady gushing of a water fountain or waterfall; both these sounds can have a calming effect on the mind of the meditator.

In your meditation, face a wall, curtain, or divider that is unpatterned. A plain beige, tan, or cream color is most restful for the eyes, which are best kept half open. (See "Eyes and Hands.") A distance of two to three feet from the wall to your knees is best. If you sit too close, you may strain you eyes.

POSTURE

For a normal, healthy person, a stable sitting posture either on a mat on the floor or in a chair is best. With your body in a stable, unmoving position, you will not have to contend with as many random thoughts as you would if you were constantly fidgeting, for such thoughts are stirred into activity through movement. If you have chosen to sit on a mat, begin by taking a comfortable posture sitting on a firm cushion, preferably in one of several cross-legged sitting positions.[21] Wear loose, comfortable clothing so that your circulation is not restricted. To stabilize your body, both knees should touch the mat or carpet. If your knees are off the mat, your body is under strain; to relieve the resulting discomfort, you will constantly move. To avoid a proliferation of random thoughts—the greatest obstacle to concentration—your back needs to be erect and your head straight, not tipped forward.

Sitting in a straight-back chair can also be an effective way to meditate. A small cushion can be inserted under your buttocks to aid in keeping your back erect and your feet firmly planted on the floor. A Scandinavian-designed kneeling chair may also be used to good effect.

Even if you are bedridden, you can derive benefits from meditation while lying in bed following these guidelines.

BREATHING

Breathing is best done naturally from your lower belly rather than your chest, with your attention directed toward a point the width of four fingers below your navel. The advantage of this is that it tends to center your body-mind in that area, thereby preventing tension from developing in your head and shoulders, reducing the number of wandering thoughts and soothing the nervous system. The breath should not be "pushed down" or manipulated in any way except at the beginning of a round of sitting, when it is advisable to take one or two deep breaths, slowly exhaling after each one, to harmonize breath and mind. While doing this, imagine you are exhaling all tension and negative thoughts. After that, let your breath take its own natural rhythm.

EYES AND HANDS

Keep your eyes half open and unfocused. ("Unfocused" means you are not trying to perceive what is in front of you.) Closing them entirely encourages sleepiness or the incidence of visions of one sort or another. The most effective position for your hands is in your lap, palms up, close to your abdomen, with your left hand in the palm of your right, thumbs lightly touching, and your elbows close to your body but relaxed. The advantage of this posture is that it establishes the maximum repose.

HOW LONG TO SIT

How long should you meditate at one sitting? This, of course, depends on the time available to you as well as on the maturity of your practice. It is advisable to start with a shorter period—say ten or fifteen minutes each day—and gradually increase the time as your body–mind accustoms itself to the routine of motionless meditation. It is better to meditate for shorter periods regularly than for a longer period sporadically.

WHEN TO SIT

Is there a best time for sitting? Although early morning is recommended—at that time of day it is quiet, there are few cars on the street, the telephone normally doesn't ring, you are rested, and you haven't eaten yet—you can meditate at any time.

CONCENTRATING THE MIND

Although there are many methods of concentrating the mind, the most common and simplest is counting the inhalations and exhalations of your breath. When you inhale, think to yourself "One," and when you exhale, "Two," and so on until ten. After that, return to one and go to ten again. Whenever you lose count or go beyond ten, return to one and resume the counting. The numbers need not be visualized; you need only concentrate fully on each number. Avoid simply counting mechanically.

Another method is to be aware of the rhythms of your breath—that is, becoming completely one with your inhalations and exhalations.

The value of these exercises lies in the fact that all reasoning is excluded and the discriminative mind put at rest. Thus the waves of thought are stilled and a gradual one-pointedness of mind achieved. Be aware that fleeting thoughts which dart in and out of the mind are not an impediment. Do not try to expel them; simply concentrate on the counting or the rhythms of the breath.

REFERENCES

INTRODUCTION

1. Marcus Borg, "Death as the Teacher of Wisdom," *Christian Century*, February 26, 1986.

2. Carl Jung, *Modern Man in Search of a Soul*, Harcourt, Brace, New York, 1955.

3. Quoted in Susan J. Smith, "When Prolonging a Life Prolongs Suffering," *Times-Union*, Rochester, N.Y., October 28, 1986.

4. W. Y. Evans-Wentz, *The Tibetan Book of the Dead*, 3rd edition, Oxford University Press, London, 1970.

5. See Karlis Osis, "Deathbed Observations by Physicians and Nurses," *Journal of the American Society for Psychical Research*, October 1963.

6. Philippe Ariés, *Western Attitudes Toward Death*, trans. Patricia M. Ranum, The Johns Hopkins University Press, Baltimore, 1975.

7. Review of *Healing the Wounds* in *Newsweek*, January 27, 1986.

8. See *Reincarnation: The Phoenix Fire Mystery*, ed. Joseph Head and S. L. Cranston, Julian Press/Crown Publishers, Inc., New York, 1977, for ample evidence that the doctrine of metempsychosis was once widely accepted in Western cultures and religions.

9. Quoted in Jung Young Lee, *Death and Beyond in the Eastern Perspective*, Gordon & Breach, New York, 1974.

10. Heinrich Zimmer writes, "It is easy for us to forget that our strictly linear evolutionary idea of time . . . is something peculiar to modern man. Even the Greeks of the day of Plato and Aristotle . . . did not share it. Indeed, St. Augustine seems to have been the first to conceive of this modern idea of time. His conception established itself only gradually in opposition to the notion formerly current." (From *Myths and Symbols in Indian Art and Civilization*, ed. Joseph Campbell, Princeton University Press, Princeton, N.J., 1971.)

11. Quoted in *Familiar Medical Quotations*, ed. Maurice B. Strauss, M.D., Little, Brown and Co., Boston, 1968.

ONE: DEATH

1. Lyall Watson, *The Romeo Error: A Matter of Life and Death*, Anchor Press/Doubleday, Garden City, N.Y., 1975.

2. Ibid.

3. Dogo and Sekiso are Japanese spellings of Chinese masters' names.

4. Zenkei Shibayama, *Zen Comments on the Mumonkan*, Harper & Row, New York, 1974.

5. "In America, Death Is a Dirty Word," *The New York Times*, June 19, 1988.

6. That is, empty of busy or distracting thoughts.

7. This remark is reminiscent of a comment by Chao-chou (778–897), an outstanding Zen master. Watching a somber funeral procession for one of his monks, he exclaimed, "What a long train of dead bodies follows in the wake of a single live being."

8. Over the centuries it was traditional for the masters to put brush to paper shortly before death in the form of an edifying verse.

9. George Santayana (1863–1952).

10. Quoted in Philip Kapleau, *The Wheel of Death*, George Allen & Unwin, Ltd., London, 1972.

11. Quoted in *Reincarnation: The Phoenix Fire Mystery*, ed. Joseph Head and S. L. Cranston, Julian Press/Crown Publishers, Inc., New York, 1977.

12. *The Wheel of Death*, op. cit.

13. That is, solids (earth), liquids (water), heat (fire), gas (air).

14. All the foregoing accounts are taken from *The Wheel of Death*, op. cit.

15. Adapted from Zen master Hakuun Yasutani, Commentary on the Koan Mu, in Philip Kapleau, *The Three Pillars of Zen*, Anchor Press/Doubleday, Garden City, N.Y., 1980.

16. See Philippe Ariés, *Western Attitudes Towards Death*. trans, Patricia M. Ranum, The Johns Hopkins University Press, Baltimore, 1975.

See also "Nothing More Beautiful than Death?" *Christian Century*, December 14, 1983, in which Dr. H. Paul Santmire writes, "[In the nineteenth century] symbolically, the cemetery came to be a kind of peaceable kingdom, and the dead themselves were less and less regarded as aliens and strangers, but instead as fellow travellers in an idealized world of peace and bliss in nature."

17. *Chuang Tzu,* trans. Herbert A. Giles, George Allen & Unwin, Ltd., London, 1961.

18. Quoted in *Kahawai,* Vol. 6, No. 1, Winter 1984.

19. That is, "The grief within me is beyond outward appearances, beyond the trappings of black mourning apparel."

20. Zen is not contrary to what is natural. When one is in a fearful situation, it is natural to be afraid. But facing death is not considered a fearful situation for a spiritually developed person.

21. Quoted in Francis Dojun Cook, *How to Raise an Ox,* Center Publications, Los Angeles, 1978.

22. Engaku Monastery. Soyen Shaku was in the United States in 1905–6.

23. Quoted in *Zen Comments on the Mumonkan,* op. cit.

24. Appolonius of Tyanna, first century A.D.

25. *Chuang Tzu,* op. cit.

26. By an anonymous writer. After "Dear Abby" attempted to find the author of this poem, she wrote in her newspaper column, "More 'authors' surfaced than I can mention here."

27. Johann Gottfried von Herder (1744–1803) was a German critic, theologian, philosopher, and poet.

28. *The Three Pillars of Zen,* op. cit.

29. Carl Jung, *Modern Man in Search of a Soul,* Harcourt Brace Jovanovich, New York, 1955.

30. From an article in the *Albuquerque Journal,* August 17, 1986.

31. *The Romeo Error: A Matter of Life and Death,* op. cit.

32. Plato, *Apology,* trans. Benjamin Jowett, quoted in *The Wheel of Death,* op. cit.

33. Ignace Lepp, *Death and Its Mysteries,* trans. Bernard Murchland, Macmillan Publishing Co., New York, 1976.

34. Ibid.

35. Charles A. Garfield, "Consciousness Alteration and Fear of Death," *Journal of Transpersonal Psychology,* Vol. 7, No. 2, 1975.

36. Quoted in Harold S. Kushner, "Why I Am Not Afraid to Die," *Reader's Digest,* August 1986.

37. Moses Maimonides (1135–1204), rabbi, physician, and philosopher.

38. C. S. Lewis, *The Problem of Pain,* Collins, London, 1940.

39. *Letters to a Friend,* ed. C. F. Androus, quoted in John Bowker, *The Problems of Suffering in Religions of the World,* Cambridge University Press, London, 1970.

40. Quoted in *The Wheel of Death,* op. cit.

41. *Reincarnation: The Phoenix Fire Mystery,* op. cit.

42. This presentation of the five aggregates is adapted from Lama Anagarika Govinda, *Creative Meditation and Multi-dimensional Consciousness*, The Theosophical Publishing House, Wheaton, Ill., 1978.

43. Philip Kapleau, *Zen: Merging of East and West*, Anchor Press/Doubleday, Garden City, N.Y.., 1989.

44. Quoted in Arthur Koestler, "Whereof One Cannot Speak . . . ?" in *Life After Death*, by Arnold Toynbee et al., Weidenfeld & Nicholson, London, 1976.

45. Chinese Zen master Mumon (1183–1260).

46. In Roman mythology, Janus was a god shown as having two faces, one in front and the other at the back of his head.

47. Masao Abe, *Zen and Western Thought*, ed. William R. LaFleur, University of Hawaii Press, Honolulu, 1985.

48. Huston Smith, *The Religions of Man*, Harper & Row, New York, 1958.

49. Zen master Bassui (1327–87), quoted in *The Three Pillars of Zen*, op. cit.

50. Abraham a Sancta Clara, an Austrian Augustinian monk and prolific author of theological writings.

51. Zen master Yasutani, *Reflections on the Five Ranks, the Three Refuges, the Three Resolutions, and the Ten Precepts*, from an unpublished partial translation by Kenneth Kraft.

52. Deuteronomy 30:19.

53. "One Against the Plague," *Newsweek*, July 21, 1986.

54. *Zen Comments on the Mumonkan*, op. cit.

55. Zen master Soen Nakagawa.

56. John C. H. Wu, *The Golden Age of Zen*, United Publishing Center, Taipei, Taiwan, 1975.

57. Adapted from Masao Abe, "The Problem of Death in East and West," *The Eastern Buddhist*, Vol. 19, No. 2, Autumn 1986.

58. From a current translation of the New Testament titled *Good News for Modern Man*, 3rd edition, American Bible Society, 1971.

59. Daniel Goleman, "The Mind Over the Body," *The New York Times*, September 27, 1987.

60. "The Barbie Trial: J'Accuse," *Newsweek*, May 11, 1987.

61. Hasidim are members of a sect of Judaism founded in Poland in the eighteenth century and characterized by emphasis on mysticism, prayer, religious zeal, and joy.

62. Quoted in Milton Melter, *Never to Forget: the Jews of the Holocaust*, Harper & Row, New York, 1976.

63. Ibid.

64. Mihajlo Mihajlov, "Mystical Experiences of the Labor Camps," in *Kontinent 2*, ed. Vladimir Maximov et al., Anchor Press/Doubleday, Garden City, N.Y., 1977.

65. Ibid.

66. Quoted in Lisa Carlson, *Caring for Your Own Dead*, Upper Access Publishers, Hinesburg, Vt., 1987.

67. Quoted in Edward Conze, *Thirty Years of Buddhist Studies*, Bruno Cassirer Ltd., Oxford, 1967.

68. "The Problem of Death in East and West," op. cit.

69. Quoted in Lynne Ann DeSpelder and Albert Strickland, *The Last Dance: Encountering Death and Dying*, Mayfield Publishing Co., Palo Alto, Calif., 1983.

70. Adapted from George Bond, "Buddhist Meditations on Death," *The History of Religions*, Vol. 19, No. 3, February 1980.

71. See "But Isn't a Corpse Dead?" for the full passage.

72. Quoted in Rollo May, *Love and Will*, Dell, New York, 1969.

73. Zen master Hakuin (1686–1769), quoted in Philip B. Yampolsky, *The Zen Master Hakuin: Selected Writings*, Columbia University Press, New York, 1971.

74. Quoted in Museo Universitario, Universidad Nacional Autonoma de México, *La Muerte: Expresiones Mexicanas de un Enigma* (Death: Mexican Expressions of an Enigma), Mexico City, 1975.

75. Ibid.

76. Ta Hui, *Swampland Flowers*, trans. Christopher Leary, Grove Press, New York, 1977.

77. That is, "I stand ready to sacrifice not merely my present life but my next six lifetimes on behalf of the emperor."

78. *Death and Its Mysteries*, op. cit.

79. Earth, water, fire, ether: the basic elements of the universe, according to the ancients.

80. See "The Evolution of Ego" and Glossary.

81. Quoted in Arthur Osborne, *Ramana Maharshi and the Path of Self-knowledge*, Rider & Co., London, 1963.

82. Arunachala is the name of the mountain next to Sri Maharshi's ashram, and, for the master, was another name for True-nature. Shiva is one of the Hindu deities.

83. *Ramana Maharshi and the Path of Self-knowledge*, op. cit.

84. The appellation the Buddha used in referring to himself.

85. That is, present-day Bodh gaya, the city in India where the Buddha attained supreme enlightenment at the age of thirty-five.

86. Quoted in *The Wheel of Death*, op. cit.

Two: Dying

1. Fred Wistow, "Death in the Family: Healing the Loss of a Parent," in *The Family Therapy Networker*, The Family Therapy Network, Inc., 1986.

2. *Visuddhimagga*.

3. Jacques Lusseyran, *And There Was Light*, trans. Elizabeth R. Cameron, Parabola Books, New York, 1987.

4. Zen master Yasutani, quoted in Philip Kapleau, *The Three Pillars of Zen*, Anchor Press/Doubleday, Garden City, N.Y., 1980.

5. See "Concentration and Euphoria: Mind Functioning at Peak Can Produce Altered States," *The New York Times*, March 10, 1986.

6. Leonardo da Vinci (1452–1519), *The Notebooks*, Vol. 1, Ch. 1.

7. Mihajlo Mihajlov, "Mystical Experiences of the Labor Camps," in *Kontinent 2*, ed. Vladimir Maximov et al., Anchor Press/Doubleday, Garden City, N.Y., 1977.

8. *And There Was Light*, op. cit.

9. "Mystical Experiences of the Labor Camps," op. cit.

10. Quoted in "First Do No Harm: The Making of a Neurosurgeon," *Reader's Digest*, November 1987.

11. Quoted in a review of *Nikos Kazantzakis: A Biography Based on His Letters*, by Helen Kazantzakis, in *Newsweek*, October 11, 1968.

12. P. T. James, *Cover Her Face*, Warner Books, 1982.

13. Quoted in Morton Hunt, "Body and Mind," *The New York Times*, March 27, 1988.

14. The Life Center is a nonprofit organization providing group and individual services for children and adults experiencing serious illness or loss, at no charge.

15. John Bowker, *The Problems of Suffering in Religions of the World*, Cambridge University Press, London, 1970.

16. Huston Smith writes of the Buddha: "He was undoubtedly one of the greatest rationalists of all times, resembling in this respect no one as much as Socrates . . . The remarkable fact, however, was the way this objective critical component of his character was balanced by a Franciscan tenderness so strong as to have caused his message to be subtitled 'a religion of infinite compassion.' " *The Religions of Man*, Harper & Row, New York, 1958.

17. See "The Evolution of Ego."

18. Quoted in *The Problems of Suffering in Religions of the World*, op. cit.

19. *The Religions of Man*, op. cit.

20. The word "nothing," when written with a capital *N*, has the metaphysical sense of the viable Void out of which all forms emerge and to which they return according to causes and conditions. With a small *n* it can be taken to mean little or no worldly possessions in this context.

21. The original word is *nirvana*, which here can be understood to mean release from the chain of causation and re-becoming.

22. Quoted in *The Problems of Suffering in Religions of the World*, op. cit.

23. Ibid.

24. John Blofeld, *The Zen Teaching of Hui Hai*, Samuel Weiser, New York, 1972, Introduction.

25. *The Problems of Suffering in Religions of the World*, op. cit.

26. Ibid.

27. *The Religions of Man*, op. cit.

28. Lama Anagarika Govinda, *The Psychological Attitude of Early Buddhism*, quoted in *The Problems of Suffering in Religions of the World*, op. cit.

29. Ronald Melzack and Patrick D. Wall, *The Challenge of Pain*, Basic Books, New York, 1982.

30. Robert G. Twycross and Sylvia A. Lack, *Symptom Control in Far Advanced Cancer: Pain Relief*, Pitman, London.

31. "Pain and the Dying Patient," an audio tape made under the auspices of St. Christopher's Hospice, Sydenham, England.

32. Karen Quinlan went into a coma in her twenties as a result of brain damage. She was the subject of court cases when her parents sought to have her respirator turned off. Paul Brophy was a fire fighter who fell into a coma, also as a result of extensive brain damage, and was also the subject of legal action when his wife sought to have his feeding tube removed. A court order permitted the Quinlans to have the respirator removed from their comatose daughter, who ironically, continued to live in that state for a number of years. The Massachusetts Supreme Court ruled in favor of Mrs. Brophy, and her husband was removed from the hospital that had refused to stop feeding him; he died of pneumonia eight days later.

33. Andrew H. Malcolm, "Choosing to Die," *New York Times Book Review*.

34. *Random House College Dictionary*, ed. Jess Stein, revised edition, Random House, New York, 1975.

35. Edwin S. Shneidman, quoted in the pamphlet *Suicide: The Will to Die*, National Association of Blue Shield Plans, 1973.

36. Lynn Ann DeSpelder and Albert Strickland, *The Last Dance: Encountering Death and Dying*, Mayfield Publishing Company, Palo Alto, Calif., 1983.

37. Edwin S. Shneidman, quoted in Ibid.

38. Anne Fadiman, "The Liberation of Lolly and Gronky," *Life*, December 1986.

39. Ibid.

40. Susan J. Smith, "A Matter of Life & Death," *Times-Union*, Rochester, N.Y., October 29, 1986.

41. Ignace Lepp, *Death and Its Mysteries*, trans. Bernard Murchland, The Macmillan Company, New York, 1968.

42. Quoted in *Encyclopaedia of Religion and Ethics*, ed. James Hastings, Charles Scribner's Sons, 1951, Vol. 12.

43. Ibid.

44. Ibid.

45. Ananda K. Coomaraswamy, *Buddha and the Gospel of Buddhism*, G. P. Putnam's Sons, New York, 1916.

46. *Encyclopaedia of Religion and Ethics*, op. cit.

47. *Suicide: The Will to Die*, op. cit.

48. *Random House College Dictionary*, op. cit.

49. Sy Safransky, *The Sun*, Issue 148.

50. Susan J. Smith, "In the Era of the 'Negotiated Death,' When to Start—and End—Treatment?" *Times-Union*, Rochester, N.Y., October 27, 1986.

51. "Is It Wrong to Cut Off Feeding?" *Time* magazine, February 23, 1987.

52. "Back from the Dead," *Time* magazine, October 6, 1986.

53. "Euthanasia and Religion," *Times-Union*, Rochester, N.Y., October 31, 1986.

54. James Rachels, *The End of Life: Euthanasia and Morality*, Oxford University Press, New York, 1986, as reviewed in "Choosing to Die," op. cit.

55. Quoted in Sandol Stoddard, *The Hospice Movement: A Better Way to Care for the Dying*, op. cit.

56. Quoted in Ibid.

57. Adapted from Philip Kapleau, *The Wheel of Death*, George Allen & Unwin, Ltd., London, 1972.

58. One of the most admired of Zen writings, written by the Third Zen Patriarch, Seng Tsan. This English translation was done by members of The Zen Center, Rochester, N.Y.

59. Quoted in *High Holiday Prayer Book*, ed. Morris Silverman, Prayer Book Press, Hartford, Conn., 1939.

60. From the Book of Psalms, *The Holy Bible*.

61. Lama Anagarika Govinda, *Foundations of Tibetan Mysticism*, E. P. Dutton, New York, 1960.

62. Quoted in Richard Blodgett, "Our Wild, Weird World of Coincidence," *Reader's Digest*, September 1987.

63. Michael Talbot, "Does Objective Reality Exist, or Is the Universe a Phantasm?" *The Village Voice*, September 22, 1987.

64. "Dying: The Last Taboo," a British Broadcasting Company television program.

65. Zen master Bassui, quoted in *The Three Pillars of Zen*, op. cit.

66. Deborah Whiting Little, *Home Care for the Dying*, Dial Press/Doubleday, Garden City, N. Y., 1985.

67. Dr. John La Puma, writing in *Archives of Neurology*, January 1988.

68. From an audio tape made by Dr. Richard Lamm and issued by St. Christopher's Hospice, Sydenham, England.

69. *Symptom Control in Far Advanced Cancer: Pain Relief*, op. cit.

70. Patrick Irvine, M.D., "Sounding Board: The Attending at the Funeral," *The New England Journal of Medicine*, June 27, 1985.

71. Ernest Morgan, *A Manual of Death Education and Simple Burial*, 10th edition, revised and expanded, Celo Press, Burnsville, N.C., 1984.

72. David Owen, "Rest in Pieces," *Harper's*, June 1983.

73. Lisa Carlson, *Caring for Your Own Dead*, Upper Access Publishers, Hinesburg, Vt., 1987.

74. Quoted in Editors of Consumers Reports, *Funerals: Consumers' Last Rights*, W. W. Norton & Co., Inc., New York, 1977.

75. Ibid.

76. From an NFCA pamphlet, *With the Body Present*, quoted in *Funerals: Consumers' Last Rights*, op. cit.

77. Quoted in Glenn H. Mullin, *Death and Dying: The Tibetan Tradition*, Arkana, Boston, 1986.

78. Paul E. Irion, *Cremation*, Fortress Press, Philadelphia, 1968.

79. Ibid.

80. Ibid.

81. Emanuel Thorne and Gilah Langner, "The Body's Value Has Gone Up: Who Should Profit from Organs?" *The New York Times*, September 8, 1986.

82. An article in *Insight*, January 18, 1988, states: "To ensure that U.S. citizens who need transplant organs are not being passed over in favor of patients in other countries, the United Network for Organ Sharing has set restrictions for hospitals receiving organs through its computer network . . . Any center found to be supplying more than 10% of its organs to people outside the U.S. will be investigated by the network's Committee on Foreign Relations . . ."

83. See "The Key Figure Is the Organ Donor," *Santa Fe Reporter*, April 9, 1986.

84. Joe Queenan, "A Send-off from This 'Vale of Tears,' " *The New York Times*, November 1, 1987.

85. Ambrose Bierce, *The Devil's Dictionary*, Hill and Wang, New York, 1957.

86. *The Religions of Man*, op. cit.

87. Lyall Watson, *The Romeo Error: A Matter of Life and Death*, Doubleday & Company, Inc., Garden City, N.Y., 1975.

88. As rebirth within forty-nine days is not fixed, in many Buddhist countries the services are repeated at specific intervals beyond the end of the sixth week up to a period of fifty years.

89. A word derived from "cremation" and "remains," which is becoming increasingly accepted in general English usage.

90. The names of all the deceased in these sections have been changed.

91. Adapted from a Japanese poem, author unknown.

92. These verses are an abbreviated version of the full text and convey its core meaning.

93. On the level of transcendental wisdom.

94. The elements of existence.

95. Quoted in *The Wheel of Death*, op. cit.

96. Hakuun Yasutani, *Eight Bases of Beliefs in Buddhism*, trans. Eido Tai Shimano, Youval Tal Ltd., Jerusalem, 1966.

97. "The Blending of Religion and Medicine," *The Christian Science Monitor*, December 29, 1987.

98. Adapted from "The White-Cloud Fox," *Buddhist Stories for Young and Old*, by Ven. Sumangalo, Poh Ern Monastery, Singapore, 1960.

99. Arthur Osborne, *Ramana Maharshi and the Path of Self-knowledge*, Rider & Company, London, 1963.

THREE: KARMA

1. According to classical Indian philosophy rooted in Hinduism, the wheel of life contains twelve spokes: (1) ignorance (blindness to the true nature of existence) leads to (2) karma-producing actions; these actions lead to (3) consciousness; consciousness leads to (4) material form and mental functions; material form and mental functions lead to (5) the six senses (the faculties of thinking, seeing, hearing, smelling, tasting, and feeling); the six senses lead to (6) contact; contact leads to (7) sensation; sensation leads to (8) craving; craving leads to (9) clinging; clinging leads to (10) formation of being; formation of being leads to (11) birth; birth leads to old age

and (12) death—and it starts all over again. In these twelve links or cycles of causation and becoming, it is impossible to say which one is the first cause, because the twelve make a circle, a wheel. Circles, of course, have no beginning and no end.

2. Ananda K. Coomaraswamy, *Buddha and the Gospel of Buddhism*, G. P. Putnam's Sons, New York, 1916.

3. John Walters, *The Essence of Buddhism*, Thomas Y. Crowell, New York, 1964.

4. D. T. Suzuki, *Outlines of Mahayana Buddhism*, Schocken Books, New York, 1963.

5. Francis Dojun Cook, *How to Raise an Ox*, Center Publications, Los Angeles, 1978.

6. Garma C. C. Chang, *The Buddhist Teaching of Totality*, Pennsylvania State University Press, University Park, Pa., and London, 1971.

7. Quoted in Philip Kapleau, *The Wheel of Death*, George Allen & Unwin, Ltd., London, 1972.

8. Narada Thera, *The Buddha and His Teachings*, Vajrirama, Colombo, Sri Lanka, 1964.

9. Lynn Rosellini, "Learning to Live Again," *Reader's Digest*, May 1986.

10. Zenkei Shibayama, *Zen Comments on the Mumonkan*, Harper & Row, New York, 1974.

11. Junjiro Takakusu, *Essentials of Buddhist Philosophy*, ed. Wing-tsit Chan and Charles A. Moore, 3rd edition, Office Appliance Co., Ltd., Honolulu, 1956.

12. Adapted from *The Wheel of Death*, op. cit.

13. *The Buddhist Teaching of Totality*, op. cit.

14. The ideas are that discarnate consciousness can produce a change in the objective world through the power of karma, which is ever at work among all sentient beings—and that by the power of karma there are certain relationships created in the external world. Birth itself is conceived as really due, not to an external power which produces it, but to the inner working of the karma principle—the principle of cause and effect—which produces the state of consciousness in human beings on their being born into the world. In other words, the world of form is nothing less than the product of mind considered individually or collectively. Most of the environment of men is due to their individual karma, but there is also a collective, or social, karma at work as well; taken together, these two types of karma explain the existence of the world as we know it. See Coates and Ishizuka, *Honen's Life and Teaching*, Chionin, Kyoto, 1925.

15. Tadeusz Borowski, "The Death of Schillinger," in *In a Dark*

Time, ed. Robert Jay Lifton and Nicholas Humphrey, Harvard University Press, Cambridge, Mass., 1984.

16. J. Glenn Gray, *The Warriors*, Harper Colophon Books, New York, 1970.

17. Arthur J. Dyck, *On Human Care*, Abingdon Press, Nashville, Tenn., 1977.

18. Susan J. Smith, "Kidney Dialysis: Learning to Accept a Life of Limitations," *Times-Union*, Rochester, N.Y., October 29, 1986.

19. Quoted in John C. H. Wu, *The Golden Age of Zen*, United Publishing Center, Taipei, Taiwan, 1975.

20. Quoted in *The Wheel of Death*, op. cit.

21. Quoted in *Family Circle*, October 1, 1987.

22. Arthur Osborne, *Ramana Maharshi and the Path of Self-knowledge*, Rider & Company, London, 1963.

23. *Zen Comments on the Mumonkan*, op. cit.

24. Quoted in "Goblins and Bad Girls," *New York Times Book Review*, April 3, 1988.

25. Huston Smith, Introduction to *The Three Pillars of Zen*, by Philip Kapleau, Anchor Press/Doubleday, Garden City, N.Y., 1980.

FOUR: REBIRTH

1. See "phoenix" in "A Note on the Drawings."

2. Henry David Thoreau, *The Writings of Henry David Thoreau*, Houghton Mifflin, Cambridge, Mass., 1894.

3. Hakuun Yasutani, *Eight Bases of Beliefs in Buddhism*, trans. Eido Tai Shimano, Youval Tal Ltd., Jerusalem, 1966.

4. *The Tibetan Book of the Dead*, W. Y. Evans-Wentz, trans., 3rd edition, Oxford University Press, London, 1957.

5. John Blofeld, *The Wheel of Life*, Shambala, Berkeley, Calif., 1972.

6. Sir James Frazer, *Belief in Immortality*, The Macmillan Co., New York, 1913.

7. George Gallup, Jr., with William Proctor, *Adventures in Immortality*, McGraw-Hill Book Co., New York, 1982.

8. *Encyclopaedia of Religion and Ethics*, ed. Rabbi Moses Gaster, Scribner's Sons, Hames Hasting, N.Y., 1955, Vol. 12, quoted in *Reincarnation: The Phoenix Fire Mystery*, ed. Joseph Head and S. L. Cranston, Julian Press/Crown Publishers, Inc., New York, 1977.

9. William Ralph Inge (1860–1954), English theologian; dean of St. Paul's Cathedral, London, 1911–34.

10. John Blofeld, *The Zen Teaching of Hui Hai*, Samuel Weiser, New York, 1972.

11. Quoted in *Reincarnation: The Phoenix Fire Mystery*, op. cit.

12. These thoughts or mental processes result from our conscious awareness of external or internal stimuli. Eastern psychology identifies seventeen stages in the thought process. They consist of (1) the unconscious, which can be likened to someone in a deep, dreamless sleep; (2) vibrations of the unconscious, which take place during sleep when the senses receive stimulation from an external object, or in the waking state between conscious thoughts; (3) arrest of the unconscious, which happens when the unconscious is stopped and the conscious arises, but the catalyst is not yet recognized; (4) thought-moment, which is the vague awareness of a disturbance from any stimulus; (5) fivefold consciousness, which is consciousness relating to a particular sense, that is, what appears is merely sensed; (6) reception, in which the sensed stimulus is received; (7) investigation, or the discriminating intellect, which investigates the stimulus; (8) decision, when a decision is made with regard to the stimulus; (9–15) thought impulses, full perception, introspection, and action, the stages during which conscious decisions can be made with regard to a particular course of action—these stages are the point at which we create karma; (16–17) registration of the experience, which occurs only if the impression was very strong. Adapted from V. F. Gunaratna, *Rebirth Explained*, The Wheel Publications No. 167/169, Buddhist Publication Society, Kandy, Sri Lanka, 1971.

13. Francis Story, *The Case for Rebirth*, The Wheel Publications No. 12/13, Buddhist Publication Society, Kandy, Sri Lanka, 1959.

14. Francis Story, "Rebirth and the Western Thinker," *Light of the Dhamma*, Vol. 5, No. 2, April 1958. (*Dhamma* is the Pali rendering of the Sanskrit work *Dharma*.)

15. T. R. V. Murti, "Radhakrishnan and Buddhism," in *The Philosophy of Sarvepalli Radhakrishnan*, Tudor Publishing Co., New York, 1952.

16. Ananda K. Coomaraswamy, *Buddha and the Gospel of Buddhism*, G. P. Putnam's Sons, New York, 1916.

17. Adapted from John Bowker, *The Problems of Suffering in Religions of the World*, Cambridge University Press, London, 1970.

18. Gary Zukav, *The Dancing Wu Li Masters: An Overview of the New Physics*, Bantam Books, New York, 1980.

19. Robert Jastrow, *God and the Astronomers*, Warner Books, New York, 1980.

20. Jung Young Lee, *Death and Beyond in the Eastern Perspective*, Gordon & Breach, New York, 1979.

21. Swami Vivekananda, *The Yogas and Other Works*. Vivekananda was the most distinguished disciple of Sri Ramakrishna and founder of the Ramakrishna (Vedanta) Order in America.

22. *The Questions of King Milinda*, trans. T. W. Rhys Davids, Dover Publications, New York, 1963, Part 1.

23. *Rebirth Explained*, op. cit.

24. Joe Fisher, *The Case for Reincarnation*, Bantam Books, New York, 1985.

25. Lama Anagarika Govinda, *Foundations of Tibetan Mysticism*, E. P. Dutton, New York, 1960.

26. Ian Stevenson, M.D., *Twenty Cases Suggestive of Reincarnation*, American Society for Psychical Research, New York, 1966.

27. From an interview with Ian Stevenson in *OMNI*, January 1988.

28. This phenomenon, called *xenoglossy*, is extremely rare, but there are a number of well-documented cases of both children and adults who have displayed this ability. In some cases the language spoken was an obscure ancient tongue known only to a few linguists.

29. From Zen master Dōgen, *Shobogenzo*, trans. Francis Dojun Cook, in *How to Raise an Ox*, Center Publications, Los Angeles, 1978.

30. From a letter to Madeleine Slade, quoted in *Reincarnation: The Phoenix Fire Mystery*, op. cit.

31. Owen Rutter, *The Scales of Karma*, quoted in Christmas Humphreys, *Karma and Rebirth*, Curzon Press, London, 1983.

32. Max Müller, *Three Lectures on the Vedanta Philosophy*, Longman, Green, London, 1984, quoted in *Reincarnation: The Phoenix Fire Mystery*, op. cit.

33. Quoted in *Reincarnation: The Phoenix Fire Mystery*, op. cit.

34. "Rebirth and the Western Thinker," op. cit.

35. *Twenty Cases Suggestive of Reincarnation*, op. cit.

36. G. H. Beale, lecturer in genetics, Edinburgh University, quoted in *The Case for Rebirth*, op. cit.

37. *The Case for Rebirth*, op. cit.

38. Private communication February 1988, Barbara Handelin, Ph.D.

39. *Rebirth Explained*, op. cit.

40. Leslie D. Weatherhead, *The Case for Reincarnation*, reprint of a lecture given to the City Temple Literary Society, New York, 1957.

41. From an article by Michael Geczi in the *Wisconsin State Journal*, July 6, 1986.

42. From an article in *Newsweek*, July 12, 1976.

43. Ibid.

44. Swami Paramananda, *Reincarnation and Immortality*, The Vedanta Centre, Cohasset, Mass., 1961.

FIVE: SUPPLEMENTS

1. Derek Humphrey and Ann Wickett, *The Right to Die: Understanding Euthanasia*, Harper & Row, New York, 1986.

2. David McQuay, "Life in Limbo: Coma," *The Sunday Denver Post*, July 21, 1985.

3. A Legal Guide to the Living Will, quoted in "The Right-to-Die Controversy," *Changing Times*, July 1984.

4. Ibid.

5. Ibid.

6. Andrew H. Malcolm, "AIDS Brings Expanded Debate on Rights of the Terminally Ill," *The New York Times*.

7. David McQuay, "A One-in-a-Million Miracle," *The Sunday Denver Post*, July 21, 1985.

8. This group also publishes an updated "Legal Guide to the Living Will."

9. Drawn up by ethician Sissela Bok in *The New England Journal of Medicine* and reprinted in the magazine *America*, September 5, 1981.

10. Cicely Saunders, M.D., director of St. Christopher's Hospice near London, quoted in Sandol Stoddard, *The Hospice Movement: A Better Way to Care for the Dying*, Vintage Books, New York, 1978. This supplement is heavily indebted to Stoddard's fine book, which is highly recommended to anyone wishing to learn more about the hospice movement.

11. Ibid.

12. Ibid.

13. Ibid.

14. From W. M. Markel and V. B. Simon, "The Hospice Concept," *Ca-A Cancer Journal for Clinicians*, Vol. 28, No. 4, 1978; and Sylvia A. Lack, "Philosophy and Organization of a Hospice Program," available from the Hospice of Metro Denver, Denver, Colo.

15. *The Hospice Movement: A Better Way to Care for the Dying*, op. cit.

16. *Ca-A Cancer Journal for Clinicians*, op. cit.

17. Ernest Morgan, *A Manual of Death Education and Simple Burial*, 10th edition, revised and expanded, Celo Press, Burnsville, N.C.

18. Deborah Whiting Little, *Home Care for the Dying*, Dial Press/Doubleday, Garden City, N.Y., 1985.

19. Compiled by the Compassionate Friends, an organization of families who have lost children.

20. Thich Nhat Hanh, Buddhist monk and peace activist.

21. For detailed descriptions and illustrations of various meditation postures and their significance, see Philip Kapleau, *The Three Pillars of Zen*, revised and expanded edition, Anchor Press/Doubleday, Garden City, N.Y., 1980.

GLOSSARY

Abbreviations: *Skt.: Sanskrit; Ch.: Chinese; Sp.: Spanish; J.: Japanese; Tib: Tibetan*

Ars Moriendi (The Art of Dying): a medieval text on dying, reprinted in part in the modern book *The Craft of Dying*.

bardo (Tib.): the intermediate state between clinical death and rebirth. See also "The Intermediate Realm."

becoming: stands against "being"; constant change.

birth and death: see *samsāra*.

bodhisattva (Skt.): literally, "wisdom being"; a spiritually awakened individual who, having attained enlightenment, dedicates himself or herself to helping others do the same.

Buddha (Skt.): a word used in two senses: (1) ultimate Truth or absolute Mind, and (2) one awakened or enlightened to the true nature of existence. *The* Buddha refers to a historical person with the given name of Siddhartha and the family name of Gautama, who was born around the year 563 B.C. He was the son of the ruler of the Shakyas, whose small kingdom lay at the foothills of present-day Nepal. Siddhartha was married at sixteen and had a son, who later became his disciple. At the age of thirty-five, after six years of hard search and struggle, Siddhartha became supremely enlightened. Thereafter, until his death at eighty, he preached to all who would listen, always suiting his exposition to the capacity of his hearers' understanding. He is regarded by Buddhists neither as a supreme deity nor as a savior, but is venerated as a fully awakened, fully perfected human being who attained liberation of body and mind through his own human efforts.

Buddhism: or more precisely, the way of the Buddha. It has two main branches: the Theravada, mainly found in Southeast Asia, and the Mahayana. The latter arose in India, whence it spread to Tibet, Mongolia, China, Korea, and Japan. Zen is a sect of the Mahayana.

calaveras (Sp.): "living" skeletons; in the Mexican culture *calaveras* are beings who are alive but in another dimension.

chanting: intoning of religious works in a blend of harmonic monotones. To be effective, chanting must be clear, wholehearted, and concentrated, with the voices of the various chanters merging harmoniously.

cremains: a word entering common usage, coined from "cremation" and "remains," to denote the remains of a person whose body has been cremated.

Dharma (Skt.): a fundamental Buddhist term having several meanings, the broadest of which is "phenomenon." All phenomena are subject to the law of causation, and this fundamental truth comprises the core of the Buddha's message.

Dukkha (Skt.): a word frequently translated as "suffering" or "unsatisfactoriness," but implying much more: pain, grief, affliction, distress, or frustration.

Egyptian *Book of the Dead:* one of several ancient Egyptian texts dealing with death and the hereafter.

enlightenment, Self-realization, awakening: spiritual awakening to one's True-nature and to the Truth lying beyond all dualism and discrimination. This term has no connection with the eighteenth-century philosophic movement.

ESP: extrasensory (paranormal) perception.

Essential-nature: see **True-nature.**

euthanasia: originally an easy and painless death; now refers chiefly to "the art or method of causing death painlessly so as to end suffering."

five aggregates, five *skandhas:* form, sensation, perception, mental formations, and consciousness. See also "The Evolution of Ego."

Four Noble Truths: (1) The Universality of Suffering, (2) The Causes of Suffering, (3) The Cessation of Suffering, and (4) The Path Leading to the Cessation of Suffering. See also "The Dilemma of Pain."

hospice: originally a medieval place of shelter for travelers, pilgrims, and the sick, often run by monks or nuns; now either a residential facility or home care for the terminally ill. Hospice programs in the United States generally accept only those patients with six months or less to live. See also Supplement 2: "The Hospice Movement."

karma: literally, "doing" or "acting"; our thoughts and actions and the consequences flowing from them; cause and effect. See also "Karma" section.

koan (J., pronounced "ko-an"; Ch. *kung-an):* in Zen, a formulation, in baffling language, pointing to ultimate Truth.

mantra: a sacred sound or syllable used to meditate on. See also *Om.*

meditation: from the Latin *meditatio,* a "thinking over," "contemplation." There are many kinds of meditation, but essentially the term denotes one-pointed concentration on a sacred word or image that is visualized, or on a concept (such as God or love) that is thought about or reflected on, or both.

metempsychosis: transmigration; the passing of a soul after death into some other body, either human or animal.

myth: not an untrue story, but a truth so majestic, so all-encompassing that it cannot be embraced within mere fact. For Joseph Campbell, author of *The Power of Myth,* it is "a metaphor for what lies behind the visible world."

mystic: according to *Webster's New World Dictionary,* "a person who professes to undergo mystical experiences by which he intuitively comprehends truths beyond human understanding." In Zen a mystic is one who has awakened to the nonduality of the world of phenomena and the world of no-form, and whose life has been transformed by this unique experience.

nirvāṇa (Skt.): extinction of ignorance and craving, and awakening to inner peace and freedom. *Nirvāṇa* (with a small *n*) stands against *saṃsāra,* that is, birth and death. See also "Gautama the Buddha."

Noble Eightfold Path: the Buddha's formula leading to awakening. See also "The Dilemma of Pain."

no-mindedly: with the mind totally void of random or distracting thoughts.

Om (Skt.), also spelled *Aum:* a sound-symbol of the energy powering the universe—the energy of which all things are a manifestation; an object of religious meditation to harness cartain energies for healing or enlightenment purposes.

oneness: with a small *o*, absorption to the point of self-forgetfulness. With a capital *O*, the experience of the Void, or no-thing–ness.

palingenesis: from the Greek *palin*, "again," and *genesis*, "generation"; the doctrine of successive rebirths.

parinirvāṇa (Skt.): literally, complete extinction of craving and ego. *Parinirvāṇa* usually refers to the state of perfect emancipation reached by Gautama the Buddha upon his passing away. See also "Gautama the Buddha."

reincarnation: rebirth of a soul in another body. See also "Rebirth Distinguished from Reincarnation."

repentance: in the Christian tradition, connected with sin, remorse, condemnation. In Buddhism, sin is ignorance of the true nature of existence; repentance is deep regret for one's basic ignorance and the determination to overcome it.

Roshi (J.): a title in the Zen sect that means, literally, "venerable teacher" or "master." It implies long training and the approval to teach of one's own teacher.

samadhi power: the energy that arises through the complete absorption of the mind in itself; heightened and expanded awareness; a state of intense yet effortless concentration. See also "What Is Samadhi?"

saṃsāra (Skt.): birth and death; the world of relativity, of impermanence, of constant change.

Self, original Self: see **True-nature**.

shunyata (Skt.): the viable Void. See also "True-nature Is Not Soul."

skandhas (Skt.): see "**five aggregates**."

soul: "generally taken to mean the sum total of an individual personality, an enduring ego-entity that exists more or less independently of the physical body and survives it after death . . . the 'soul' is considered to be the personality-factor which distinguishes one individual from another . . ." —Francis Story

Sri (Skt.): a Hindu title of address, equivalent to the English "Mr."; also, an honorific title applied to a religious or spiritual teacher in the Hindu tradition.

tanha (Skt.): commonly translated as "thirst for," "craving," "desire." See also "The Four Noble Truths of Suffering."

Tao (Ch.): see "**Way**."

Tathagata (Skt.): the appellation the Buddha used in referring to himself. It literally means "Thus-come," the "Thus" indicating the enlightened state.

Tibetan *Book of the Dead:* a traditional Tibetan text of instructions for the dead and dying. According to Tibetan tradition, it is the work of the ancient sage Padmasambhava; it tells how to prepare oneself for death and the passage to rebirth.

transmigration: the passing of a soul into another body after death. See also "Rebirth Distinguished from Reincarnation."

True-nature: see "True-nature Is Not Soul."

Visuddhimagga: a text written in the fifth century A.D. by Buddhaghosa, a Buddhist monk-teacher.

Way, Tāo: the fundamental principle and reality of the universe; ultimate Truth. See also "True-nature Is Not Soul."

Zen (J.): an abbreviation of *Zenna*, which is a transliteration of the Chinese *Channa* (or *Chan),* which in turn is a transliteration of the Sanskrit *Dhyana*. This last has many meanings in Hinduism; in Zen Buddhism, however, the term Zen generally refers to the cultivation, chiefly through meditation, of one-pointedness, stillness, and stability of the body-mind.

Zen Buddhism: a sect of Buddhism that is free of dogmas and creeds and whose teachings emphasize the fundamental, personal experience of awakening and its integration into one's life.

Zen master: a person of deep, awakened understanding and compassion who has integrated his understanding into his life and whose actions reflect this.

AUTHOR'S NOTE

Without the active support and help of many friends, this book would not have come into being. In particular, I'm grateful to Dr. Peter Auhagen, who encouraged and prodded me to undertake the extensive revision and expansion of the slim ancestor to the present volume—*The Wheel of Death*. I also want to thank him for the many medical books on death, dying, and pain that he supplied me with, all of which were valuable in my research. In our free-ranging discussions of these subjects we were often joined by his wife, Dr. Christina Auhagen, and the Ven. Bodhin Kjolhede, the present abbot of The Zen Center, Rochester, New York. The ideas that surfaced in these bull sessions became the building blocks for the structure of the book.

My debt to the Ven. Sunyana Graef is considerable. An authorized teacher of Zen Buddhism with twenty years of training, she was an indefatigable collaborator in the preparation of the sections on karma and rebirth. Were it not for her able assistance, these important sections of *The Wheel of Life and Death* would not be nearly as complete as I believe them now to be.

The Ven. Mitra Mello has worked long and arduously through the many stages of this book. Besides acting as my secretary, she carried out research, wrote the first draft of portions of the book, was a friendly critic, and data-processed the whole text. I'm exceedingly grateful to her for her unstinting efforts.

Tom Roberts, my longtime friend and attorney, did a yeoman's job in overseeing many aspects of the book, from handling of the contractual arrangements to participating in the editing of the manuscript. Because of his perceptive comments and criticisms, this book is much better than it otherwise would have been. I can't thank him enough for his tireless exertions.

In their reading of the manuscript of *The Wheel of Life and Death*, Chris Pulleyn, Donna Jacobs, Ken Kraft, Dr. Mary Wolfe, Michael Millard, Rafe Martin, deLancey Kapleau, and Allan Clevenger pruned much excessive verbiage, refined a number of ungainly sentences, and offered suggestions that have had a strong influence on the present form of the book. I am enormously grateful to them.

Thanks are due Greg Mello for his excellent draft of the biography of Socrates and his article on the hospice movement.

To supplement my limited involvement with dying patients, I consulted a number of health care professionals. They include Drs. Leonard Wheeler, Jon Sheldon, Maike Otto, and Robert Goldmann, all of whom took time from busy schedules to tell me about their experiences with dying patients. The following people generously gave of their time in answering my many questions about terminally ill patients: nurses Penny Townsend, Geoffrey Lister, Carolyn Jaffe, Nathan Hanks and Jeffrey Estes, and pharmacist David Vandertie. My deepest thanks to all of them for their pertinent comments, all of which were of great value in enabling me to round out the section on dying.

Patricia Meyer made a substantial contribution to the book at an early stage—aiding in the coordination of research, operating the data processor, and attending to many secretarial duties. I thank her for her conscientious labors.

Lastly, I wish to express my thanks to Marjorie Miller, director of the Life Center for Attitudinal Healing in Santa Fe, New Mexico, who kindly made available to me audio- and videotapes of certain clients of her center.

In expressing my profound gratitude to all of the people who have aided me in this (largely) labor of love, I absolve them of responsibility for any deficiencies that may appear in the book. These last are exclusively my own.

BIBLIOGRAPHY

DEATH AND DYING

ARTICLES, PAMPHLETS, REPORTS:

Abe, Masao, "The Problem of Death in East and West," *The Eastern Buddhist*, Vol. 19, No. 2, Autumn 1986.

"Back from the Dead," *Time*, October 6, 1986.

"The Barbie Trial: J'Accuse," *Newsweek*, May 11, 1987.

"The Blending of Religion and Medicine," *The Christian Science Monitor*, December 29, 1987.

Blodgett, Richard, "Our Wild, Weird World of Coincidence," *Reader's Digest*, September 1987.

Bond, George, "Buddhist Meditations on Death," *The History of Religions*, Vol. 19, No. 3, February 1980.

Borg, Marcus, "Death as the Teacher of Wisdom," *Christian Century*, February 26, 1986.

"Concentration and Euphoria: Mind Functioning at Peak Can Produce Altered States," *The New York Times*, March 10, 1986.

Deciding to Forego Life-sustaining Treatment, President's Commission for the Study of Ethical Problems in Medicine and Biomedical and Behavioral Research, 1983, reprinted by Concern for Dying, New York.

Earnshaw-Smith, Elisabeth, "Emotional Pain in Dying Patients and Their Families," *Nursing Times*, November 3, 1982.

"Euthanasia and Religion," *Times-Union*, Rochester, N.Y., October 31, 1986.

Fadiman, Anne, "The Liberation of Lolly and Gronky," *Life*, December 1986.

"First Do No Harm: The Making of a Neurosurgeon," *Reader's Digest*, November 1987.

Garfield, Charles A., "Consciousness Alteration and Fear of Death," *Journal of Transpersonal Psychology*, Vol. 7, No. 2, 1975.

Goleman, Daniel, "The Mind over the Body," *The New York Times*, September 27, 1987.

Holden, Ted, "Patiently Speaking," *Nursing Times*, June 12, 1980.

Hunt, Morton, "Body and Mind," *The New York Times*, March 27, 1988.

Irvine, Patrick, M.D., "Sounding Board: The Attending at the Funeral," *The New England Journal of Medicine*, June 27, 1985.

"Is It Wrong to Cut Off Feeding?" *Time*, February 23, 1987.

Kahawai, Vol. 6, No. 1, Winter 1984.

"The Key Figure Is the Organ Donor," *Santa Fe Reporter*, April 9, 1986.

Khantipalo, Bhikku, *The Wheel of Birth and Death*, The Wheel Publications No. 147/148/149, Buddhist Publication Society, Kandy, Sri Lanka, 1970.

Kushner, Harold S., "Why I Am Not Afraid to Die," *Reader's Digest*, August 1986.

"The Nature and Nurture of Pain Control," *World Medicine*, February 21, 1984.

"One Against the Plague," *Newsweek*, July 21, 1986.

Osis, Karlis, "Deathbed Observations by Physicians and Nurses," *Journal of the American Society for Psychical Research*, October 1963.

Owen, David, "Rest in Pieces," *Harper's*, June 1983.

Parabola: Myth and the Quest for Meaning, Vol. 2, No. 1, Winter 1977.

Queenan, Joe, "A Send-off from This 'Vale of Tears,' " *The New York Times*, November 1, 1987.

Santmire, H. Paul, "Nothing More Beautiful than Death?" *Christian Century*, December 14, 1983.

Smith, Susan J., "In the Era of the 'Negotiated Death,' When to Start—and End—Treatment?" *Times-Union*, Rochester, N.Y., October 27, 1986.

———, "A Matter of Life & Death," *Times-Union*, Rochester, N.Y., October 29, 1986.

———, "When Prolonging a Life Prolongs Suffering," *Times-Union*, Rochester, N.Y., October 28, 1986.

Suicide: The Will to Die, National Association of Blue Shield Plans, 1973.

Twycross, Robert G., *Principles and Practice of Pain Relief in Terminal Cancer*, Sir Michael Sobell House, Churchill Hospital, Headington, Oxford, 0X3 7LJ, England.

BOOKS:

Books that are especially recommended are indicated with an asterisk.

*Abe, Masao, *Zen and Western Thought,* ed. William R. LaFleur, University of Hawaii Press, Honolulu, 1985.

Allen, John, ed., *One Hundred Great Lives,* Greystone Press, New York, 1948.

Anderson, Ray S., *Theology, Death and Dying,* Basil Blackwell, Oxford and New York, 1986.

Anthony, Dick, Bruce Ecker, and Ken Wilber, eds., *Spiritual Choices,* Paragon House Publishers, New York, 1987.

*Ariés, Philippe, *Western Attitudes Toward Death,* trans. Patricia M. Ranum, The Johns Hopkins University Press, Baltimore, 1974.

Bankei, *The Life and Teaching of Zen Master Bankei,* Introduction by Norman Waddell, North Point Press, Berkeley, Calif., 1984.

Bendit, Laurence J., *The Mirror of Life and Death,* 2nd edition, The Theosophical Publishing House, Wheaton, Ill., 1968.

Birnbaum, Raoul, *The Healing Buddha,* Shambala, Boulder, Colo., 1979.

*Blofeld, John, *The Zen Teaching of Hui Hai,* Samuel Weiser, New York, 1972.

*Bowker, John, *The Problems of Suffering in Religions of the World,* Cambridge University Press, London, 1970.

Brown, Norman O., *Love's Body,* Random House, New York, 1966.

Budge, E. A. Wallis, trans., *The Egyptian Book of the Dead,* Dover Publications, Inc., New York, 1967.

*Carlson, Lisa, *Caring for Your Own Dead,* Upper Access Publishers, Hinesburg, Vt., 1987.

Carse, James P., *Death and Existence,* John Wiley & Sons, New York, 1980.

*Chang, Garma C. C., *The Buddhist Teaching of Totality,* Pennsylvania State University Press, University Park, Pa., and London, 1977.

Childress, J. F., and J. Macquarrie, eds., *The Westminster Dictionary of Christian Ethics,* Westminster Press, Philadelphia, 1986.

Conze, Edward, *Thirty Years of Buddhist Studies,* Bruno Cassirer Ltd., Oxford, 1967.

——, ed., *Buddhist Texts Through the Ages,* Philosophical Library, New York, 1954.

*Cook, Francis Dojun, *How to Raise an Ox,* Center Publications, Los Angeles, 1978.

*Coomaraswamy, Ananda K., *The Buddha and the Gospel of Buddhism*, G. P. Putnam's Sons, New York, 1916.

David-Neel, Alexandra, *Buddhism: Its Doctrines and Its Methods*, Avon Books, New York, 1979.

*DeSpelder, Lynne Ann, and Albert Strickland, *The Last Dance: Encountering Death and Dying*, Mayfield Publishing Co., Palo Alto, Calif., 1983.

Dossey, Larry, M.D., *Beyond Illness*, New Science Library, Shambhala, Boston, 1984.

*Editors of Consumer Reports, *Funerals: Consumers' Last Rights*, W. W. Norton & Co., Inc., New York, 1977.

Elias, Norbert, *The Loneliness of the Dying*, Basil Blackwell, Oxford and New York, 1985.

Engel, George, "Pain," in *MacBryde's Signs and Symptoms*, ed. Robert S. Blacklow, J. B. Lippincott Co., Philadelphia, 1983.

Evans-Wentz, W. Y., *Tibetan Yoga and Secret Doctrines*, 2nd edition, Oxford University Press, London, 1958.

———, ed., *The Tibetan Book of the Great Liberation*, Oxford University Press, London, 1954.

———, trans., *The Tibetan Book of the Dead*, 3rd edition, Oxford University Press, London, 1957.

Fairley, Peter, *The Conquest of Pain*, Charles Scribner's Sons, New York, 1978.

Ford, Charles V., M.D., *The Somatizing Disorders: Illness as a Way of Life*, Elsevier Biomedical, New York.

Frazer, Sir James, *The Golden Bough*, abridged edition, The Macmillan Co., New York, 1945.

Fremantle, Francesca, and Chogyam Trungpa, trans., *The Tibetan Book of the Dead*, Shambala, Berkeley, Calif., 1975.

Fromm, Eric, *The Heart of Man*, 2nd edition, Perennial Library, Harper & Row, New York, 1980.

Fulton, Robert, Eric Markusen, Greg Owen, and Jane L. Scheiber, ed., *Death and Dying*, Addison-Wesley Publishing Co., Reading, Mass., 1978.

Giles, Herbert A., trans., *Chuang Tzu*, George Allen & Unwin, Ltd., London, 1961.

Govinda, Lama Anagarika, *Creative Meditation and Multidimensional Consciousness*, The Theosophical Publishing House, Wheaton, Ill., 1978.

*———, *Foundations of Tibetan Mysticism*, E. P. Dutton, New York, 1960.

Gray, J. Glenn, *The Warriors*, Harper Colophon Books, New York, 1970.

Grollman, Earl, *When Your Loved One Is Dying*, Beacon Press, Boston, 1980.

———, ed., *Concerning Death: A Practical Guide for the Living*, Beacon Press, Boston, 1974.

Gunaratna, V. F., *Buddhist Reflections on Death*, The Wheel Publication No. 102/103, Buddhist Publication Society, Kandy, Sri Lanka, 1966.

Hampton, Charles, *The Transition Called Death*, The Theosophical Publishing House, Wheaton, Ill., 1979.

Harmer, Ruth Mulvey, *The High Cost of Dying*, Collier Books, New York, 1963.

Hastings, James, ed., *Encyclopaedia of Religion and Ethics*, Vol. 12, Charles Scribner's Sons, New York, 1951.

Hodson, Geoffrey, *Through the Gateway of Death*, The Theosophical Publishing House, London, 1976.

Humphrey, Derek, and Ann Wickett, *The Right to Die: Understanding Euthanasia*, Harper & Row, New York, 1986.

James, P. T., *Cover Her Face*, Warner Books, New York, 1982.

*Jung, C. G., *The Undiscovered Self*, The New American Library of World Literature, Inc., New York, 1958.

Kamath, M. V., *Philosophy of Death and Dying*, Himalayan International Institute of Yoga Science and Philosophy, Honesdale, Pa., 1978.

Kapleau, Philip, *The Wheel of Death*, George Allen & Unwin, Ltd., London, 1972.

Kierkegaard, Søren, "The Decisiveness of Death: At the Side of a Grave," in *Thoughts on Crucial Situations: Three Discourses on Imagined Occasions*, trans. David F. Swenson, 2nd edition, Augsburg Publishing House, Minneapolis, 1941.

Kothari, Manu L., and Lopa A. Mehta, *Death: A New Perspective on the Phenomena of Disease and Dying*, Marion Boyars, London and New York, 1986.

*Kübler-Ross, Elisabeth, *Death: The Final Stage of Growth*, Simon & Schuster, New York, 1986.

———, and Mal Warshaw, *To Live Until We Say Goodbye*, Prentice-Hall, Inc., Englewood Cliffs, N.J., 1978.

Ladd, John, ed., *Ethical Issues Relating to Life and Death*, Oxford University Press, New York, 1979.

*Lee, Jung Young, *Death and Beyond in the Eastern Perspective*, Gordon & Breach, New York, 1974.

*Lepp, Ignace, *Death and Its Mysteries*, trans. Bernard Murchland, The Macmillan Co., New York, 1968.

Levine, Stephen, *Who Dies?* Anchor Press/Doubleday, Garden City, N.Y., 1982.

Lewis, C. S., *The Problem of Pain*, Collins/Fontana Books, London, 1959.

*Lifton, Robert Jay, and Eric Olson, *Living and Dying*, Praeger Publishers, New York, 1974.

Lipp, Martin R., M.D., *Respectful Treatment: A Practical Handbook of Patient Care*, 2nd edition, Elsevier, New York.

*Little, Deborah Whiting, *Home Care for the Dying*, Dial Press/Doubleday, Garden City, N.Y., 1985.

Lunceford, Ron and Judy, *Attitudes on Death and Dying*, Hwong Publishing Co., Los Alamitos, Calif., 1976.

Lusseyran, Jacques, *And There Was Light*, trans. Elizabeth R. Cameron, Parabola Books, New York, 1987.

*————, *The Blind in Society* and *Blindness, A New Seeing of the World*, Proceedings No. 27, The Myrin Institute, New York.

Maguire, Daniel, *Death by Choice*, Image Books/Doubleday, Garden City, N.Y., 1984.

*Maslow, Abraham H., *Toward a Psychology of Being*, D. Van Nostrand Co., Inc., Princeton, N.J., 1962.

Maximov, Vladimir, et al., eds., *Kontinent 2*, Anchor Press/Doubleday, Garden City, N.Y., 1976.

May, Rollo, *Love and Will*, Dell, New York, 1969.

Melter, Milton, *Never to Forget: The Jews of the Holocaust*, Harper & Row, New York, 1976.

Meltzer, David, ed., *Death*, North Point Press, San Francisco, 1984.

*Melzack, Ronald, and Patrick D. Wall, *The Challenge of Pain*, revised edition, Basic Books, Inc., New York, 1983.

*Morgan, Ernest, *A Manual of Death Education and Simple Burial*, 11th edition, Celo Press, Burnsville, N.C., 1988.

Mullin, Glenn H., *Death and Dying: The Tibetan Tradition*, Arkana, Boston, 1986.

Museo Universitario, Universidad Nacional Autonoma de México, *La Muerte: Expresiones Mexicanas de un Enigma*, (Death: Mexican Expressions of an Enigma), Mexico City, 1975.

Neale, Robert E., ed., *The Art of Dying*, Harper & Row, New York, 1973.

Nelson, Leonard J., ed., *The Death Decision*, Servant Books, Ann Arbor, Mich., 1984.

Osborne, Arthur, *Ramana Maharshi and the Path of Self-knowledge*, Rider & Company, London, 1963.

Paramananda, Swami, *The Problem of Life and Death*, 2nd edition, The Vedanta Centre, Boston, 1917.

Parrish-Harra, Carol W., *A New Age Handbook on Death and Dying*, De Vorss & Co., Marina del Rey, Calif., 1982.

Pelgrin, Mark, *And a Time to Die*, ed. Sheila Moon and Elizabeth B. Howes, The Theosophical Publishing House, Wheaton, Ill., 1962.

Porath, Samuel, *Life Beyond the Final Curtain*, KTAV Publishing House, Inc., Hoboken, N.J., 1985.

Rachels, James, *The End of Life: Euthanasia and Morality*, Oxford University Press, New York, 1986.

Rawlings, Maurice, M.D., *Beyond Death's Door*, Bantam Books, New York, 1978.

Ring, Kenneth, *Life at Death*, Quill, New York, 1982.

Sabom, Michael B., M.D., *Recollections of Death*, Harper & Row, New York, 1982.

Sahler, Olle Jane Z., M.D., ed., *The Child and Death*, The C. V. Mosby Co., St. Louis, 1978.

*Saunders, Dame Cicely, M.D., "Pain and Impending Death," in *Textbook of Pain*, ed. Patrick D. Wall and Ronald Melzack, Churchill Livingstone, London, 1984.

Schwiebert, Pat, R.N., and Paul Kirk, M.D., *When Hello Means Goodbye*, University of Oregon Health Sciences Center, Portland, Ore., 1981.

*Shibayama, Zenkei, *Zen Comments on the Mumonkan*, Harper & Row, New York, 1974.

Shibles, Warren, *Death: An Interdisciplinary Analysis*, The Language Press, Whitewater, Wis., 1974.

Silverman, Morris, ed., *High Holiday Prayer Book*, Prayer Book Press, Hartford, Conn., 1939.

Simonton, O. Carl, M.D., Stephanie Matthews-Simonton, and James Creighton, *Getting Well Again*, J. P. Tarcher, Inc., Los Angeles, 1978.

Simpson, Keith, consultant, *The Mysteries of Life and Death*, ed. Martin Schultz, Crescent 1980 edition, Crown Publishers, Inc., New York.

Singh, Kirpal, *The Mystery of Death*, Ruhani Satsang, Delhi, India, 1968.

Smith, Huston, *The Religions of Man*, Harper & Row, New York, 1958.

Snellgrove, D. L., *Four Lamas of Dolpo*, Harvard University Press, Cambridge, Mass., 1967.

Spiro, Howard M., M.D., *Doctors, Patients, and Placebos*, Yale University Press, New Haven, Conn.

*Stoddard, Sandol, *The Hospice Movement: A Better Way to Care for the Dying*, Vintage Books, New York, 1978.

Strain, James J., M.D., and Stanley Grossman, M.D., *Psychological Care of the Medically Ill*, Appleton-Century-Crofts, New York.

Strauss, Maurice B., M.D., ed., *Familiar Medical Quotations*, Little, Brown and Co., Boston, 1968.

Sumangalo, Ven., *Buddhist Stories for Young and Old*, Poh Ern Monastery, Singapore, 1980.

Toynbee, Arnold, and Daisaku Ikeda, *Choose Life*, ed. Richard L. Gage, Oxford University Press, London, 1976.

Twycross, Robert G., and Sylvia A. Lack, *Symptom Control in Far Advanced Cancer: Pain Relief*, Pitman, London.

*von Franz, Marie-Louise, *On Dreams and Death*, Shambala, Berkeley, Calif., 1986.

Walshe, M. O'C., *Buddhism and Death*, English Sangha Trust Ltd., London, 1970.

Ward, Milton, *The Brilliant Function of Pain*, Optimus Books, New York, 1977.

*Watson, Lyall, *The Romeo Error: A Matter of Life and Death*, Anchor Press/Doubleday, Garden City, N.Y., 1975.

Zaleski, Carol, *Otherworld Journeys*, Oxford University Press, New York, 1987.

The following books and articles are recommended under the topic of moral philosophy and medical ethics:

Dyck, Arthur J., *On Human Care*, Abingdon Press, Nashville, Tenn., 1977.

Frankena, William K., *Ethics*, 2nd edition, Prentice Hall, Englewood Cliffs, N.J., 1973.

Kohl, Marvin, "Understanding the Case for Beneficent Euthanasia," *Science, Medicine and Man*, Vol. 1, 1973.

Reiser, Stanley, Arthur J. Dyck, and William Curran, eds., *Ethics in Medicine*, MIT Press, Cambridge, Mass., 1977. This is an anthology of considerable scope, covering many topics and containing essays by medical professionals, moral philosophers, lawyers, and religious ethicists.

Karma and Rebirth

Articles, Pamphlets, Reports:

"Goblins and Bad Girls," *New York Times Book Review,* April 3, 1988.

Gunaratna, V. F., *Rebirth Explained,* The Wheel Publications No. 167/169, Buddhist Publication Society, Kandy, Sri Lanka, 1971.

Jayatilleke, K. N., *Survival and Karma in Buddhist Perspective,* The Wheel Publications No. 141/142/143, Buddhist Publication Society, Kandy, Sri Lanka, 1969.

Nyanatiloka, Mahathera, *Karma and Rebirth,* The Wheel Publication No. 9, Buddhist Publication Society, Kandy, Sri Lanka, 1964.

"Reincarnation and Renewed Chances," *The Christian Agnostic,* Abingdon Press, Nashville, Tenn., 1965.

Rosellini, Lynn, "Learning to Live Again," *Reader's Digest,* May 1986.

Smith, Susan J., "Kidney Dialysis: Learning to Accept a Life of Limitations," *Times-Union,* Rochester, N.Y., October 29, 1986.

Stevenson, Ian, M.D., *The Evidence for Survival from Claimed Memories of Former Incarnations,* M. C. Peto, Tadworth, Surrey, England, 1961.

Story, Francis, *The Case for Rebirth,* The Wheel Publications No. 12/13, Buddhist Publication Society, Kandy, Sri Lanka, 1959.

————, "Rebirth and the Western Thinker," *Light of the Dhamma,* Vol. 5, No. 2, April 1958.

Weatherhead, Leslie D., *The Case for Reincarnation,* reprint of a lecture given to the City Temple Literary Society, New York, 1957.

Yamamoto, Kosho, "Karma," *Young East: Japanese Buddhist Quarterly,* Summer 1956.

Books:

Books especially recommended are indicated with an asterisk.

Abhedananda, Swami, *Doctrine of Karma,* 4th edition, Ramakrishna Vedanta Math, Calcutta, India, 1965.

————, *Reincarnation,* Ramakrishna Vedanta Math, Calcutta, India; distributed by Vedanta Press, Hollywood, Calif.

Aurobindo, Sri, *The Problem of Rebirth,* Sri Aurobindo Ashram, Pondicherry, India, 1952.

*Blofeld, John, *The Wheel of Life,* Shambala, Berkeley, Calif., 1972.

Borowski, Tadeusz, "The Death of Schillinger," in *In a Dark Time,* ed. Robert Jay Lifton and Nicholas Humphrey, Harvard University Press, Cambridge, Mass., 1984.

Carse, James P., *Death and Existence*, John Wiley & Sons, New York, 1980.

Carus, Paul, *The Dharma*, The Open Court Publishing Co., La Salle, Ill., 1943.

————, *Karma/Nirvana*, The Open Court Publishing Co., La Salle, Ill., 1973.

Cerminara, Gina, *Many Lives, Many Loves*, William Sloane Associates, Inc., New York, 1963.

*————, *Many Mansions*, William Sloane Associates, Inc., New York, 1950.

*Chang, Garma C. C., *The Buddhist Teaching of Totality*, Pennsylvania State University Press, University Park, Pa., and London, 1977.

Ch'en, Kenneth K. S., *Buddhism: The Light of Asia*, Barron's Educational Series, Inc., Woodbury, N.Y., 1968.

Conze, Edward, ed., *Buddhist Texts Through the Ages*, Philosophical Library, New York, 1954.

Davids, T. W. Rhys, trans., *The Questions of King Milinda*, Part 1, Dover Publications, New York, 1963.

*Evans-Wentz, W. Y., trans., *The Tibetan Book of the Dead*, 3rd edition, Oxford University Press, London, 1957.

Fisher, Joe, *The Case for Reincarnation*, Bantam Books, New York, 1985.

Frazer, Sir James, *Belief in Immortality*, The Macmillan Co., New York, 1913.

Fremantle, Francesca, and Chogyam Trungpa, trans., "The First Six Days of the Bardo of Dharmata," *LOKA, a Journal of the Naropa Institute*, Anchor Press/Doubleday, New York, 1975.

————, trans., *The Tibetan Book of the Dead*, Shambala, Berkeley, Calif., 1975.

Gallup, George, Jr., with William Proctor, *Adventures in Immortality*, McGraw-Hill Book Co., New York, 1982.

Gaster, Rabbi Moses, ed., *Encyclopedia of Religion and Ethics*, Vol. 12, Scribner's Sons, Hames Hasting, N.Y., 1955.

Govinda, Lama Anagarika, *The Psychological Attitude of Early Buddhist Philosophy*, Rider & Company, London, 1961.

Hall, Manly P., *From Death to Rebirth*, The Philosophical Research Society Inc., Los Angeles, 1972.

Hanson, Virginia, and Rosemarie Stewart, *Karma: The Universal Law of Harmony*, 2nd edition, The Theosophical Publishing House, Wheaton, Ill., 1981.

*Head, Joseph, and S. L. Cranston, ed., *Reincarnation: The Phoenix*

Fire Mystery, Julian Press/Crown Publishers, Inc., New York, 1977.

Humphreys, Christmas, *Karma and Rebirth*, The Theosophical Publishing House, Wheaton, Ill., 1983.

Jastrow, Robert, *God and the Astronomers*, Warner Books, New York, 1980.

*Jung, C. G., *Memories, Dreams, Reflections*, ed. Aniela Jaffe, trans. Richard and Clara Winston, Pantheon Books/Random House, New York, 1963.

Kapleau, Philip, *The Three Pillars of Zen*, Anchor Press/Doubleday, Garden City, N.Y., 1980.

————, *Zen: Dawn in the West*, Anchor Press/Doubleday, Garden City, N.Y., 1980.

Kelsey, Denys, and Joan Grant, *Many Lifetimes*, Doubleday & Company, Inc., Garden City, N.Y., 1967.

*Küng, Hans, *Eternal Life?* trans. Edward Quinn, Doubleday & Company, Inc., Garden City, N.Y., 1984.

Langley, Noel, ed., *The Hidden History of Reincarnation*, A. R. E. Press, Virginia Beach, Va., 1965.

*MacGregor, Geddes, *The Christening of Karma*, The Theosophical Publishing House, Wheaton, Ill., 1984.

————, *Reincarnation in Christianity*, The Theosophical Publishing House, Wheaton, Ill., 1978.

Moody, Raymond A., Jr., M.D., *Life After Life*, Bantam Books, New York, 1976.

Narada Thera, trans., *The Dhammapada*, Varjirarama, Colombo, Sri Lanka, 1972.

Neufeldt, Ronald W., *Karma and Rebirth: Post Classical Developments*, State University of New York Press, Albany, N.Y., 1986.

Paramananda, Swami, *Reincarnation and Immortality*, The Vedanta Centre, Cohasset, Mass., 1961.

Perkins, James S., *Through Death to Rebirth*, The Theosophical Publishing House, Wheaton, Ill., 1961.

Prabhavananda, Swami, *The Spiritual Heritage of India*, Doubleday & Company, Inc., Garden City, N.Y., 1963.

*Rahula, Walpola, *What the Buddha Taught*, Grove Press, New York, 1959.

Rastrapal Bhikshu, *An Exposition of Kamma and Rebirth*, Buddhist Research and Publication Society of India, 1965.

*Sangharakshita, *The Three Jewels*, Rider & Company, London, 1967.

Schilpp, Paul Arthur, ed., *The Philosophy of Sarvepalli Radhakrishnan*, Tudor Publishing Co., New York, 1952.

*Stevenson, Ian, M.D., "Twenty Cases Suggestive of Reincarnation," *Proceedings of the American Society for Psychical Research*, Vol. 26, September 1966.

Suzuki, D. T., *Essays in Zen Buddhism, First Series*, Grove Press, Inc., New York, 1961.

*Takakusu, Junjiro, *The Essentials of Buddhist Philosophy*, ed. Wing-tsit Chan and Charles A. Moore, 3rd edition, Office Appliance Co., Ltd., Honolulu, 1956.

Tatz, Mark, and Jody Kent, *Rebirth: The Tibetan Game of Liberation*, Anchor Press/Doubleday, Garden City, N.Y., 1977.

*Toynbee, Arnold, et al., *Life After Death*, Weidenfeld & Nicholson, London, 1976.

Trungpa, Chogyam, *Cutting Through Spiritual Materialism*, Shambala, Berkeley, Calif., 1973.

Warren, Henry Clarke, *Buddhism in Translations*, Harvard Oriental Series, Vol. 3, No. 9, Harvard University Press, Cambridge, Mass., 1947.

Yasutani, Hakuun, *Eight Bases of Beliefs in Buddhism*, trans. Eido Tai Shimano, Youval Tal Ltd., Jerusalem, 1966.

Zukav, Gary, *The Dancing Wu Li Masters: An Overview of the New Physics*, Bantam Books, New York, 1980.

INDEX

THE VEN. PHILIP KAPLEAU, founder of The Zen Center, in Rochester, N.Y., is the author of *The Three Pillars of Zen, Zen: Merging of East and West*, (formerly *Zen: Dawn in the West*), *To Cherish All Life*, and *The Wheel of Death*, which is the precursor to this volume. His first book, *The Three Pillars of Zen*, now near its twenty-fifth year of publication, has been published in ten languages.

In his youth, Kapleau studied law and became a court reporter, serving for many years in the state and federal courts of Connecticut. At the end of World War II he was appointed chief reporter for the International Military Tribunal at Nuremberg, then was sent to cover the International Military Tribunal for the Far East in Tokyo.

In 1953 he gave up his business in America and left for Japan to undergo Zen training. After five years he came to an awakening, then went on to complete eight more years of formal study and training. He was ordained by his teacher Zen master Yasutani during that time, and was authorized by him to teach.

Kapleau returned to the United States in 1966 to found the Zen Center in Rochester. The Center has since grown to include affiliated centers in a number of cities in the United States, Canada, Europe, and Central America. In 1986, after twenty years as abbot, Kapleau transmitted the teaching to the Ven. Bodhin Kjolhede and appointed him his successor. Kapleau, no longer based in Rochester, continues to teach from time to time at the Rochester center and other Buddhist centers.